MW00568923

CJ West

Taking Stock

22 West Books, Sheldonville, MA
www.22wb.com

Requests for permission to make copies of any part of the work should be mailed to the following address: Permissions, 22 West Books, P.O. Box 155, Sheldonville, MA 02070-0155

The following is a work of fiction. The characters and events are of the author's creation and used fictitiously. This book in no way represents real people living or dead.

Cover photo and design by Sarah M. Carroll

Author photo by Gloria West

ISBN10: 0-9767788-1-5
ISBN13: 978-0-9767788-1-3

Other Books by C.J. West

Sin and Vengeance October 2005*

* Brad Foster meets Charlie Marston, the hero of Sin and Vengeance, mid-way through this book.

Acknowledgements

As I write novels I am forever grateful for the opportunity to research so many facets of life in this world. It is exceedingly interesting to learn about different professions, cultures, and life situations and I am greatly indebted to those who spend so much time sharing their life experience with me.

Special thanks to George Devin a seasoned internal auditor and audit manager for his help with Herman, Sarah, and Stan. He helped me understand their profession and how the personalities of real-life auditors relate to their successes and failures.

Thanks to Monique Houde, author of *Blinded by Love,* for her help understanding the ramifications of domestic abuse and how it impacts the lives of people real and fictional. Erica shares traits with many successful women as she strives too hard to become all that her mother was not.

Thank you to my pre-release readers Paul Babin, Jady Bernier, and Jay Brooks. My utmost thanks to my wife Gloria who still manages to get excited about my work somehow.

Dedicated In Loving Memory to:

Edgar L. Martin, Sr.   1921 – 2006

Mildred E. Martin 1922 – 2007

Chapter 1

A single monitor glowed among the racks of black cabinets abuzz with the stirring of three hundred tiny electric fans. The server farm was hard at work crunching the day's results down into thousands of reports for the investment managers to digest the next morning. The people who attended these machines and the $44 billion they guarded had long gone home. The constant drone of the two-ton compressor and the fans blowing cold air beneath the floor drowned out any sound beyond the glass walls and left him completely isolated in this narrow walkway between cabinets. His early fears had been replaced by a polished routine, a well-rehearsed alibi, and a knowledge that very few people remained in the office this late at night.

The machine finished its work with spectacular results, but this was not the time for celebration. Calmly his fingers tapped on the keys and the machine went to work erasing every trace of his work here tonight. Seconds later, the CD ejected and he slipped it into his bag. He arranged the server desktop the way he had found it, locked the glass cabinet door and slipped to the end of the row. There against the wall he watched for movements in the myriad reflections. He waited and listened nearly a minute before slipping down the ramp and out the door.

The cubicles beyond were silent, office lights switched off.

He eased down the hall ten feet to the security room door, slid the key into the lock and slipped in, gladly out of sight again. He'd be done in another few minutes. Very few people had access to this room, and those who did rarely stepped inside. Another series of cabinets lined two walls.

These were filled with wires rather than computers. The single PC monitored the comings and goings at every entrance the company controlled. A few doors, like the one to this room, operated with keys, but most required a plastic access card. When someone opened an electronic lock their identity was captured here. He scrolled down the list looking for the problem he'd found several times before.

Here it was again.

She couldn't enter nineteen and then get up here to twenty-two ten minutes later. None of the exits downstairs had been opened in that time. A few clicks and the evidence of her visit to nineteen vanished. It would be impossible to know who passed out the doors when she eventually left; impossible for anyone to piece together what he'd done.

He turned to the VCR and ejected the tape. The one he replaced it with looked old enough to have been around a few months. It had, although everything on it had been erased, just as the one in his hands would be before he returned it to the stack.

The monitor on the wall showed an empty computer room then several dim hallways around the building. She was there somewhere and it would be just his luck for her to get her face recorded coming in rather than out. Damn workaholic. If he was lucky, he'd get out before she left nineteen. The last thing he needed was to bump into her as he left the room. If the bitchy do-gooder got suspicious, getting in and out would be a nightmare and the whole thing would come to a halt. He couldn't afford that.

The computer didn't record his exit from the security closet. The only evidence he'd been there was in his black leather bag and that would be short-lived. He strode briskly for the lobby, far too intent for the hour. Alerted to his presence in the hall, the motion sensor unlocked the door with an audible click. The tiny electric device hummed as the latch was held open for him. The security computer logged an exit that could only belong to Erica Fletcher.

Down the elevator and into the Boston spring air he went.

Chapter 2

In two strides, Gregg's footsteps on the industrial carpet faded into the cacophony of perky, placating voices. Tones of assurance and stability emanated from the fuzzy gray cubicles that stretched to the glass-encased horizon. Marissa watched dozens of sleek black headsets bob confidently. Unseen fingers clicked plastic keys to contact the electronic oracle on the twenty-second floor. Marissa's new computer screen and matching perfect-bound manual seemed mystical indeed. Four days training with Gregg had passed quickly. Calls had been answered, customers appeased, but somehow it had been surreal with Gregg at arms length. Alone now the LEDs on her phone lay dark, waiting for a multi-tentacled machine to decide it was time for her to join the clamor of forced-smiling voices, time to deliver efficient and caring servitude, time to prove she could earn her own way.

The red light flashed silently at first then was joined by a buzzing that sent her hands grasping for the receiver. Lifting it didn't stop the noise. Finally, she remembered to flip the switch that activated her headset.

Fumbling, heart racing, she paused a bit too long after the line came live. "Thank you for calling Boston Financial Services. My name is Marissa. How can I help you?" She forgot to identify herself as a member of the client services group. Whoever reviewed her tapes would catch such a basic mistake on her first call.

"I'll be amazed if you can, but you can give it a try. This is Hank Johnson and I have a problem with an order I placed on December twenty-eighth." The gravelly, rumbling voice conjured an image of a large, powerful man.

"Can you describe the problem for me, Sir?"

"Glad to," he spat. "Your company's cheating me. Actually, my wife convinced me to give you one last chance. Honestly, I don't see how you can straighten this out short of admitting you're thieves. When you prove me right, I'm moving every cent to Fidelity."

This had to be a test. Someone from client services, a supervisor or a manager, was hiding in another room and playing angry to see how well she could handle a difficult call. She vowed to shine.

"I'm sorry you feel that way, Sir," she answered evenly. "Let's walk through your order and figure out where we've gone wrong."

He plunged in without a second's hesitation. "I moved ten thousand dollars into your Penguin Small Cap Growth Fund. I bought it at nineteen point two five." He spoke calmly, his anger bubbling beneath the surface.

Marissa wanted to ask for the ticker, but didn't dare interrupt. The other CSRs would have known it offhand.

"I'd been watching that fund for months and when it finally dropped below twenty, I placed my order."

"Ok."

"Not really. My statement shows the shares were priced at twenty-three point five. I never would have paid that much. I won't stand for this. I want the shares I have coming or you'll hear from the attorney general."

She'd heard the numbers, but his hostile intonation of 'attorney general' chased them from memory. Down by her mouse were several blank sheets of scratch paper. She should have been using them to make notes. She glanced up at the idle computer screen as time ticked by. Mr. Johnson was waiting for a reply. He wouldn't stay quiet long.

Marissa quickly searched for an account with the last name Johnson. There were several screens full. She asked again for his first name, Hank, and found two Hank Johnsons. She asked where Mr. Johnson lived, Marlborough, and found no Hank Johnson there. Confused, she felt the heat building in her cheeks, a bead of sweat forming under her bangs, unsure what she had done wrong. When Mr. Johnson rudely suggested she could find him easier with his account number, which he rattled off from the printed statement in his hands, his information flashed up on the screen. The account owner was Elizabeth Johnson of Marlborough. Hank was listed as joint tenant. Each mistake, each delay, brought a harsher tone to Mr. Johnson's voice as if her uncertainty were a mask for the company's unwillingness to help him. If this were a training exercise, she'd failed. Unfortunately, the dread she felt affirmed that this was more important to Mr. Johnson than a mere exercise.

Seconds passed as she stared at the screen.

There was no transaction on December 28th, but there was a transaction for the 29th. Marissa reviewed a purchase of PSCX, the mutual fund Mr. Johnson was referring to.

"Are you still with me?"

"Yes, Sir. I was just reviewing your purchase on the twenty-ninth."

"Damn it, I didn't purchase anything on the twenty-ninth, that's what I've been trying to tell you for the last five minutes. What's wrong with you people? This is so simple. How can you get it so screwed up?"

"Sir, I see a transaction on the twenty-ninth. You purchased four hundred twenty-five point five three shares."

Johnson hollered so loud Marissa yanked off her headset to save her eardrums. Whatever he said next was unintelligible with the headphones in her outstretched hand. He was still ranting when she re-fitted the earpieces over her ears. "…believe you can actually say that to me with a straight face. I have proof that I called on December twenty-eighth at two o' seven precisely. If you can't get that through your head, I'll fax you my phone bill so even you can see it. I know how simple you are over there!"

The transaction on the screen showed the time of Mr. Johnson's call as 3:45 P.M. on the 28th, well after the three o'clock deadline for mutual fund orders. She was certain he was mistaken. This was the most common problem new customers had. They placed an order after the trading deadline and were annoyed when they were given the following day's closing price. This should have been a simple problem. It would be for a seasoned CSR.

"Sir, it seems you placed your order after our trading deadline."

Johnson exploded. "Aren't you listening? I did no such thing! I placed this order at two o' seven! What part of that don't you understand?"

"Sir, our system shows–"

"I don't give a damn what your system shows. I placed this order at two o' seven and I can prove it. Your firm owes me three thousand dollars and if you can't get that through your head, I'll sue you along with your slimy, thieving company."

Marissa stared at the transaction on her screen knowing that if she didn't come up with some sort of answer, Johnson would start yelling again. She'd felt so proud at the beginning of this day, her last day of training, the day she would receive her first real paycheck. This job hadn't impressed her parents or her college friends, but Boston Financial Services was a real company. Coming to the thirty-story building in a suit each day had buoyed her pride. An hour ago, she'd thought she was going somewhere, but now she stared numbly at her screen, terrified to speak, unsure about the problem she faced or what to do next.

Johnson lit into her again and she felt a tear inching its way toward the microphone. Strangely, the tears protected her against the stream of insults screaming over the line. Letting go of the professional status she'd been clinging to somehow gave her immunity. She asked him to hold on for her supervisor and set the headset down on the desk, dabbing her eyes as she stood up. She wandered through the blurry maze of gray cubicles to find Gregg.

An hour before, she was eager to win his approval and build from there toward affection. The half-dozen years between them were never a concern. Now she'd be glad for him to save her from the angry man on the phone so she could go back to being the young girl he supplied with fatherly advice.

Chapter 3

When Marissa stood up the voices around her dropped to a murmur in respect for a wounded comrade. She retreated from the frenzy of the front lines, fighting to cover the signs of defeat. She refused to dab her eyes as she walked, crumpling the tissue deep inside her fist instead. She refused to sniffle or convulse under the weight of the tears she held back. They all knew. Had they expected her to wash out after ten minutes? Had they heard her fear over the low partition walls? Did her frustration and anxiety clang over the reassuring voices of the veterans? She wondered if this would be her last day at BFS.

The people behind the disapproving glances were no more to Marissa than the churning masses that bustled down the sidewalks. Gregg was the only person that mattered. He was the perfect intersection of potential friend, boss, and wistful after-hours companion. She hunched in his doorway with her eyes on the carpet and waited for him to finish his call. Everyone here seemed to be on the phone constantly.

The high partitions of Gregg's cubicle made a U shape against the wall of glass that ringed the office. Far below tiny cars and people hurried along under a crystal spring sky. Gregg was secluded from the chaos inside and out. Even standing he'd be barely visible to anyone among the low warren of identical desks beyond. The only person who could watch Gregg work was Jane Wheeler, a manager whose cubicle also abutted the glass and opened toward Gregg's. Her slow polite nod held more compassion than she'd felt from anyone she'd passed on the way here. Maybe compassion came with the position or vice-versa.

Once Gregg saw Marissa's face, he abruptly ended his conversation and left his chair. Her makeup was a disaster, but Gregg was at her elbow and there was no place to turn except back through the maze of prying eyes. She wasn't eager to make that walk alone just now.

"Tough call?" he asked without prompting. "Can I help?"

"He's holding for you."

Gregg reached for a notepad. "What do I need to know?"

She related the few details she could remember. An experienced agent would have come with the facts, but Gregg didn't mind. His eyes held no disappointment for her failure just minutes after being left alone. He made no complaint about the sparse details she offered. He listened calmly, thoughtfully and when she was done, he led her back to her desk.

Gregg took her chair, put on the headset he wore around his neck, and plugged it in. He muted Marissa's headset and handed it to her, tethering her to the conversation, but requiring nothing except that she listen. There wasn't room for a second chair and her skirt wouldn't allow sitting on the desktop. She stood silent and tall amid the cubes like a lone sidewalk tree attracting the attention of every dog that passed.

Gregg began in a strong, soothing voice, "Good morning, Mr. Johnson. Sorry to keep you waiting. I'm Gregg Turner, a client services supervisor here at BFS. I understand you're concerned about a recent transaction. I want you to know I'll do everything I can to help."

"I'll believe that when I've got my money back."

"Before we get to that, please help me understand something?"

"Why not?" he scoffed.

"Our records show that you spoke to one of our brokers on December twenty-eighth at three forty-five P.M. Marissa tells me we've got it wrong. Can you tell me how you know?"

"I told your girl already. I have my phone bill in my hand. I called you at two o' seven and believe me I wasn't on the phone with you until three forty-five. The call lasted six minutes and change."

"My apologies if we've made a mistake, Mr. Johnson. Would you mind faxing that bill to me? That would help speed this along."

With a few well-chosen words, Gregg turned the hostile maniac into a rational customer that was still displeased, but cooperative. The man that drove Marissa out of her cubicle on the edge of tears was no challenge whatsoever for Gregg. He instructed Mr. Johnson to fax in the phone bill and he did as asked. As they waited, Gregg printed a few pages of the Johnsons' account information and signaled Marissa to fetch them. By the time she returned, Gregg had logged their call into the system and was out of the chair waiting for her.

He motioned her to sit.

"Sorry you got such a difficult problem for your first solo call."

The problem hadn't seemed difficult for Gregg.

"Don't worry about it. You can't fix every problem on your own. Even experienced CSRs need help sometimes. That's why I'm here. You did exactly the right thing."

"Didn't seem that way," she sniffed.

"Trust me. You won't get many of those. Remember you can't win an argument. Just offer to help. Be positive and stick to the facts."

"Easy for you."

"Believe me it wasn't at first." Gregg's attention swung across the room. "Listen, I'm going to go chat with someone from IT about this. Stay off the phone for a while. Go get a coffee. When I get back, we'll listen to the tape and talk about what happened."

"You're going to do fine. Don't worry."

Gregg smiled and zigzagged off through the cubicles.

Chapter 4

Halfway across the call center Gregg stepped into the most popular work area at BFS. Bob Hicks managed this group from a cubicle just spitting distance from the corner office. On paper Gregg and Bob were peers, but Bob had relationships with the executive team that Gregg might never achieve. His location between the coffee station, the printer station, and mahogany row may have gained him his popularity, or else it was his penchant for hiring women with looks that drew a flood of male loiterers to his area. These stunning employees garnered more rapid salary increases than any team on the floor. Gregg's team consistently scored the best customer satisfaction ratings in the department yet their salaries lagged behind Bob's employees. If the customers had met Bob's team in person, the satisfaction numbers would have been closer, too.

Gregg closed in on Brad Foster, vice president of information technology, who also happened to be the CEO's brother-in-law and Bob's inspiration to work his way into senior management. Brad was never too busy to trot down to the nineteenth floor if someone on Bob's staff needed help, but when Gregg had a problem, his repeated calls went unanswered. If not for Gregg's relationship with Erica Fletcher, Brad's ace technologist, he'd be sunk.

Brad leaned over the printer station wall, engaged in an intimate conversation with a new blonde that Bob had undoubtedly prepped for his arrival. She was enthralled by whatever Brad was saying, thrilled to be talking to a vice president on her first day. She'd be having dinner with him by midweek.

Brad was telling the woman how critical the relationship between systems and service was and why he spent so much time down here servicing Bob's needs. It seemed like the reverse to Gregg as he stopped outside the cubicle entrance and got a look at the silk blouse Brad was talking to. Gregg excused himself and waved the papers in his hand. Brad reluctantly shifted his attention to Gregg with a penetrating glare that said he didn't appreciate the interruption at such an inopportune moment. The young lady seemed disappointed as well, though next week when she'd come to her senses, she'd welcome this same intrusion.

Brad made no move to examine the papers Gregg extended. Seconds passed awkwardly and Gregg pulled them back. Brad's audacity was infuriating. He took every liberty being the CEO's brother-in-law afforded.

Gregg explained the serious nature of the problem and the customer's threats to file suit and a complaint letter with the attorney general's office. Brad's eyes returned to the young blonde's neckline unencumbered by the weight of Gregg's words. Brad was similarly unmoved by the tale of Marissa's distress and Gregg's assertion that the problem was systems related. He didn't flinch at the mention of criminal negligence. Gregg dropped his voice to a whisper and warned, "This kind of attitude will get us a class action suit or an SEC probe for sure. You can't ignore legitimate complaints. It's your responsibility to protect our customers. If you don't, you're putting the entire firm at risk."

Brad didn't even turn to face him. It was as if he believed the systems staff was infallible and that any issue that arose had to be of Gregg's creation. That or he had no interest in his job other than the fringe benefits it provided. He deserved a hard right to the side of the head.

Gregg paused, appalled by Brad's stonewalling. He stood tall, hands on hips, and waited. He wasn't leaving without an assurance that something would be done.

The young woman turned away from Brad and measured Gregg, trying to understand if he was some sort of crackpot or if someone in Brad's position could so completely shirk his responsibilities.

Brad couldn't ignore him any longer, not if he wanted any chance with the girl. "What exactly do you want from me?"

"Help me track this down. This guy's phone bill shows he called before the deadline on the twenty-eighth. I need to know if our records agree. If they do, and I think they will, I need to know why we didn't get his order in until the twenty-ninth."

"How much does he want?"

"Three thousand plus."

"Good motive to doctor up your phone records, don't you think?"

Gregg waved the statement. "This complaint is legit."

"You want me to have someone spend hours searching through phone records? For what? You know the policy. You know this happens a dozen times a day. Deal with it. Don't come to me because you can't have a difficult conversation with a client."

"Don't tell me how to do my job. I can't just shoo this guy away. He has a legitimate gripe and I need to know what went wrong."

"Nothing went wrong. I just told you what happened."

The young girl was learning about Brad's cooperation with the CSRs.

"You guessed. You don't know. Tell me precisely when the call was taken and when it was entered. Then I can go back to this guy, not before."

"Gregg, I know it's tough for you, but sometimes you need to do what's right for the firm. Do you have any idea how much time this kind of research takes? Do you think I can tie up one of my developers every time some kook screams at one of those college drop-outs you put on the phones?"

The girl reeled back in her seat. Brad didn't notice.

"I am doing what's right for the firm. You're the one who's confused. Brendan took the original call. He's one of my best reps. There's no way he waited over two hours to enter the order. No way."

Brad ripped the sheets from Gregg's hand, took two steps to his left and dropped them in the shredder. The motor clicked on automatically. Even so, Gregg nearly got around him in time to get hold of the pages before the machine sliced them into two dozen indecipherable strips.

Gregg stared at the paper going into the machine, dumbfounded.

"That's what's right for the firm," Brad mocked.

Gregg felt half a dozen sets of eyes on him.

The paper disappeared and Brad clicked off the shredder.

"What kind of shit is that?" Gregg asked. He wasn't looking forward to asking angry Mr. Johnson for another copy of the phone bill. He couldn't tell him what happened. When he didn't explain, Johnson would assume Gregg was even more incompetent than before.

Brad stepped around the corner and rested a hand on Gregg's shoulder. He wasn't especially tall, but Brad was an exercise fanatic. His biceps bulged and his pectorals pressed outward to form a resting place for his tie.

Brad's voice was barely a whisper, "Listen, sit on it a few weeks, then call the guy back and tell him our records show exactly what they show. He called late. It'll save you and me a lot of trouble."

Gregg had a clear shot, a strong right to the abdomen. His father would have decked him already and he'd expect Gregg to do the same. Brad would never know what hit him, but it would cost Gregg his job.

Humiliated, he turned back toward his desk without a word.

Chapter 5

Gregg wished he'd had the foresight to copy the phone bill or at least write down the Johnsons' number and the time of the call before offering his only copy to Brad. Mr. Johnson wasn't pleased, but he accepted Gregg's explanation of a coffee spill without his earlier animosity and faxed it again without complaint. A minute later, phone bill in hand, Gregg went outside to cool down. He remembered the astonished looks of the two girls nearest him when Brad ran the documents through the shredder. They expected him to fly off in a fit of rage and even he wasn't sure why he hadn't. He was embarrassed, a bit ashamed, maybe, but it was what he needed to do to survive here. Father would have grabbed a handful of Brad's shirt, dropped him and probably gotten a date with the hot blonde in the process. He would have been fired of course, exactly why father worked for himself on the farm. Gregg wondered how valuable a job was that required him to humble himself to strangers day after day. Was this opportunity worth the softening his brothers teased him about?

He walked across Franklin Street and into Post Office Square Park. It was little more than a tiny patch of grass surrounded by shrubbery and fruit trees to screen out the passing cars and city bustle. The fountain and surrounding benches were the main attraction in summer, but the water had yet to be turned on for the season. It was warm enough for the hordes of office dwellers to venture out and cram every square inch of grass during lunchtime, but the landscape looked pristine. The ropes around the lawn kept the people on the brick walks and benches and allowed the grass to soak up the spring sunshine without being trampled. The winter respite wouldn't last much longer.

An SUV appeared from under the park. The bushes screened the ramp that led to six stories of underground parking buried beneath his feet. It was the latest thing in Boston. Bury the infrastructure and cover it with grass. Workers from the Big Dig had done the same with the expressway, burying the northbound and southbound traffic in tunnels and preparing to build a green park for kids to play in. Unfortunately, they ran out of money before they finished. City people got excited about grass. Grass meant relaxation, vacation, time to play. Odd the things people latched on to. Gregg lived here, but he wasn't one of them, far from it. He came from a place that was green as far as you could see. Green in every direction. He belonged there. He was at home there. City life was a necessary stop on his road to something bigger.

On his second lap around the park, his anger cleared and he thought of the one person who could help. His body turned on its own to face her office up on twenty-two as if some sort of spiritual magnetism drew his soul to hers whenever she came to mind. His hands began to sweat as he crossed Franklin Street. He weaved among the flowerbeds that subtly doubled as bomber barriers and strode back into the lobby. Gregg wasn't a rube like his brothers, who lost control whenever a woman of the appropriate age entered the room. They latched onto the first pretty girl who returned their flirtations and they were both married before they were twenty. There were thousands of women at S.M.U. and Gregg had dated his share. He could charm a girl off a barstool as well as he could calm an angry customer on the hotline, but he wasn't willing to settle for any girl.

Working six months with Erica was enough to know she was different from any woman he'd ever met. She made it clear that she needed nothing from anyone. That made getting close to her evermore difficult. She had to know she was gorgeous, but she never used that power over anyone, man or woman. She had the body of a dedicated runner, but kept it concealed beneath loose-fitting clothes that almost allowed Gregg to keep his thoughts on a professional level. He was riding the elevator to her now because she was the only person upstairs kind enough to help him voluntarily. Gregg considered himself quite a catch, but he'd devote himself to her completely if she would only agree to accept him.

The elevator doors opened on twenty-two. Gregg slid his white plastic card through the reader and stepped inside. The quiet was a striking contrast to the constant chatter on nineteen. The hall snaked around the computer room with its rows and rows of glass-fronted racks filled with colonies of blinking LEDs. There was an empty desk at the front of the room, a remnant from the days when computers needed to be constantly attended. Now the systems were smart enough to summon help on their own.

The few staffers Gregg passed were intent on their monitors, deep in thought as if puzzling out a mystery of one sort or another. Not one conversation could be heard anywhere.

Erica's door was open. Gregg filled the doorway and tapped his knuckles against the metal frame. Erica's fingers clicked away. Her shoulders turned slightly toward him, but her eyes remained focused on the screen. Behind her the Boston skyline glistened in the spring sunshine.

She clicked a final button and her gaze shifted from her work to Gregg so smoothly he didn't notice the transition. One second she was looking at the monitor, the next she squarely faced him. Her intensity reminded him of one of their first encounters. They were talking together in the office after work. Some of the other CSRs were horsing around with a Nerf football. Bob threw the ball full strength and sent it whistling over the cubicles too fast for his friend to handle. The ball hurtled directly at the back of Erica's head. Gregg flinched and Erica spun into action, her outstretched arm was ready faster than Gregg could see it move. She caught the ball by its point, an impressive demonstration of reflexes and coordination, even more so when he learned her skill was the result of ten years of Karate.

Looking at him now she smiled a warm, relaxed smile that brightened her features. "Hey," she said without a hint of the tension or nervous expectation Gregg felt.

"What do I have to do to get an office like this?"

"Learn dot Net. I could use you tomorrow, maybe sooner."

16

"Easier said than done, I'm sure."

"No problem for a guy as smart as you." Her mischievous smile hinted that she'd enjoy working closely with him again. She knew why Gregg came to her so often. At least she didn't object.

Gregg felt a twinge of embarrassment and more than a bit confused. The boundaries had been settled two years ago. Erica was dating Simon. Still, he couldn't help feeling there was almost as much interest on her part as his. He wanted to believe there was, but he knew this was just Erica's way. This wasn't an invitation to romance. Romance rarely crossed her mind. What he'd take for innuendo from another woman was simply the unvarnished truth coming from Erica. There was no hidden meaning to delve for. Looking for one only brought frustration.

He tried to shake the thought from his mind.

"I've got a tough one for you today," he said. "You should know I've already had a run-in with your boss and lost."

"Do I seem like the type of girl who takes on a problem after her boss has said no?"

"You're not the type of girl who turns away someone in need."

"Especially not you."

Gregg explained Marissa's conversation with Mr. Johnson and the discrepancy between the two documents in his hand; the phone bill which showed a call at 2:07 P.M. and the Johnsons' account statement which showed an order placed at 3:45 P.M.

"So you want to know who to believe?"

"Yeah. Can you poke around the database? Maybe check the phone system and make sure it all looks kosher? I'm sure I'm going to have to pay this guy, but I'd like to have something concrete to point to in case someone asks. Having our phone records would make me feel a lot better."

"I don't have access to the phone system. It's in the security room and Brad's the only one of us who can get in there. You're going to need his help."

"That's not going to happen."

"Why? What did he say?"

"He said I should do what's right for the firm, meaning he was too busy ogling some new chick that works for Bob to even listen to me."

Erica smiled knowingly.

"He spends more time down there than up here. You'd think he could spare five minutes when I have a problem."

"He must have said something. What reason did he give?"

"Reason? He's not capable of reasoning. He's a testosterone overdosed monkey. If his sister hadn't married Marty, he'd be working in a toll booth."

"Serious hostility." She chuckled.

"He took my only copy of this guy's phone bill and ran it through the shredder. Right in front of everyone. Made me look like a moron."

Erica's hand rushed to cover a smile. "You should've decked him."

"I wanted to, believe me. Of course I'd be unemployed by now. You'd miss me, wouldn't you?"

"Wow. How could he do that? I don't get it."

"All he said was the order missed the three o'clock deadline. He didn't check anything. He didn't look at my paperwork. He just shredded it."

"That's gutsy even for him."

"Can you do some poking?"

"You know I'll take any chance to show Brad for the dufus he is."

"But?"

"But that dufus has no clue what goes on around here. The only time he comes to see me is when he's adding something to my workload or taking away one of my resources."

"So you're busy?"

"If I had double the staff I'd be busy. I'm barely surviving."

"Anyone else who might look at it?"

Erica reached out and took the pages. "After Brad told you to drop it? What do you think? Everyone up here drinks the Kool-Aid."

"So you're my only hope."

"A dim hope. I'll have some breathing room after the rollout. Will your customer wait that long?"

"What choice have I got? Besides poking around in the database myself that is?"

"That's a frightening thought."

Erica stood and came around the desk.

Gregg hesitated. She was dismissing him, but he didn't want the conversation to end. This was the recurring theme in all their interactions, but he couldn't help himself. "How's Simon these days?"

She almost seemed not to remember him. "He's fine," she said after a long hesitation. "I haven't seen him much lately. This project's killing me."

Gregg took his cue, thanked her and left twenty-two with a spark of hope.

Chapter 6

The sun disappeared behind the buildings leaving the streets blanketed in long damp shadows. A few hours earlier, office workers had been penned up in row after row of ten-by-ten boxes, twenty, thirty, even forty stories high. The sidewalks that had brimmed with primped masses were mostly empty now. Moms and dads had scurried out to the suburbs to get the kids. The younger crowd that remained churned energetically in bars scattered every block or two throughout the financial district.

Erica rounded the corner carrying a warm box of veggie smothered pizza that would sustain her through the late hours and into the morning. Jovial voices drew her attention halfway down the block. A group of twenty revelers spilled out of the International and onto Pearl Street. She recognized two women in their early twenties that had worked for her in client services and she detoured over to say hello. Other familiar faces appeared in the group as she drew near. Soon Gregg pushed his way through the crowd and stopped a few feet from Erica.

The women moved along reluctantly as if they'd been given some secret signal to get lost, but didn't want to. Erica and Gregg stood firm in the middle of the jostling, joking group that enveloped them as it moved along Pearl Street.

"You're going the wrong way aren't you?" Gregg asked.

"That depends where you're headed."

"It's seven thirty on Friday night. You're not going back?" Gregg indicated the gray concrete building across the street.

Two younger girls drifted back from the group to watch their conversation from a safe distance.

"Your fans are waiting."

"This is the client services crew. We do this every couple months. Same as ever."

"I know who they are. No one from Bob's group though, shame."

"Funny. We're meeting Bob at The Rack. You should come."

"You already have both hands full of twenty-somethings. How are you going to have time to talk to me?"

"I don't date women from the office," he choked.

"Really. I wasn't sure that was a problem for you."

"You know everyone here works in client services. If they worked in another department it might be different."

"Convenient. Sounds plausible, but not too limiting."

"You love making me suffer, don't you?"

"You make it way too easy."

"The Rack will be fun. You could let loose for a change. Whatever you're going back for can wait."

"Looks like you're going to have plenty of fun without me."

"Don't you want to see all your old pals?"

"Yeah, but I want to keep my job more." She raised a hand to her forehead in a mock salute. "I've got bugs up to here and I'm running out of time. Even working seven days a week I don't think we'll be ready for go-live."

Gregg took a half step toward the office. "I am your number one beta user. We could talk systems stuff if that would make you feel better. You know how much I love veggie pizza."

For a second Erica thought he was going to invite himself upstairs, and for a second she thought she wanted him to. He waited then took one tentative step back and then another. The girls behind him released a collective sigh.

"Sbarro's only two blocks from The Rack," she said.

Gregg wished her well, turned, and joined the group waiting for him near the corner.

Erica crossed the dark street and made her way up to her office. She found herself staring at the whiteboard holding a half-eaten slice of pizza, not quite seeing the neat handwritten tasks. She'd never been the life of the party, but before joining Brad's team she wouldn't have passed up an invitation to shoot pool and listen to a new band with her friends. The career she'd chosen left room for little else. Trading security for a bit of fun had never bothered her before. This was the first time she'd noticed. She shuddered, feeling a bit like she'd noticed a huge stain on the back of her outfit after wearing it all day. This was more than a day's outfit; this was her life. She felt small sitting alone in the office.

Alert and back in the moment, Erica faced the identical laptops on her desk. With only eight days to go, the bug list was longer than ever and the testers kept finding new problems faster than her team could fix them. Erica worked her way down the list of completed items. She read through each problem report then connected into the test system and verified that the fix solved the problem completely. Checking everyone's work was monotonous, but she couldn't count on the QA person Brad assigned. Like many things on the project, Erica was doing this herself. She wasn't neurotic. It was the pressure, Brad's needless pressure and his fantasy that she could finish on time with half the resources identified in the initial project plan. She was project manager, lead developer, and quality assurance department all in one. That left little time for anything outside work except a couple hours sleep and a commute that was more about hygiene than spending time at home.

Heavy footsteps sounded in the hall shortly after nine o'clock. They stopped outside Erica's door as Brad leaned a muscled shoulder against her door casing. There was only one person who came to her office this late. She knew it was Brad before she looked up and saw the fiendish look on his face. He had a way of studying her with a smile lurking beneath the surface, a grin he couldn't let loose until he was out of view. His torment was intentional, but why her? She was driving his biggest project. If she quit or if she failed, he was in deep. Maybe he hated strong women. She posed little professional threat since he was Marty's brother-in-law. No employee was going to supersede him. His cruelty made no sense unless it was purely for sport. He was the perverse type and she wouldn't put it past him.

"I've got bad news for you," he said.

"It can't be worse than this bug list."

"Actually it can. I've reassigned Jenkins to the attribution project starting tomorrow."

Erica's face went slack in disbelief. "You can't do that. Tomorrow's Saturday. My whole team's coming in." She'd worked hours shuffling the workload so they could meet the deadline. Without Jenkins it was hopeless.

"He'll be here, but he'll be working on attribution."

"How can you do that? What are you trying to do to me?"

"I had no choice. The PMs are screaming. This business is driven by the investment team not client services."

"This isn't some diddley project. This is mission critical. We're revamping the way everyone looks at our investment history not just client services. There's no way I can bring this in on time without Jenkins."

"Don't preach to me, Erica. I know how important every project is. What you fail to recognize on the other hand, is that there is other work going on here. It's all interrelated and the schedule is set. If you can't handle this, I'll bring in Devlin to manage and you can go back to coding."

"You can't do that!"

"Nothing personal. We're all tightening our belts. You've got to slog through one more week. I can't push the schedule. Marty won't have it. If you need Devlin's help, I'll get him on board Monday, just let me know."

"No thanks."

Brad turned and disappeared. Just like him to let her work on a project eighteen months and then try to give it to someone else when it was time to hand out the credit.

Fuming, too angry to think about anything seriously except doing Brad bodily harm, Erica got up and paced around her office. Her eyes darted around her workspace, finally settling on the pages Gregg left with her. She laughed at them as if Gregg could hear then placed them on top of a pile where she could see them. No time for them in the next two weeks. No one else was going to have time for them either, but this might be the sword she could use to take a swipe at Brad. Gregg was going to have to fend off Mr. Johnson for awhile and there was nothing she could do about that. When things slowed down, she'd dig deep. If Brad had ignored a serious problem, she'd uncover every detail and she'd tell anyone who'd listen. Even Marty cared about the customers. They supported his lavish lifestyle after all.

Erica noticed the ever-blinking red light on her phone, clicked on the speaker and logged-in to check her voicemail. Half-listening, she angrily punched the delete button on the first six messages before any of them finished playing.

Impossible. She was never going to finish on time.

The next voice was Simon's, "Erica, hey, where have you been? Dating is supposed to be a two person endeavor. A contact sport if it's done right. I can't get you anywhere. Call me."

Erica deleted a few more messages.

Her mother's voice came next, "Erica, I haven't heard from you in a few weeks. Wanted to make sure everything's ok. Call me. I miss you."

Delete. Delete. Delete.

A young woman's voice played from the speaker, "Erica, Kate. Eisenstein was ripped you blew it off again. He went postal about those students who never show up for class and think they'll pass – meaning you. He says that doesn't play in graduate school. Better come next Wednesday. See ya."

Simon's voice returned, angrier than before, "Erica, this is ridiculous. Call me." She wondered how long it had been since they talked.

Erica laid her head on the desk and closed her eyes.

Chapter 7

"One o' five Marlborough."

"One o' five Marlborough, Mam."

A blurry close-up of stitched blue vinyl appeared through Erica's sore eyes. She pushed herself up. The windows of the cab were dark, the streetlights too pale for her to recognize her own block. She knew better than to let her guard down in public, especially at night in the city. Here she was in the car with a complete stranger, asleep, with no idea where she was. He could have driven her anywhere. She cursed herself for nodding off. She knew first hand what could happen and that knowledge kept her ever vigilant. She could take three guys like this scrawny cab driver, but her self defense training was worthless when she was asleep. Fortunately, she wouldn't need her training tonight.

She poked a ten through the plexiglass and rambled into the lobby and up the stairs. Her body steered its own way home, her eyes so heavy she could barely see. She pushed the key in the lock, jammed her shoulder against the door, and stumbled inside when it jerked out of her way. The stark lights jarred her to a stop. Every one of them was on and she felt every watt through her thin eyelids. The blow dryer whined loudly in the bathroom. The light and the noise blocked her advance and she wanted to lay down right there on the carpet. Eyes closed, she marched zombie-like to the hall, her shoulder rubbing the wallpaper when she reached it, guiding her, keeping her upright.

One cracked eye spied Melanie pulling a fat round brush with one hand and waving the dryer with the other. The hair on one side hung down straight, the other waved with curls that would only become more pronounced if allowed to dry. Nine on Saturday night, Melanie was going out. Erica wouldn't last another five minutes.

Erica stumbled on, but Melanie's voice pulled her back, forcing her to remain standing longer than she thought possible. Her joints longed to sprawl out beneath the sheets. The dryer thankfully ceased.

"Where've you been?" Melanie asked.

"Work," Erica said leaning against the wall for support.

"Let me get this straight. You worked all day Friday, Friday night and Saturday, a day most people take off, and you're just getting home at nine o'clock. No wonder you look like Hell."

"Thanks, you too."

"But I'll be glamorous in five minutes."

"You get to it, I've got to crash."

The voice followed her, but the words were too garbled to discern. At least the blow dryer was quiet. With luck she'd be asleep before it started again. Finally through the door and into the dark, her sneakers hit the floor, her jeans dropped in a lump beside the bed, her bra lofted toward the chair. She was beneath the chilly sheets, eyes blissfully closed. Even her thoughts were too tired to stir.

Erica didn't bother to open her eyes when Melanie's voice came from the doorway. The sliver of light she let in fell harmlessly on the comforter that covered her shoulder.

"Simon came by today."

"Was he mad?" she mumbled from under the blankets.

"Beyond mad. He didn't even ask for you."

"What'd he want?"

"A couple of shirts and some sweatpants. They were too big for you, so I let him have them."

"Not surprised. He seemed really–"

Melanie started talking before Erica finished, oddly rude for her. "He said to tell you he's done; he can't take it anymore. He said, and I quote: dating you is pointless. He was a nice guy. They all are."

Erica tried to tell her how important the project was, but her voice was so weak she couldn't hear her own mumbling.

Melanie kept on talking.

"You know what he said? He said he could never tell if you really liked him or not. After all that time. You were so focused on work that you tuned him out. That's what guys do to us. It really sucks."

Erica tried to tell her how much she tried with Simon. How she'd gone to dinners and movies, really spent time with him. How he should've known how she felt. None of it got past her heavy lips.

Melanie kept on.

"You keep pushing them away. You make yourself positively undateable. If I did that, I'd be alone forever. I swear all that running you do is to get away from them faster. It works, but someone's got to tell them to stop lining up. What's the point?"

What did Melanie know? She'd spend the next half hour straightening her hair so men would take her seriously. Then she'd go out with her friends to some sports bar, desperate to get noticed in spite of the televisions every six feet and the two dozen other women trolling the same waters.

Erica drifted off. Melanie might still have been talking, but she couldn't hear her anymore.

Simon walked in and stood at the foot of the bed. Next came Derek, who took his place shoulder to shoulder with Simon. A procession of men formed a line that extended through the wall and into the blackness. None of them could lift his arms from his side. All wanted to come take hold of her, but none could. The line continued to a dark hall, where a man walked toward her. He was noticeably shorter than the others, about twenty, dressed in a shabby T-shirt stretched tightly over his muscles. He had a dirty, drunken look about him and he still had the scar Erica saw the morning he died.

Chapter 8

The electronic buzz pulsed through Brad like an ice pick piercing his
frontal lobe. He groped toward the bedside table, the stabbing pain behind
his eyes intensified by the dim light that glowed through the blinds. Hours
earlier he'd started the night with a string of Bass drafts in at least four
different bars around Faneuil Hall. He drained a Bass with each woman he
approached. Some lasted five or ten minutes, some only two. None resulted
in a second shared drink. When he deemed the night an utter failure he
veered sharply toward tequila shooters with an occasional Bass for taste.

He didn't want to admit he was losing his touch; that the women he
pursued recognized his motives almost on sight and that even he himself had
become tired of the never ending quest for the next meaningless physical
interlude. He was as muscled as ever. Mid-forties with a great job, he was a
prime candidate for marriage-minded women of a certain age and he played
the prospective husband and father routine well. Ending up alone night after
night was devastating his ego.

Worse than the pain in his head and lonely pit in his chest was his dread
of the man who'd be on the other end of this call. No one else dared call this
early on Sunday morning. He'd always thought he was his own man; that he
could walk away from anything if he didn't like the course it was taking, but
he didn't have the luxury of such options now. He'd made a mistake and
gotten in deep. The man on the other end of the phone was a pro of the
worst kind. He could end this for Brad in a dozen ways, none of them
pleasant. His only hope was to play along, do what he was told, and do it

skillfully enough so the results never surfaced. So far, he'd done it, but keeping things quiet was getting more difficult by the day.

Brad picked up.

"You shouldn't drink so much, Foster. With all the money you're taking down you can afford a pro. It'd be much easier than hitting on half the women in Boston. More successful, too."

Brad opened an eye, but he couldn't focus on the tiny LED panel well enough to see the number. He groped for the record button and clicked it. The man was sending a message: he was close by and he knew everything Brad did no matter when or where. Brad was out of his league and if he defied orders, the end would be brutally swift.

"How are we doing?" the voice asked.

Even after a good run the night before, the results weren't going to satisfy the boss. Brad knew better than to lie. "Fourteen mil."

"Pitiful. You leave in two weeks." The angry voice confirmed there would be no forgiveness for coming up short. He was caught between the boss' wrath and the ever-increasing likelihood of being caught if he took too much too fast. "I need the last six, Foster. This is our last chance. Get me to twenty. I don't care how."

Skimming that much in two weeks would make waves Brad couldn't cover. "We're not getting there. Things are way too hot. Turner's pissed. He'll do anything to screw me now."

"Forget him, Mr. V.P. What is he? A damn clerk for God's sake."

"It's not just him. Erica's helping him and she's trouble."

"You can't handle one whiny chick? I'm tired of you complaining about her. You're her freaking boss. Find some backbone."

"Backbone? What more can I do? Nothing affects her. I've taken half her team so what does she do? She works day and night to keep up, and puts herself right in the middle of it. She's too damn close. I'd be better off is she was a nine to fiver. She strays one step in the wrong direction and she's going to trip over us."

"It's her or you. She trips, knock her down."

"Easy for you to say from the sidelines. We've got nearly two hundred mil. Enough is enough."

"No, it's not enough. This is an expensive operation. If you want to quit, you can finance the shortfall. I'm not going to."

"She's there day and night. How am I supposed to keep getting in and out of the computer room without her seeing me?"

"Just don't do anything stupid like you did with Tinsley. You have every right to go into the computer room. We've kept this hidden for three years. She's not going to figure it out in two weeks. She's not that smart. Don't give her time to breathe and everything will be fine."

"There's nothing more I can do. If I take anyone else, the project will crash and burn. I don't need that kind of attention right now."

"Idiot. Can't you think of another way to keep her busy? What would happen if one of her programs started acting funny? That might take quite a bit of time to fix, no? And it'll drive her nuts."

"I'll think of something."

"I just did. Do it quick and get me my last six million."

"Impossible."

"Get it! You've got two weeks."

The line went dead.

Brad stared down at the white box a moment before ejecting the mini cassette. He carefully dated it and put it in his brown leather bag with the others. This would be his payback for three years of torment. Threatened every day with discovery and a rough ride to jail, Brad dreamed of standing toe to toe with him in an alley somewhere and making him pay. Getting even with the bastard was the last thing he'd do before making his break for France.

Chapter 9

Melanie picked up the cardboard tube, peeled back the label and worked her fingernail into the seam. The lasagna in the oven was made with canned sauce and the bread came from a tube, but Melanie felt good about the sly dinner party she'd arranged. Nothing could keep Gregg away. Erica would be uncooperative, but Melanie had a feeling she'd at least come. She pondered what she might have to do to keep the party together once Erica realized what was up. She diced tomatoes and strategized. She sliced a cucumber and combined it with the lettuce she'd chopped into bite-sized chunks. As she sprinkled shaved carrots and a bit of red onion over the top, footsteps rushed down the hall. The door jerked open and Erica walked in looking nearly as harried as she had the night before. She sniffed the air, gave an approving nod and let her eyes dart around the room suspiciously.

It wasn't as if Melanie never cooked. When she first moved in, Melanie was so grateful for the free room she cooked almost every night. At some point in the last few months things had changed. Erica had started spending more nights in the office than at home and Melanie had stopped playing homemaker. This was the first dinner she'd made in a long time, but Erica's mind wasn't devious enough to smell out what Melanie had concocted. Melanie convinced her that a relaxed Sunday meal would be the perfect stress reliever after all the long hours she was putting in. Erica went off to the shower unaware that her true dinner companion was yet to arrive.

Soon the lasagna was out of the oven and the small table was set for three. The security system beeped and Melanie buzzed Gregg into the lobby.

She kept one eye toward the bathroom, wondering if she should have warned Erica. The shower was still running. If she ducked into the kitchen before she finished dressing they'd both be shocked, but that might be the catalyst they needed. Melanie considered sending him in to wash his hands and starting the fireworks herself. Erica would be appalled and Gregg would be mortified. Melanie remained nervously silent until he knocked.

With a quick look over her shoulder, she pulled the door wide and welcomed Gregg in. The loafers and red crewneck sweater dressed up his jeans enough so they didn't look hickish, but not so much that his intention was obvious. He handed Melanie a bottle of white wine and looked past her for Erica. He knew she was as likely to work through the night as to come home for dinner, invitation or not.

"She's getting dressed," Melanie said.

Gregg's body language was all jumbled as if he wasn't sure what to make of the news. His eyes lit up, but the rest of him tensed. He might have been relieved to learn she was still at work.

"What? No flowers?"

"I thought that was a bit over the top."

"Kidding. Good call. Now lighten up or your face is going to crack."

She put him to work opening the wine to calm his nerves.

When he was done, he had trouble deciding whether to sit at the table or on the couch facing the windows. The blow dryer started whining at the back of the apartment. His posture stiffened and he plopped down on the couch with his back to the noise, lest he see something he shouldn't. Yes, she was half naked back there and his imagination was running wild. He was the kind of guy Melanie could fall for: strong and smart, polite and deferent. He was marriage material and he was completely gaga over Erica. Otherwise, Melanie would have thrown herself at him by now. If she couldn't have him, she'd bring Erica around before he got tired of waiting. No sense letting a hunk like Gregg go to waste.

A few minutes later, Erica padded down the hall barefoot in sweatpants and an old Northeastern T-shirt. She saw the back of Gregg's head over the couch, pointed and mouthed, "What's he doing here?"

Melanie stepped closer and whispered, "I saw him downtown and invited him. Simon's history, why not?"

"It's been one day. I don't need a fix up," Erica whispered louder.

"It's not a fix up. He's been under your nose five years. If I was going to fix you up I'd bring home someone new for you to trample."

"Ouch. Simon really got to you."

"It's not Simon I'm worried about." She looked down her nose at Erica, but she didn't seem to understand who Melanie was trying to help. "Let's eat. I want to get some lasagna before I get kicked out."

Erica smirked. That wasn't going to happen.

The whispers grew loud enough for Gregg to hear, but he wisely faced the windows. Erica snarled, spun back toward her room, probably considering changing her sweat pants for something more appropriate, but she turned again and crossed the kitchen toward Gregg. This wasn't a date for Erica. She hadn't known he was coming and she wouldn't validate Melanie's meddling by dressing up.

Melanie watched him turn and meet Erica's eyes.

Her protest was lost on him.

Erica stopped a foot from the couch. "What brings you here?"

"I heard the food was good," he said.

"It's ready," Melanie chimed from the kitchen, heading off Erica's sarcastic retort. She watched Gregg as she delivered the salad to the table. He was entranced by Erica. Less than five minutes out of the shower, no make-up, wearing sweatpants and a ratty old T-shirt, she looked amazing. Eleven years younger, Melanie wished she could look as good.

Gregg chose the middle seat, so he'd be next to Erica whichever end she chose. He asked about the project. Erica rambled on about her work the previous sixty hours and how Brad had taken away another member of her project team. The technical gibberish was meaningless to Melanie, but she watched how easily they talked. Putting the two of them together couldn't have been more natural.

Gregg spent his weekends on the family farm from May to October. They needed all the help they could get, so he rarely visited the office on a weekend except during the winter. He shared a few country stories and had Erica enthralled, but when he asked about her family, the conversation came to a dead stop and nothing he said could revive it.

"Not much to say. It's just me and my mom," was all she said.

She offered nothing more in spite of his prompting.

He asked about things they did together when she was young; games, sports, movies, anything to spark a conversation or give him an idea for a date. She deftly reflected the conversation back at him, learning about his family, his work, his politics, all the while revealing nothing of herself. Listening to this, Melanie realized Erica routinely did the same with her. Melanie idolized her father and adored her mother. They had talked for hours about Melanie's family, but not five minutes about Erica's.

After dinner Erica claimed the sole armchair in the living room before Melanie could think to occupy it herself. Erica relaxed with the increased distance between them, but Gregg's mood sunk so low Melanie didn't dare leave them alone. She added her own stories to brighten the mood, but the awkward dance toward the door had begun.

An hour later, Erica escorted him out from three feet away. Gregg was dying to close in, but she sent no clear sign what she'd do if he did. He had to face her at work in the morning and his anguish was clear. He wanted to try again, but facing the embarrassment every time he saw her at work was too much. Melanie wished she could walk over and shove them together.

They faced each other for a pregnant moment.

Neither moved toward the other and he left with his head low.

Melanie followed him into the hall and shut the door.

"Thanks for trying, Mel. It's just not there." He slumped against the rail looking shattered, not sure where to go or what to do.

Melanie felt responsible. "Don't give up. She has feelings under there, honest. She'll come to her senses if I have to smack them into her."

She watched him trudge downstairs. Even if she did come around, he'd probably end up dejected after a few weeks. They always did.

Chapter 10

He sat on the cold concrete for an hour after she left, watching the building from the park in case she decided to return. Only the front doors were open on weekends, so if she'd gone for dinner and come back, she'd have passed right in front of him. She didn't. She was probably sleeping after working forty hours in the last three days. It was Sunday after all.

No one was there to see him casually cross the street and slip through the lobby. The guard sympathized with the late hours as they usually did. The elevator carried him up to twenty-two and he strode around the entire floor, poking his head in every cubicle and office before setting to work. He was positively alone when he slipped inside Erica's office and flicked on the light. Stacks of documents covered every square inch of her desk, credenza, and filing cabinets, not surprising given the tremendous load he'd assigned. Still, the clutter diminished her achievements somewhat. He valued order. Organization meant clear-headedness and discipline.

The computers on the desk were running as usual. A tap on the nearest keyboard brought a password box up on the screen. He entered her password, surprised, or maybe a bit disappointed that she'd stopped changing it so often. No matter, the little program his partner supplied allowed him to impersonate her anytime he wished. In the beginning she changed it every month or so. Her paranoia made him wonder if she knew about his incursions into her virtual territory. It seemed she had only been following protocol. The information assets under her stewardship warranted extraordinary measures of protection, but now the pressure had overshadowed her professionalism. Fatigue overtook good judgment. To her credit, she was worn down to the point of exhaustion and still hadn't made a blunder big enough to justify getting rid of her. He routinely covered mistakes for the other developers, but he'd give Erica no such leeway. He'd take any chance to move her out, but she gave him no justification, a wonder in this chaos.

The bug list was on top of the pile to the left of her laptop. He browsed down the page, checking her scribbles to find problem after problem she'd certified as resolved and ready for production. On the computer, he tapped his way into the programs she'd fixed then stopped and studied. Toying with her was an art. She needed to believe these new problems were her mistakes. Tired as she was and with the load she carried, the assumption would be natural. He wouldn't make errors so obvious as to tip her off, or so severe that she'd restore from backup and make her changes again. He spent nearly an hour changing several files, adding the wrong numbers together to get information that looked good, but wasn't accurate. How he'd enjoy pointing these problems out later, or even better, seeing her reaction when the system went live and the users began screaming all at once. He'd relish that moment.

Finished, he returned the computer to the exact state he found it in and rose to leave. As he straightened a pile he'd ruffled with his elbow, he noticed a form marked-up with highlights and red pen. It was a phone bill; the same one Gregg had thrust upon him. That one died in the shredder. He took this new copy and a few pages of account history beneath it and steamed out.

Chapter 11

Sarah Burke handed her paperwork to the human resources coordinator with a flourish and watched her circle the three younger recruits as they struggled with the stack of forms. She was eager for her new beginning; eager to forget the married partners knocking on her hotel room door; eager to work in the same place every day with people she could leave each night; eager for the normal life she would build here in Boston. Never again would she search for ways to pump up her billable hours. Never again would she cover for an inept sponsor because he signed the check for a consulting gig. This new life would be different. This job was about finding the truth. She relished the opportunity to proclaim it to all who would listen.

Herman Richards appeared at the conference room door, barked a single word, "Sarah," and stood tensed and ready as if he expected her to snap to attention, salute, and run toward him. She rushed out as quickly as she could without risking a fall in front of her new coworkers. Herman had been intense in the interview room, but she never imagined this was his day-to-day persona. He gave the host a curt nod, and led Sarah down the hall without acknowledging the three young men at the table.

Matching his long strides in two-inch heels was a challenge. If not for the short elevator ride and the pauses when he stopped to hold the doors open, she might have lost sight of him. She was winded when Herman disappeared into a small office behind the elevators. The room abounded with cherry-finished furniture that was new employee, first day clean. This office was hers. The bookcases, desktop, and even a small round table with two chairs looked new and shiny-smooth, ready for her to dig in. There was no window and the elevator would vibrate up and down all day, but this was her first walled office. The confidential nature of her work was the reason she had solid walls, but that didn't steal the pride she felt for her new surroundings. Coming to this small office would be a pleasure.

Herman motioned her to sit. He stood across the desk, his bald head and intense eyes even more menacing from three feet above.

"I know this is your first internal audit position," he said, "so I'm going to make the rules painfully clear. This is not a democracy and it's not the Wild West. We have unfettered access throughout the firm, but we do not intrude whenever it suits our fancy. Is that understood?"

Sarah could only nod.

"We have a plan." He picked up a thick blue binder from the table and thrust it at her. "Read this today and tonight. Follow it and you'll be successful. Stray from it and I'll be explaining to the audit committee why *I* failed to execute. I've never had that conversation and I don't expect to."

Sarah opened the binder and flipped for the table of contents.

"Stan Nye is your partner. He'll come by and show you around. Get comfortable. Tomorrow we'll get you into the flow."

Herman stepped back toward the door and hesitated there. "One more thing: nothing goes to the audit committee unless it goes through me – and I mean nothing. If you have a discussion with any member that goes beyond the weather and whatever you do outside this building, your ass will hit the pavement faster than you can say take me back to PFCC. Understand?"

"Completely."

Herman left her with the binder and a roomful of empty furniture.

Halfway through the table of contents, she stopped and stared at the page. Herman was not at all what she expected. She had yearned for the comfort of working in the same place each day. She assumed she'd still have the latitude to do things her way. As a consulting manager, she was turned loose for months at a time with a few goals and an introduction to her customer contact. Maybe working for a company meant they cared more about what you actually did, rather than focus on the fees. She hoped

Herman's speech was first-day posturing and that he'd lighten up when he got to know her, but deep down she felt a bit rattled. She opened the binder and read to crowd the worry from her thoughts. The crisp pages described an investigation of human resources and accounts payable practices in excruciatingly mundane detail.

A chirping sound from the hall broke her trance on the book. A head of thick dark hair extended inward horizontally from the door casing, followed by bushy eyebrows, a generous nose, and a puckered face that continued to chirp as he scanned her expression from several feet away. She couldn't imagine why the office crazy had chosen her doorway for his roost.

He stepped inside, short, stocky, smiling now that his chirping was done. He introduced himself as Stan Nye, her partner, the only other person who worked for Herman. The contrast from Herman to Stan was astounding. If he could survive here, certainly she could, too.

"Boy, not much going on here. Let's take a spin. I'll show you who's who and what's what." This was the welcome she expected from Herman.

On the ride to the twenty-third floor, Stan summed up working for Herman simply. "Do what he tells you, keep quiet, and life is grand."

If his meandering pace and his advice were any indication, Herman's requirements for Stan weren't terribly stringent.

Technically there weren't any places they couldn't go, but Stan lowered his voice as they passed the boardroom where Sarah had started her workday. He marched down the mahogany hall past rows of sharp, efficient-looking assistants and pointed out Herman's closed door. His crisp steps said what he did not. Stan was intimidated up here among the executives so much so that he forced himself to walk professionally, a vast improvement over his earlier bird impression.

The wide rectangular hallway paralleled the perimeter of the building. He pointed out Marty Finch, the company CEO, and indicated a large area of offices for the money managers. Their offices were less ornate than Marty Finch's, but even their assistants had better views than Sarah.

At the corner, Stan unceremoniously slipped into the stairwell and descended to the floor below.

Stepping out onto the twenty-second floor, Stan relaxed. He let himself into the computer room and showed her around the rows of glass paneled cabinets. He couldn't tell her what the machines behind the glass did exactly, but he was proud that he could slide his card in the reader and walk inside whenever he wanted to. The cramped room next door was full of wires and one single computer. Stan bragged that only four people had keys to get in. Sarah would be the fifth when she earned Herman's trust.

Back in the hall, she wondered how reliable Stan could possibly be.

Stan pointed out Brad Foster, who was glad to stop and chat about the accomplishments in IT. She pegged him for a decent guy, but when they were out of earshot Stan told her that everyone hated Brad with the possible exception of Marty, his CEO brother-in-law. Next they visited Erica Fletcher, who seemed tense and high-strung. She gave a genuine smile, but was either too busy or too arrogant to take a minute and say hello. Stan couldn't have been more positive about Erica as they headed for the elevator. Sarah wondered if his admiration and her arrogant attitude both stemmed from the elegant lines of her face and her perfect smile.

The next three floors blended together. The noise level grew subtly with each floor they descended until they stood on the nineteenth floor in the middle of a long strip of gray cubicles that made up client services. People talked everywhere you looked. It was one constant blabbering, yammering of voices, each one clear if you stood nearby, but trailing off into a jumble of noise as you moved away.

Sarah had made a solemn promise to herself the night before not to get involved with another man at work. Dating coworkers at her last job had been catastrophic. The isolation of a traveling project team worked wonders for productivity, since there wasn't much else to do alone in a strange city. Playing with company men was a hazard she was warned about early on, but it became a bit too convenient. One short-lived road romance led to numerous invitations for more, some legitimate and some that begged the utmost discretion.

Here, on her first day, she'd already met a man who could make her break that promise. Gregg Turner was different. He had a solid hunky physique like many of the consultants she worked alongside, but Gregg's job demanded compassion. He solved customer problems and coached fresh college graduates through their first professional years. He was part babysitter, part kindergarten teacher, part mountain man. They shook hands outside the cubicle of a customer service person, a kid with a headset who looked nineteen. He and Stan both admired Gregg reverently.

Sarah wanted to learn more.

The intersection of their work lay in a file drawer of customer complaints. Stan admitted he hadn't researched anything in that drawer in the eight years he'd been at BFS. It was tricky business. Angry customers had to be called and Stan had little taste for that. Surely some of the complaints were founded and she wondered what had been done with those. An investigation would get her closer to Gregg and possibly win her favor with Herman. Glad for the help, Gregg made a copy of the latest complaint letter. The drawer held hundreds more that had been researched and responded to. This one drawer held more promise than anything in Herman's plan about human resources and accounts payable and there was enough work to keep her within sight of Gregg for the next three months.

Chapter 12

Brad grunted as he locked out two forty-five. He let out a whoosh and eased it down for another rep. The dweeby guy in the corner with the pot belly and receding hairline was struggling with a lat pull-down of forty-five pounds. He was as much a total joke as his trainer was smoking hot. Five-ten with long legs and an ass only a teenager or an aerobics instructor could maintain. The whole package was wrapped so tight in spandex she'd hold Brad's attention over anything else that walked in. She urged the middle-aged guy on as if managing forty-five pounds was some sort of accomplishment. The real accomplishment was paying attention to this guy long enough to earn her fee.

In the other corner a muscle-head was curling sixty-five pounds with one hand, as intent on the bicep in the mirror as he was on curling the weight. Footsteps droned on a treadmill in the next room broken by a CNN newscast that had repeated the same stories for about the fifth time since Brad arrived. He pressed the weight up and rested it on the holder, his eyes locked on the spandex-clad buns in the mirror.

A figure in sharply-creased blue pants blocked his line of sight.

"Impressive. That's gotta be over two hundred."

"Yeah. Two forty-five." Brad sat up and faced Ray from accounting, a pretty solid guy, but dry and more than a little uptight.

"Amazing what you can do when you're down here all day."

"Hey, the clock never stops in IT."

"Apparently there's a substantial pause between twelve and two."

Brad grabbed a worn white hand towel and dabbed his face to hide a chuckle. He sprayed a fine mist from the water bottle and wiped off the bench as if that might remove twenty minutes of heavy sweat from the black cushion. "Say what you want, but when you bean counters run home for dinner we're just getting going."

Brad slid off the weights one by one and replaced them on their holders. Ray watched. "What's the good word upstairs? You guys still hacking my budget?"

Ray's face tensed. Why did mention of the budget process make him nervous? He was the one who spent his time uncovering the boondoggles and trying to kill everyone's pet projects. "Computers are kind of important in the mutual fund business," Brad said.

"Hysterical. You and those guys in investment management and their six-figure software packages are going to spend us out of existence."

"Not likely."

"If my brother were CEO, I wouldn't worry either. The rest of us are a bit closer to the layoff line."

Brad replaced the last of the weights and led Ray toward the locker room. "We haven't had a layoff in sixty-two years and we're not going to start. Don't go around scaring people. It's not healthy."

Ray trailed silently along the cinderblock hall. He said nothing even after they entered the rows of lockers, likely out of fear that someone might overhear. Brad's relationship with Marty sheltered him from the scrutiny Ray feared. He performed well, but he did things his way, unencumbered by policies he didn't like or didn't care to enforce. Ray had no such luxury; he had to play by the rules.

Ray retrieved a business card from his locker and headed back to work. Brad headed for the sauna.

Forty minutes later Brad reclined in his overstuffed leather chair facing the harbor. He disregarded an inbox full of messages and a slew of project status reports he'd been neglecting. Instead he watched a series of jets land two minutes apart. Staring out the window he imagined the country farmhouse he'd tear down and the life he'd build when this was finished. The time was coming soon and sadly, Brad would be making the trip alone.

The phone rang. Brad instinctively punched the button. "Brad Foster."

The metallic voice squawked a single word, "Speaker."

Brad hopped from his chair, breezed across the room and closed the door. Returning to his desk, he hesitated for a breath before picking up the phone. When the receiver touched his ear, the voice blared.

"Where have you been? Marty can't fire you, but you could at least pretend to care about your job."

"That's none of your damn business," Brad retorted.

"Careful, Tough Guy. Everything about you is my business. I own you. You screw up, you expose this thing before I'm ready and the world will crash down around you in a heartbeat. The package is always ready."

The shiny briefcase left inside his apartment had changed his life. The shock that someone could slip inside and leave without a trace was disquieting, but that was nothing compared to what the case held. The contents still had Brad terrified two years later. The recordings were made when Brad was just beginning to trust his new friend. Brad took a few hot stock tips. He sold Worldcom short and made a killing then did the same with Tyco. He was on top of the world until he listened to himself being told these companies were in trouble with the SEC by a voice he didn't recognize. The tapes were dubbed, but sounded so authentic Brad couldn't tell what he'd said and what had been clipped together. From then on he listened to unabashed demands and did what he was told. For three years the commands from his demonic partner had become increasingly forceful and the burning in his stomach had become decidedly more intense.

"That's better. Now, how did we do last night?"

"The market's been quiet. I'm waiting for a swing."

"What? You need to run this thing every night. And you need to turn it up. Get on it," the voice said.

"If the market's flat it's not worth the time." Brad was thinking risk.

"This thing needs to be grabbing anything it can. This isn't the time to be shy. Speaking of time - how's our friend? Plenty stressed I hope."

"My maneuver on Sunday cost her a day. She's frantic. I can't believe she hasn't gone screaming to HR."

"Keep her distracted. Tired angry women don't make good decisions. That'll be important when you get back."

"Nothing to do but wait. I don't see how she's going to make it, but if she does, she won't have an ounce of energy left."

What would happen if Erica failed? The ramifications would surely hit him, but how hard?

"Have you met the new auditor yet? I hear she's a real stickler. Wouldn't want her investigating me," the voice said.

"I'll leave that to you."

"She's a bulldog. When she gets a sniff of what's going on, she'll never let it go. Just don't go propositioning her and everything'll be ok."

She was a bit chunky for Brad's taste. He preferred a woman who enjoyed the gym as much as he did, though his lack of recent success had loosened his standards. He didn't feel guilty or embarrassed about his woman chasing or the results, but the jab stung. Each barked order, each insult he bore and every retort he swallowed built a hunger to get even.

He'd take care of that when the financial matters were settled.

For now he'd do as he was told.

Chapter 13

The book popped shut abruptly and mom kissed the top of Erica's head to make amends for interrupting the story midway. She patted the quilt smooth and stood up in response to something Erica asked. Strangely, Erica couldn't hear the request now. She could only watch as mom nervously glanced toward the front window twice, afraid of something out there. Erica couldn't see anything beyond the glass and she couldn't hear anything at all, inside or out. Mom turned in place scanning the tiny room. She was torn between whatever was at the window and whatever she had lost. Not finding it she flashed a final look toward the window and rushed for the hall.

Erica wanted to tell her to forget whatever it was. She didn't need to bother. Erica was a big girl and she could take care of herself. Mom disappeared down the stairs and instantly she was back with Mr. Purple Bunny. She slipped him under the covers and tucked the quilt right up to his chin. He was warmer that way and just having him there made Erica feel safe. Nothing could hurt her if Mr. Purple Bunny was there next to her.

Mom held a finger to her lips, asking, no, begging for Erica be quiet.

Then mom was gone.

Erica felt her father's angry screams downstairs. She hid under the covers, her warm breath nearly suffocating Mr. Purple Bunny. She remembered creeping to the stairs, listening. Any scary sound would have sent her scampering back to bed or maybe to the closet where she often hid among the shoes and clothes. She found herself on the stairs where she heard nothing then or now. She slid down the stairs one by one. Her bum thumped each carpeted tread. She stopped on each one, listening, and exploring the reaches of the living room and the kitchen that had just come into view. Thump, another foot closer.

Now she stood frozen in the middle of the living room, her feet rooted to the floor through the plastic soles of her feety pajamas. Mom kneeled on the kitchen floor rocking with huge silent sobs. One side of her face was red and puffy, and her shirt hung open for lack of buttons. They'd been neatly fastened when she was in Erica's room. She wondered where they went.

Father lay sprawled on the floor, the red pool around his head growing and growing. Mom looked at Erica and in that second she understood they were free. Erica's heart raced with the remembered terror of the police taking her mother from her, leaving her alone with the couple next door. She gasped, but could not breathe.

She gasped again and bolted upright. The dark outline of her computer confronted her. The fabric walls of the cubicle across the way were lit by the dim security lights. Time and place settled over her, comforting in spite of the pressure of a looming implementation deadline.

She hadn't had this dream for years. Karate lessons, hours of extra homework and an unwavering commitment to her career had guaranteed she'd never end up like her mother. So why did the dream come back now? She could still see the yellow-striped wall paper and the bright-colored polka dots. The scene was real, but Erica had escaped this fate. It was behind her. Now, in the middle of the night she was defined by her escape. She'd poured herself into her work and excelled beyond even her own expectations. She'd jumped over, around or through every obstacle the men had thrown up in front of her, defying any attempt to hold her back. She needed no one. She was free, but so much of her life played out isolated in this sterile room, safe from the dangerous tangle of relationships outside.

A door closed down the hall. Erica checked the time. 11:46 P.M.

She crept to the door and peered into the darkness. She didn't understand why she was afraid. She'd always felt safe here, but not on this night. Maybe it was leftover energy from her dream. She went back to her computer and printed something down the hall, an excuse to roam around.

Chapter 14

Sitting here during the first few runs with the numbers flashing on the screen, Brad had been so terrified he couldn't enjoy the massive accumulation of wealth. He thought the fear would eventually subside, but instead his nervousness spread to the rest of his waking hours and even his dreams, thanks to the manufactured evidence that had arrived on his doorstep. The feds were hot to prosecute insider trading and the audio tapes would give them more than enough to put him away. He was powerless to refuse any request now, no matter how absurd or how dangerous. Demoralized, he sat in the cold room, forced to be on guard, forced to satisfy another man's greed.

Collecting six million in a week was impossible even if he came here every night, but the boss refused to listen. Crossing him meant going to jail, so Brad would do what he was told until the scheme came to a close. He needed the boss to pin this on Erica. It wasn't a perfect plan, but Brad hadn't come up with anything better in three years of ruminating. She'd go to jail and he'd resign in disgrace for letting it happen. Sharon and Marty would never look at him the same, but his only alternative was to run and never come back. If he did that, they'd never look at him at all.

Columns of changes whizzed by too fast to read.

One day Erica would understand Brad's machinations were more than the random thrashings of an egomaniacal, bully boss. Left alone she would have connected his late night computer room visits to the seemingly inexplicable problems in client services. He gave her twice the workload of his best developer and added as much pressure as possible. She had no time for anything but the project at hand. She hadn't discovered his motives and she was running out of time. Soon there'd be an investigation and it'd be pointed directly at her. Hopefully, she'd put it all together right before she was hauled away in cuffs. She'd go squirming, knowing what happened, but she'd be unable to fight back.

Did taking delight in her sorrow make him evil? Not delight, it was self-preservation. Her naïve prying threatened to expose him. Discovery meant going to jail, losing his job, and being forever separated from the only family he had left. Sharon had been a domineering older sister; the only parent he'd known since he was 13. He wouldn't risk losing his last link to the family, not for Erica, not for anyone.

Even if things went well, Sharon would blame him for the damage to her husband's company, another huge disappointment from her little brother. She wouldn't offer him another job and he wouldn't want one. Another thread between them would be severed, leaving their relationship more tenuous than ever, but she'd still take his calls and she'd still read his Christmas cards. Maybe that was enough.

Brad was destined to be alone.

He forced himself to focus on the numbers to push away the image of a long solitary life. The empty hole in his chest grew until the numbers stopped and gave him something else to concentrate on. Two hundred fifty-one thousand, not his best, but not a flop either. He needed a gigantic swing in the market. That or he'd have to make big changes, risky changes that wouldn't go unnoticed.

No time for that now. Time to cover his tracks.

After hundreds of repetitions the procedure was second nature. In moments, the program was deleted, the CD was in his bag, and the server desktop looked exactly as it had when he arrived. He slipped down the row of glass-fronted cabinets and eased around the corner to where he could get a view over the cubicles outside. A blast of frigid air sent a chill up his leg, but he didn't step off the vented tile. Her office was dark. Surprising she'd be gone before midnight with her deadline looming. Maybe she'd given up.

CJ West

Emboldened he stepped through the glass doors. A few steps down the hall he slipped the key into the security room door and disappeared inside.

The console came to life. With a few taps he knew she hadn't opened a door since four o'clock. She usually went for dinner around six, but there was no entry for her return. There were scarcely any others in that time, no one to let her tailgate through security. Strange. He left the record as it was with her entry into the computer room at 10:04 P.M. and an exit at 11:40 P.M. He switched the video tape with a blank from his bag and left.

He froze one step into the hall.

Her light was on. The printer whirred. Footsteps padded on the other side of the cubicles. Brad couldn't breathe. She knew. She had to. Why else would she wait for him to finish then turn on her light? If she was logged into the same system she could have collected every change he'd just made. No one could help him if she did.

His eyes turned toward the elevator. His body wanted to run, get in the elevator and never come back, but his shoes remained still, three feet outside the security room door. His eyes darted for escape routes.

Brad reminded himself of his authority over everyone and everything on this floor. Slowly, tentatively, he headed for his office. His knees refused to bend; his facial muscles hardened in an expression of shock. He rounded the cubicles. There she was taking up pages that spewed from the Laserjet. She had her own printer. She didn't come here to print. She was here to collect proof, to see for herself who was running the program.

How could he get enough to satisfy the boss now? How could he do this the next five nights with her watching? Irritating that many customers would send a shock wave through client services. The rumblings would head directly to her. She'd echo their outrage for all to hear, her voice booming to Marty, the auditors, the feds. Brad was caught between the uncompromising thief and the brilliant rookie. One of them would be his undoing.

Erica sensed his fear immediately. "Working pretty late for someone who's taken two-thirds of my team," she snipped.

Brad slowed as he reached her, but didn't stop. "You're not the only one who works hard around here."

"Apparently not."

He walked past, his eyes straight ahead, his face neutral, his walk slow. He could feel her watching, but didn't look back. He waited thirty minutes in a chair by the door, listening to every movement in the hall. The evidence in his bag was irrefutable. He didn't dare return the CD to its hiding place. He couldn't give her another chance to get her hands on it. It was time to go.

Back at his apartment he pulled the leather bag from his closet. Two changes of clothes, the mini cassettes, his passport and enough cash to get him anywhere in the world, all ready in an instant. He added the video tape and the CD and called a cab. He'd feel safer at the airport. He'd wait there for the next plane to France no matter how long it took.

The cab picked him up on Devonshire and zipped off through empty streets. The Corvette would sit idle until the landlord worked through the eviction process. Could they sell his abandoned belongings to pay the rent? He couldn't give them away. Sharon would scoff at his things and he could think of no one else to give them to. He'd miss the Corvette and he couldn't risk buying another. He'd find another fast car to fall in love with.

The cab swerved to a stop in the tunnel. A black SUV blocked the road ahead. Brad hadn't seen it until the cabbie slammed on his brakes. The men were out in an instant and running toward them. They surrounded the cab. The fat muzzle of a handgun tapped the driver's window. The driver could have thrown the cab into reverse, but he was too frightened to resist. He raised his hands and remained completely still. The back passenger's door flung open. One of the men grabbed Brad's bag and motioned him out. Brad didn't move. This wasn't a robbery. They were here for him.

The cabbie lowered the front window and the man outside talked deep and easy. No mistake in what he wanted or the consequences of disobedience. He asked for a driver's license and the cabbie complied with a trembling hand.

"Our friend will ride with us."

The man pointed his gun at the radio. "Don't even think about calling this in. Everything will be fine. Our friend's just a little confused about where he's supposed to be right now."

Brad wasn't going to make it to the airport.

No one had stopped behind them. Not a soul on the road to help. With men on both sides of the cab he wouldn't make thirty yards on foot.

The man up front was still talking to the driver.

"We'll be monitoring your frequency. Call this in and we'll visit your nice little house on Agawam Road. It won't be tomorrow or next week, but we'll come. You have kids?"

The driver swore he wouldn't call the cops. No one would know Brad was gone until his body turned up on a garbage barge.

"Out Foster!" the man at the back door yelled.

The gun came out of his jacket or his pants. The barrel pressed into his ribs forcing him toward the back of the SUV. Brad climbed in and they sped off. They burst out of the tunnel and weaved through narrow streets. Soon Brad was lost. Both men were eerily calm. They'd kidnapped him in the ideal spot between his apartment and the airport as routinely as he ordered coffee. Amazing since he'd only decided to run forty minutes ago.

"Scared the shit out of you, didn't she?"

They couldn't mean Erica. How could they know?

"Don't worry. She doesn't know what she saw."

The car headed downtown.

"Don't believe us? Listen, what do you think we do all day?"

Brad hadn't known these guys existed. The guy in back looked like someone he'd passed on the street a thousand times. Maybe he was.

"We listen to you and Fletcher and a few others. We skip the boring stuff, but we hear pretty much everything you say."

If they were telling the truth, getting around them was going to be tough, but they couldn't know everything. He spent his days in dozens of different places. They couldn't bug them all.

"You're not going to bully me. I'm not going to jail for you."

"That's right. You're not going to jail. You're going to do what you're told and we'll all come out of this rich."

"I'm done. I'm out. I can't go back."

The driver spoke for the first time. "Don't be stupid. You say that to the boss and we'll be dumping your carcass in an alley in Chelsea."

"It's over."

"It's not over. Everything's fine. She's a zombie. If she makes it through next week, she'll go home and sleep for four days."

"You don't know that."

"Brad, listen, the last time you had sex was six weeks ago. She had long straight hair and red lingerie. She was incredible, but you got her so drunk I bet she had the nastiest hangover of her life. No wonder she never called back. Now, the blonde in the pink Red Sox hat last Saturday, wow! She was hot. A little young for you maybe. She had her eye on some guy across the bar. Too bad, I was looking forward to seeing her naked."

"What's your point?"

"We know even more about Fletcher. She's nothing to worry about."

They pulled to a stop on Devonshire. All three men got out.

Brad took back his bag feeling lucky they hadn't looked inside.

A fist to the kidney from nowhere dropped him to his knees. Before he knew what happened they hauled him up and had both hands clasped behind his back. The guy behind him hadn't looked that big, but Brad couldn't break his grip. The other guy punched away at his ribs, punishing him in a place that would never show.

"That's for making us chase you. That's about enough of that bullshit. Do your job and stop whining."

They left him flat on the curb, tires squealing away. He dragged himself upstairs and started hunting for microphones and miniature cameras.

Chapter 15

Erica slipped into class fifteen minutes early and took the best seat in the room. Up in back against the wall she plugged her laptop into the only power outlet within reach of the student desks. Paying her own way instilled a drive to get her money's worth that was uncommon in her fellow students. She devoured newfound knowledge like a starving animal, but this last course she'd taken solely for credit. She needed three to complete her master's degree and didn't have the time or energy to put into something new. Erica programmed .Net twelve hours a day, six days a week. The professor couldn't teach her anything she didn't already know.

She still couldn't believe she'd abandoned the team to come here. Not that their work would come to a halt when she left. It was more a statement of solidarity, eeking out every last minute before go-live on Monday. Everyone was putting their life aside for the next four days and she'd come simply to show her face and placate Dr. Eisenstein. Two hours of email and bug list review weren't a total loss, but working through class couldn't assuage her guilt.

The stirring in the aisles didn't distract Erica from her laptop as students dotted the middle rows of the classroom. She expected more competition for the back, but for the uninitiated .Net could be difficult. The muddy explanations from the windbag up front made mastering the language an even greater feat. Eisenstein and his comrades were the only link these kids had to the technology. Without him, they'd be sunk. Even so, he had to threaten deductions for poor attendance to fill the seats.

"Hey, I thought you dropped out."

Erica turned toward a blue tie adorned with white marble columns and fountains. Jim slipped into the seat beside hers and gave a broad smile. She'd come to this class three times and all three times he'd sat next to her. Jim didn't look any older than the kids in T-shirts and torn jeans, but he was comfortable in his dark suit. There were half a dozen professionals in class, some lucky enough to have a company sharing the cost.

"This stuff comes easier to some of us," she said. "Maybe you should sit closer so you don't miss anything."

"I like the view back here."

Why did she attract unattached guys everywhere she went? She wasn't advertising. Two women sat together on the opposite side of the room. Their tight jeans and clingy tops showed more than Erica revealed at the beach, hence every seat around them was occupied. Even in the baggy pantsuits she wore for work, guys like Jim sidled up to her whenever she stayed in one place too long. She guessed that's just what guys did.

A wispy haired man shuffled across the front of the class to the lectern. From there he focused a pair of beady eyes up through the ranks of seats, prompting a flurry of books opening. Conversations ceased. He noted who came and who didn't. He was one of the few inane professors who graded homework. Eisenstein touted his final project as the pinnacle of their educational experience. Students would develop a web-based system and the projects would be graded ruthlessly, but he guaranteed that any student who received an 'A' on the final project would get an 'A' for the course. This one criterion kept the students nervous and attentive except for Erica. Her final project had been done for weeks, much of it modeled on her current client services project. She'd present a series of active pages that utilized sixteen SQL tables, a dozen forms, and provide the stringent security appropriate for a money management firm. This all but freed her from Dr. Eisenstein. Why she had come tonight, she wasn't sure.

The clack of the door latch drew every eye in the room to a young woman sheepishly slipping in toward the back. Her eyes found Erica then she made her way along the back row and parked behind her.

Erica whispered a hello to Kate and went back to days of unread email.

Eisenstein droned about the rampant abuses of proper style in the homework. He overemphasized the need for form and documentation to the point of absurdity. If he'd worked two days in industry he'd know that descriptive object and subroutine names and an observance of good structure made most code readable to a professional. The documentation he prattled on about was only necessary for peculiarities.

The room fell strangely quiet. Erica looked up from her laptop. Eisenstein stared directly at her from the front row. The entire class craned backward for a look.

"Hello, Miss Fletcher. You come so infrequently I wouldn't remember you had our previous exchanges not been so colorful. Are you going to surf the Internet for the entire lecture or will you be tuning in occasionally?"

"I'm an excellent multi-tasker."

"We've noticed. So would you mind answering a simple question?"

"Shoot." She nearly returned to the email she was reading while he asked his question, but thought better of it.

"It seems you missed our discussion of object inheritance last week. I assume you've done the reading. Could you tell me when you might use classes to define custom objects and when it would make sense to use inheritance from those objects."

Eisenstein assumed a confident pose waiting for her to fumble and then beg forgiveness. He stood ready to explain what she could not.

Erica grinned. "Have we covered classes? Is everyone comfortable with what classes are and why they're used?" Not one of the students nodded.

"If you were here more often you'd know," Eisenstein said.

"I'm quite comfortable with classes and inheritance."

"Do tell."

"We use classes to define objects that we use over and over. In a production shop, you'll have pre-defined classes that apply to your specific vertical industry. You won't define these as a rookie programmer. Someone will hand you a listing that will guide you through what all the objects are."

Eisenstein was steamed that she addressed her response to the class rather than to him.

"I work in financial services, so we have classes that apply to all sorts of financial objects. A mutual fund is a good example. We have an object called fund that carries certain basic information like the inception date, manager's name, etcetera. We use inheritance to push these common attributes to various types of funds: stock funds, bond funds, index funds, what-have-you. Each different type of fund needs different types of information stored, but they all have the same basic information from the fund class. The benefit of inheritance is this: say we hire a new fund manager and his name is Thurston Montgomery-Wadsworth and our fund manager name is only twenty characters long. Because we used inheritance, we change the fund object and the change propagates down through all the various types of fund objects that derive from fund.

"That's how we use inheritance. Is that what you were looking for, Professor?"

Eisenstein didn't even look in her direction. He wandered behind the podium and said, "So it seems even Miss Fletcher is clear on custom classes and inheritance and that means it's time to move forward."

At least half the class looked at each other hoping someone would speak up, but no one did. Eisenstein didn't volunteer to elaborate, probably out of fear Erica would correct him from the back of the room. Instead he launched into a discussion about connecting to SQL databases to retrieve information and display it on a web page. Erica went back to work undisturbed for the remainder of the two hour lecture.

Chapter 16

Sarah sat alone in the conference room on twenty-one, waiting for Stan to meander in and for Herman to come down from twenty-three. Herman invariably arrived twenty minutes late, according to Stan, and they were expected to be ready and waiting. Eleven minutes before two and all seventy-two pages of the blue binder sat in front of Sarah, like a weight dragging her away from the work that held her future. Investigating the letters would bring her and Gregg together. She'd been plotting ways to get his attention though she'd promised herself she wouldn't let it get physical anytime soon. It was more than Gregg. Every one of those letters held a story of something gone wrong at BFS, something she could fix. Since childhood she'd been the family soother, mediator, relationship fixer. This was the work she was born for.

The binder held little promise of fixing anything.

The plan described a most excruciatingly detailed work effort that would take the entire year to finish. Following it would earn Herman his bonus, but accomplish little else.

Stan burst into the room dramatically, "dunt, dunt, dunt-dunt-dunt-dunt." The tune was unfamiliar.

These outbursts relegated them to windowless offices on twenty-one, while Herman sat on twenty-three with the execs. What kind of idiot was he? She didn't want anyone speaking of her and Stan in the same breath. She planned to move up in BFS and that meant breaking away from Stan Nye. The further, the faster, the better.

"C'mon. You know where that's from. I know you do."

"No idea."

"You're kidding! Rat Patrol. Desert GIs fighting the Germans. The fifty caliber mounted on the jeep." Stan held out his fists, jerking them back and forth a few inches as he spun in place firing at some imaginary foe. "A true classic. Come on. The sand blowing off the dunes and the jeep in mid-air." Stan noticed the binder on the table. "You spend too much time reading crap like that. It's rotting your brain."

"Have you read it?"

"Bits and pieces. I can only take it in small doses."

Stan swiveled a chair and sat across from Sarah with only a blank notepad and a single pencil. How could he come to a status meeting without a printed report? Would Herman tolerate such a waste of his time? He certainly disregarded theirs, but this couldn't be acceptable in a company like BFS. Stan began scribbling notes as if he sensed her displeasure with his lack of preparation.

At 2:08 P.M. Herman was still nowhere in sight. Stan had almost finished scribbling a high school caliber status report. BFS was nothing like PFCC.

She wanted to ask Stan what he thought of the binder and the work he was doing, but why? Stan was along for the ride, doing the minimum to collect his check. His opinion would be random and juvenile. Why distract him from hacking together his last minute notes? He was trying to appear more than marginal, futile as that effort was.

Sarah ignored Stan and reflected on Herman's lecture about working the plan. Getting permission to investigate the letters was going to be difficult. Touting her idea so soon meant belittling his objectives and Herman wasn't the participative management type. He wasn't looking for the best way to manage the team. He valued discipline above all.

Herman tromped in, whipped the door shut, and took a seat at the head of the table. He carried the blue binder and a stack of battered manila folders, presumably needed as he stomped from meeting to meeting intimidating various people around the company. He pulled one particular file and pushed the others to the corner of the table. He focused on her coldly, not angrily, but an emotionless measurement that said he'd make his decisions based on the facts. He'd promote her or terminate her and feel nothing. He didn't care which way it went.

"Glad you're still with us," he said to Sarah then turned to Stan. "Prepared like never before I see, Stanley. She's rubbing off on you."

The reprimand had no effect. Utterly unprepared and with little skill or enthusiasm for auditing, Stan looked squarely at his hulking boss without a hint of fear for the man others cowered from.

"Always," Stan said. "After eight years, if someone even thinks the word embezzlement, I'm on 'em." The excited tone could have been pulled from a 70's TV show where the enthusiastic rookie overestimates his ability and sails headlong into trouble. So fitting for Stan.

"Well Mr. Excitement, I wouldn't be so glib if I were you. If Miss Burke here finds something you've missed, you'll find your ass in a sling."

"Roger that ten-ninety-one control. If she finds something I'll be the first to issue the code twenty."

Stan got stranger every minute and Herman didn't look the least bit surprised. Sarah couldn't tell if he understood the gibberish or if he was avoiding being drawn into Stan's adolescent banter.

Herman grinned. "Stan spent his childhood watching Adam-12. He knows every code they used on the radio and he enjoys showing off something he knows that we don't. At least it proves he can learn with prolonged exposure."

"A good sign," Sarah said, refreshed by Herman's professionalism.

"I tried confusing him with military jargon and call signs, but that just encouraged him."

"Were you a pilot?"

"No. Army logistics."

Logistics sounded about as exciting as accounting and probably about as dangerous. Herman tired of small talk. "Ok, Stan. Tell me where you are and we can get back to work."

Stan barely glanced at the paper in front of him, "I'm ready to sign off on fifty vendors."

"Fifty? It's nearly May, Stanley."

"I've got packets out to the rest, but the follow-ups are dragging."

"Stan, the AP vendors are a forth of the plan. At this rate you won't be done until September. How are we going to finish if you can't get the vendors done by June?"

"I didn't write the plan, Boss. I just follow orders."

"Good thing Sarah's on board. At least now we've got a chance."

"Good thinking, Captain. Maybe she can fix the transporter beam while she's at it."

Herman turned away flabbergasted. "Sarah, I'm going to put you on payroll verification." He waited for a nod, but this was not a time to object. "I want you to check every employee on file. I want to know they exist for sure. Shake their hands, you understand?"

"Shake every hand. Right." How hard can that be, she thought.

"I mean every single one. Audit their hours and document which people are working their fair share and which aren't. I'm not looking for an extra fifteen minute break. I'm looking for extra weeks of vacation, people not showing up, that sort of thing. The security system on twenty-two should be a big help."

Sarah nodded half-heartedly.

"What? You have a problem with payroll?"

"No, Sir."

"C'mon spit it out."

"We're working hard to track down money leaving the firm."

"Embezzlement usually involves taking money from the firm. Computers, desks, stuff like that, they get noticed."

"But we aren't doing anything for client services or investments."

"You think we should pay more attention there?"

"Right."

"We did extensive work on client services controls last year. This year they're in the middle of a major systems implementation. Imagine the chaos down there with us and the IT guys crawling all over the place. Nothing would get done. Good thinking, but we'll give them a pass this year and hit them next year when they're more comfortable with their new system."

The explanation restored some respect for Herman's plan and his coordination with the rest of the company, but she needed to see those letters. If something was wrong at BFS, the answer was in the complaint file. She couldn't let it go.

Sarah hesitantly slipped the letter from the binder and angled it toward Herman. He knew by her reluctance that she was looking for permission to step outside the box. He didn't look pleased.

"What's this?"

"A complaint letter from client services. There are dozens more."

"Probably nothing."

"What if it isn't?"

"We screw up sometimes. Legitimate complaints get attention. The customer screams and we pay them for their loss. When that happens, you can be sure we investigate."

"Who? Stan?" she scoffed.

Herman scowled and for a second Sarah wished she'd kept her attitude in check. "Whoever's closest to the problem digs in."

She couldn't help herself, "Are they equipped to handle stuff like this?"

Herman picked up the letter. The aggravated look said she'd done enough pushing for her first week on the job.

He locked eyes with her when he was done.

"So you found a crusade already?"

"If you let me follow through on this, I've got a chance to uncover a real problem." She felt like a child begging for chocolate cake.

"Rather than follow the plan and muck through pay stubs."

"I didn't say that."

"You didn't have to. You're not going to go dig through one letter. That's not a program, that's a witch hunt. Nothing good can come of it. If you find something, it looks like Stan's missing problems left and right. If you don't, it's time we can't account for. Either way I lose."

Sarah took a deep breath to protest, but Herman stopped her.

"If you're doing this, you're going back to January one and I'm holding you personally responsible for us meeting plan. We miss plan, it's on you. I'll add your little adventure to the plan and you get yourself in gear."

Herman reaffirmed the meeting for the same time next week, stood and left almost before she realized she'd gotten what she wanted. It didn't feel like victory. She'd been tricked into working doubly hard. Herman positioned himself to share the credit and linked her success to Stan's meager output. How could he have survived eight years? His only interest was for old TV shows. Herman, on the other hand, seemed able to outmaneuver her without really trying.

Auditing was going to be different than consulting and she'd have to adjust. If Stan was slow, she'd have to pick up the slack until she learned the rules. He'd made it this long. Herman had to know his limitations.

At least she had no worries about Herman tempting her into bed. The shaved head and the age difference would see to that. He was gruff and direct, but what he wanted was clear. If she finished the plan and he got his bonus, Herman would be a happy man.

Chapter 17

Gregg had been heartsick the last three hours. Too distracted to work, he stared at the papers on his desk and waited for the office to empty. At eight he climbed the concrete stairs to the twenty-first floor landing. He froze there, looking up at the final flight that led to Erica. No one would overhear the rejection that rolled off her lips; no one would see him drag himself downstairs, dejected once again. How would he console himself if she said no? The finality of this visit had him stuck. If she said no, he'd move on. He couldn't keep embarrassing himself, not after a third rejection.

Knowing how likely that rejection was made climbing the next step painfully difficult. He'd made a similar walk two years ago, encouraged by office mates who saw the chemistry as clearly as he did. The results were disastrous. She denied feeling anything and he couldn't understand why. He felt the spark anytime they were alone together. He could see it when their eyes met, but when he moved closer, she pushed away. Years later nothing had changed. He still got the same tired questions about their relationship and he was sickened every time he said they were good friends and nothing more. He changed when she was in the room and she did, too. Feelings flowed between them without words, without movement or expression. The distance she pushed between them might have made sense when they worked together in client services, but she was upstairs in IT now. It was time to move beyond the polite excuses about work and not ruining their friendship.

She dated other men, forceful men who didn't give up. Persistence earned them a few dates, but she took no pleasure in the meals and movies they shared. Even those truly enraptured quickly understood their pursuit would be fruitless. Gregg bided his time jealously watching each relationship bud then wither from neglect. Simon was the latest. Soon another would spring up to take his place and flowers would begin to arrive in the lobby. Gregg couldn't watch that again. He should have pushed his way into her life earlier. Would he have succeeded where the others failed? Or would he have slowly soured and given up? It was time to find out.

Why was she so afraid? She knew he was thinking long term. How many women would jump for a dependable guy who wanted to settle down and raise a family? Why did he fall for the one thirty-something who wanted to stay unattached indefinitely? It couldn't be true. He looked at her and saw a loving wife and mother. And *he* wasn't someone to fear. So what was holding her back? If he knew, he could persuade her to unleash her true feelings or at least admit she had them.

Gregg took a step up.

He recalled Melanie's words. "It's obvious she's got the hots for you. Just snap her out of denial and she's yours."

She was in denial. She wouldn't admit feeling anything but friendship. The energy between them had been welling up for the last four years behind hints and glances and Gregg was brimming full. She kept from simmering with a friendly smile and an unwavering focus on all things impersonal. One kiss would change that. When their lips touched, the pressure would be released and they'd be overwhelmed with irresistible passion. Even she couldn't deny it then. Getting to that point without endangering their friendship would be tricky, but it was time to take that risk.

He took the steps faster.

His hands reached out before him. In his mind's eye he wasn't in the stairwell, but her office. Erica had thrown her work and her inhibitions aside and admitted what Gregg had known since they met. He felt her body beneath him. Her warm lips pressed into his. She finally released her libido from the emotionless prison she kept it locked up in.

Gregg touched the door handle and the image faded. The promise of intoxicating bliss and the threat of humiliating rejection lay down the hall past the silent cubicles. He looped his way around to her office unsure which he'd find.

She focused on her work with angelic determination. Her head tilted toward him as he stopped outside her door, but her eyes remained on the screen as if it had hold of them. He pushed the door open and stepped inside.

"Hey." She smiled and relaxed back into her chair. "What are you doing up here so late?"

"I thought I'd make sure you're eating."

She knew this was a continuation of Melanie's dinner party, but feigned ignorance. "Eating's optional. I've only got two days left. Sunday we go with what we've got. Brad doesn't care how broken it is. But you know he'll blame me for every little issue that comes up."

He stepped further inside, angling for a way to get closer. The office was a disaster. Several feet of carpet and a cluttered desk lay between her and the only available seat. There was no room beside her to stand and chat. Unsure what to do next, he crossed then uncrossed his arms trying to look casual. With nowhere to sit or even lean close by he was stranded in the middle of the floor facing her over the two monitors. She smiled at his uneasiness and met his eyes with the unspoken question: why are you doing this again? He wondered why he'd chosen this place for his final try. Casually getting that kiss would be impossible here. She'd never let him get that close.

"So you're too busy to stop and eat?" he asked hopefully.

She nodded toward the empty pizza box on top of the trash can. "I walked to Ossimo a while ago."

"I'm a bit late then."

"Or really early. Can I take a rain-check?"

"Sure. How long will you be in work-yourself-to-death mode?"

"Until Monday then things get ugly."

"I can't believe you volunteered for this."

"It doesn't have to be this way. Brad's taken three people off my team in the last four months. Things were fine before that."

"He have a more important project?"

"Not that I know of. He's got them doing piddley crap. They think he's punishing them for something, but they have no idea what it could be. Some of them are starting to look for ways to get even."

"He has that effect on people." If Brad wasn't related to Marty, Gregg would have dropped him on the carpet in client services a week earlier.

"Be glad you don't work for him."

The tension was gone. They were chatting like they did over the cubicles when he first started at BFS. He longed for those days. The closeness was leading to something then. Now it was pushed down below the surface. Whenever he ventured toward romance she got nervous and deflected his advances with never ending banter about work. When he backed off, everything returned to normal. They were doomed to chats about work and weather and he wondered how long he could keep it up.

"So what about that rain-check?"

"Can we play it loose? Say Wednesday or Thursday depending on how things go."

Gregg said goodbye and walked away with something he never imagined he'd get. In his mind it was a date, but only next week would tell if she'd be anything more than cordial.

He'd been waiting a long time for this chance. Another handful of days would be a breeze.

Chapter 18

The hard wooden bench hurt her bum as she concentrated on the edges of her fancy black shoes. Mr. and Mrs. Ortiz had made her stop tapping because it made too much noise, so instead she brought her little shoes closer and closer together without touching, lining up the patterns carefully. She moved them closer and closer until they touched ever so lightly. When they did, she eased them apart a few inches and started again. Closer and closer. She had a napkin in her lap that she twisted. It dropped lots of little white pieces. When she brushed them off, they fell like lost snowflakes down to her little black shoes and then the marble floor. She wasn't allowed to go down there and pick them up.

She dreaded having to sit still on the bench so long. It was impossible to be quiet when mom was so close, but she did her best so she could talk to mom at the end. Just a few minutes after it was over, that's all she ever got, but it was worth all the sitting in the world. Purple Bunny would be glad to get a hug, too.

Tired of tapping and wringing her napkin, she stood up on the bench and looked at the faces. Usually there was someone who would smile and make faces to entertain her. Lots of people had pencils and pens today. They were writing things down, messy things mostly and she couldn't figure out the words. A few people smiled at her, but they kept looking at the people up front. No one wanted to play.

She turned and looked at the man in the blue suit. Mr. and Mrs. Ortiz said he was on our side. When the man at the other little table said bad things about mom, the man in the blue suit would stand up and shout. He talked softer than the others most of the time and he always sat right next to mom. Sometimes he went up front near the man in the robe who talked really loud. Sometimes he went to talk to the people in the little pen.

He was sitting with mom now.

The men at the other little table were sitting, too.

Everyone was waiting for something.

She turned back to the people behind her. There was a woman two rows back in a blue dress. She smiled for a second, but she, too, was interested in something up front. Standing on the bench, Erica blocked her view to the man in the robe who liked to talk loud and bang his hammer when he got mad. The woman just leaned to one side and looked around.

Bang. The hammer struck.

Erica turned around quick thinking the man banged his hammer because she wasn't supposed to stand on the bench. She was ready to say she was sorry, but the man wasn't looking at her at all.

Everyone started talking at once.

Cameras flashed and mom hugged the man in the blue suit. Mr. and Mrs. Ortiz picked her up and squeezed together for a big hug that would have squished Mr. Purple Bunny if he wasn't safe on the bench.

The hammer banged some more times and then mom turned around right toward Erica. She was smiling and pushing past lots of people who wanted to talk to her. She came right to the bench, reaching, reaching...

Erica woke with a start.

The only light came from a beach scene on her computer. The room was silent except for the hum of tiny computer fans. She felt drugged, groggy, and she could still feel herself reaching for her mother across the wooden bench. It was 4:00 A.M. Time to go home and get some sleep.

Erica reached for the phone and called a cab.

Chapter 19

Stan stopped a few feet short of Sarah's door and listened for her voice on the phone. She'd asked him down to compare notes, which meant her overactive sense of duty was driving her to take control. She needed to know he wasn't slacking. He needed to squash the rookie enthusiasm before Herman raised the bar ridiculously high. Stan had enjoyed free run of the company for the last eight years. No one knew what he did on any given day, no one cared, and that's the way he liked it. There were no criminals in this tiny company and Stan wouldn't expend unnecessary energy to prove it.

Sarah's office was quiet.

He stepped up to the door jam and burst around the corner. "All right lady, we got your 911 call. What's your emergency?" He looked under her guest table, tilting the chairs aside. "Your ex-boyfriend attacked you, you say? Where's the blood? What'd you do with him?" Stan got down on his knees, looked under her desk then leaped back to his feet.

She reeled back.

He thrust an imaginary microphone in her face. "He's in the basement, isn't he? Chopped him up, didn't you? Come on admit it. It'll be easier to tell the truth now. Don't make me work you over back at the station."

She stared back, embarrassed. Not a chuckle or a smile, just a confused look that said comedy didn't fit her neat professional world of spreadsheets and task lists. She was going to be a stick to deal with, a big stick.

"Nice interview technique. No wonder the vendors don't call back."

Stan took a seat from the guest table, spun it toward the desk, and sat. "Funny. Ever try nailing down two hundred vendors?"

"No. You?" she asked.

"Good one. Didn't think you had it in you."

"What's up with you, Stan? Everything about you says you hate this job. Why do it?"

"We've all got to work. Why not have some fun?"

"Was Herman kidding about the police thing? It doesn't fit."

"Believe it or not, I wanted to be a cop since I was a kid. I studied criminal justice and accounting. Thought I'd do financial investigations, you know insider trading, investment fraud, that sort of thing, but I could never get my foot in the door."

"So you're stuck here." She raked her fingers through her long hair.

Stan felt the weight of her brown eyes on him. Drawn to them, he quashed his reaction before she noticed. He forced his eyes to the empty bookshelf. She wasn't his type at all. Why couldn't he look without staring?

"It's not that different," she said.

"Yeah, minus the criminals, the jobs are exactly the same."

"Don't think about it that way. We've only got four hundred people to police, but our busts are big time. We're not handing out parking tickets and directing traffic. Anyone we catch is going to jail."

"You're all fired up because you're new. Give it three or four years without finding anything then tell me how important this job is."

"I've already found something."

"Get real. Do you have any idea how many of those letters we get. Some old geezer lost three hundred dollars. So what?" Stan stretched his lips over his teeth and began whistling his words. "Young Feller, I bought some of them dag nab mutual funds and then you made the market go down. You sneaky no-good-for-nothins. I want my money back or I'll sue blast you. That's what I'll do. I'll have you in court 'till Betsy runs dry."

Sarah smiled at the impression, but contained her laughter. "Those letters are telling us something's wrong. We have to listen."

"Things were fine without you begging for extra work. If you get lucky and find something I'll never hear the end of it."

"You finish your half of the plan, I'll finish mine."

"I know what Herman said. If we don't make it, it's your butt. If I were you, I'd be real nice. If not, I might start showing up late, know what I mean?" He gave her a sly come-sit-on-my-lap look. If she was offended she hid it well.

She fished the letter out of a folder and pushed it across the desk. Stan stood up and reached for it. The neck of her top hung forward and down and Stan spied something he hadn't considered in his new partner. Round firm breasts trimmed with black lace hung there shadowed but clearly visible as the letter slipped toward him. He reached for the page without moving his eyes. His hand found hers. He drew back thinking himself caught, bumped the stapler and made three fumbling grabs before securing the letter.

He noticed the long straight hair again. She reached to straighten the stapler giving Stan an even better view.

"Read that and tell me there's nothing wrong."

She looked curious that he was still standing. He sat.

He browsed the letter thinking about her move to the stapler and her overwhelming drive to get caught up in this minutia. She must be some sort of compulsive neurotic. When he finished half the letter he casually nudged the stapler off kilter an inch. He peeked over the letter, pretending to read as he watched. No longer aligned with the pictures and the tape dispenser, the stapler had her full attention. She held back a moment before carefully lining it up with the other accessories.

Stan restrained a guffaw behind the letter.

Working with Sarah was going to be more fun than he thought. He didn't quite understand why he promised to finish the vendors by June, but he did. He also volunteered to evaluate the employee review system, the more difficult of the two remaining projects, so Sarah could work on her complaint letters. Odd for Stan, he left her office eager to get back to his and dig in. The work hadn't changed and he wouldn't admit why his attitude had heaved about, not even to himself.

Chapter 20

At 7:02 A.M. Erica flipped the switch and lit up the vast expanse of client services cubicles. She wasn't making a statement by arriving first. She was truly nervous. Fifty people were about to start using a system that needed two more weeks to be ready. After losing Keith and Mike midstream, it was a miracle it worked at all. As she made her way to Gregg's office, she remembered the two mornings she discovered her late night work had gone terribly wrong. Exhaustion had made her unreliable. She wondered how many similar problems would spring up today and how long they'd be fighting them. Brad's inhumane expectations had done this, but he'd take no blame for what happened today.

The table outside Gregg's office had been arranged the night before with a PC to monitor the server upstairs and enough chairs for Erica's team to gather. From there they'd watch carefully for signs of stress on the system and its users. Erica laid out enough food to keep them going all morning. A dozen bagels, a half dozen tropical fruits and four coffees, two for her if they weren't claimed soon, covered half the table. She fought the plastic top off the fruit tray and walked across the floor to fetch a handful of napkins and white plastic utensils. She arranged and rearranged the food to occupy herself. Not a soul came through the lobby.

Andy and Ganesh had another twenty minutes to arrive on time. She wondered what could be keeping them. Andy, tall with a waistline that was expanding with middle age as his hairline receded, had left at eleven the night before to drive to the suburbs. Ganesh, short and slight with a personality to match, had stayed till nearly 1:00 A.M. to help with a few final configuration changes. Both men were steady and competent. She never would have finished without their help and she feared she was going to need them desperately once the users started arriving.

Alone, Erica felt just how tired her body was. With nothing to do, she melted into her chair to wait. Fear had driven her the last weeks and now she had nothing left to give. She met Brad's deadline without begging for help. They'd skimped on testing and left out a dozen features Erica had promised, but the unrelenting pressure left her no choice. It had to be done and delivered today. She had signed off and now she sat waiting for the repercussions to come crashing down.

Ganesh arrived, gangly if that was possible for someone five feet four. Meek enough to go unnoticed in any group, he propped himself up on the seat and waited for his orders. Andy arrived next showing signs of a long commute and impossibly long hours. He slumped along to the table, thick rings underlining his eyes. A missed button had one side of his collar springing up while the other was fastened securely to his chest. Gregg strolled in next, cheerier than the rest, and took up a position between Erica and the outer wall of his cubicle.

Erica manned the computer and doled out plates and coffee before reviewing the plan. Andy and Ganesh would wander the floor, visiting the supervisors regularly, and watching the staff for signs of frustration. Erica would monitor server performance. If things went badly enough to warrant emergency changes, Erica would make them.

Shortly before 8:00 A.M., the supervisors began to trickle in. These were mostly friendly faces Erica had worked with for years. Many had volunteered for roles on the project team and they'd taken the time to be trained and retrained. They were eager for her to succeed.

Soon a flurry of five people arrived and began settling in for the day. Andy and Ganesh wandered around watching them turn on their computers and log in. Sitting still in the chair, Erica's eyelids threatened to close in spite of the pressure. If she dreamed it would have been a chaotic and turbulent nightmare, a mass of twisted silicon surrounded by angry wires.

The people in her dream would expect perfection. They wouldn't understand that the electronic beast was utterly uncontrollable.

Gregg leaned toward her. None of his staff had arrived, so they were alone with a fair amount of space between them and the nearest client services rep. "Who're you betting on?" he whispered.

"What do you mean?"

"Who's going to have the first problem?"

"You if you keep it up."

Gregg whispered even softer. "Relax, it'll be fine. Now humor me. Someone's got to have at least one problem. Who're you going to pick?"

Erica turned toward the smell of his cologne. Breathing it deeply she settled her gaze into his deep brown eyes. Only inches separated them. It may have been fatigue or maybe he'd hung around long enough to wear her down. Whatever the reason, her lips yearned to rise up and meet his. It was totally inappropriate here in the office, but she could barely resist. She would have kissed him if not for the screams from her conscience. The two forces deadlocked. Her lips pushed forward, her conscience pushed back. There she stayed measuring him from several inches. His longing eyes held steady where they'd always been. She'd pushed him away a dozen times and yet he was the one constant in her life. Compassionate, romantic, those eyes saw the struggle that held them apart, though they couldn't understand it. His eyes didn't see that a bold move would have been handsomely rewarded. Seconds passed. The eyes never faltered, but the power of the moment lost its grip.

Erica turned toward the CSRs chatting on their headsets. She couldn't remember what he'd asked and maybe neither could he. Her heart beat strongly beneath her silk top. He didn't need to see it pumping. He knew what she felt. Melanie knew, too. Erica had only hidden this from herself.

Breathing again, she watched Andy and Ganesh fritter from cube to cube. Too nervous to be hopeful, she watched a score of cordial conversations that lasted less than a minute and didn't require the men to take a single note. So far the news was good. No stress. No fingers through the hair, all smiles.

Gregg visited each of his CSRs when they arrived and came back to report that all was well. The server handled the load fine and Erica began to relax. Twenty minutes later she began to hear what she hadn't had the courage to hope for. The chatter over the cubes turned to raves.

Two hours in, a dozen old friends had stopped by to compliment her on her genius. Everyone knew how to use a browser and the old system was now described as clunky and cryptic. The young CSRs took to the system as naturally as they googled for a new website. Erica was completely at ease when Steve Harris stepped off the elevator. Steve ran all of client services from the twenty-third floor. What he didn't know he learned on visits like this one. His eyes met Erica's and he predictably veered off toward Bob Hicks' cube. A minute later his cautious stride and neutral expression were replaced by an energetic gait and an engaging smile. He walked directly to Erica and thrust out his hand.

"Excellent work, Erica. Sounds like things couldn't have gone better."

"Thank you. So far, so good."

Gregg reemerged from his cube.

"You're too modest. This was a huge project and it's come off swimmingly," Steve said. "You should go out and celebrate."

"We should," Gregg chimed in rather loudly.

Steve didn't miss a beat. "You were on the team too, weren't you, Turner? I'm appointing you CS ambassador. Take this young woman out somewhere nice for dinner. It's on my nickel. Sky's the limit."

Gregg accepted before Erica could say anything. The two men shook hands and Steve walked away.

"What just happened?" Erica asked.

"We got a free dinner."

"What about the rest of the team?"

"Buy 'em a pizza. I'm thinking you and me at Le Meridian."

The whole exchange seemed a bit too tidy. He couldn't have known things would go so well or that she'd agree to go with him. Whatever he'd done, it worked. Gregg finally had the date he'd been waiting years for.

Chapter 21

Sarah's first day off plan began as she'd dreamed every day on her new job would. She had evidence that promised results and a partner that was helpful, knowledgeable, and ruggedly handsome. It wasn't clear which excited her more, but she was brimming with anticipation for the moments to come. She hadn't felt this positive about the change since Herman came to retrieve her from the conference room on her first day.

Sarah watched Gregg through the conference room window. He stood a dozen feet from his office waiting for a young guy in one of the cubicles to finish his conversation. When he pulled his mic down below his chin, they bantered back and forth a bit. Then he pulled off his headset and they headed for the conference room together. The younger guy was nearly Gregg's height, but his body looked like it had grown a foot taller in the last few years. He was desperately in need of Oreos and milk to fill it out.

Gregg introduced Brendan Purcell who took his seat across the table, looking glad for the time away from the phones rather than fearful of the questions Sarah was going to ask. Gregg chose a seat on Brendan's side of the table. It seemed loyalty to his staff outweighed the facts she'd laid out for him earlier. She wasn't going to go easy on Brendan regardless of what Gregg thought. One way or another she was going to catch her thief.

Gregg opened the meeting belaboring Brendan's credentials. He'd received stellar ratings on the phones for three years and he'd soon be promoted to supervisor. His introduction for Sarah was decidedly less superlative and far less ominous than she would have preferred. In thirty seconds he turned Sarah's pressure packed interrogation bunker into a men's steam room where she was the one feeling exposed.

"Thanks, Gregg," Sarah said in spite of the lackluster introduction. "Brendan, we asked you here to discuss a transaction you processed on December twenty-eighth last year."

Brendan straightened in his seat and flashed a queer look at Gregg. Not squirming, not an iota of guilt on his face. Asking him about a three month old transaction seemed absurd.

Sarah handed a copy of the complaint letter across the table. "This letter is from Hank Johnson. Does the name sound familiar?"

Brendan didn't flinch. He shook his head and skimmed.

"Mr. Johnson is pretty upset and it seems he has good reason."

Brendan looked up curiously. "What about?"

"He thinks we cheated him. He thinks we pushed his transaction to the next day because we knew the price was going up."

"We're good, but we're not psychic," he laughed at his own joke until he noticed Sarah's glare. "Everything's automated anyway." His voice trailed off. His chin retreated into his neck, mortified at the insinuation.

Gregg gave Sarah a scornful look.

"Mr. Johnson is certain he called before the cut-off. Any idea how a transaction that was phoned in on time could get pushed off to the next trading day?"

The tone of the questions finally hit Brendan. He glanced at Gregg for support, but couldn't read his expression. He looked ready to bolt. "You don't think I did this on purpose? The system times these automatically. I can't change it and what good would it do me if I did?"

Brendan was on edge. His hands fidgeted on the tabletop, drifting with his thoughts. His eyes darted from Sarah to Gregg, no doubt seeing the ire in her and wondering what his boss was thinking in the seat next to him.

Gregg put his hand on Brendan's. "Whoa," he said patting the hand as if calming a spooked horse. "No one is saying you did anything wrong. Let's not get ahead of ourselves. The customer complained and we paid him what he asked. Sarah needs to know how it happened. Let's stick to that."

Sarah had her tension now. Brendan was panicky enough to tell her anything if she asked the right question. The scene had played out exactly as she pictured it, but Gregg's pragmatism left her feeling embarrassed of her own eagerness. She felt petty and confused. This kid was no criminal mastermind. Stan was right about the job. It wasn't about catching criminals, but she was positive this was more than an honest mistake. Lightning struck on her first day and she'd made a career discovery. She might never stumble on something this big again and she wasn't going to let it go, not for Gregg, Brendan, or Herman.

She took a deep breath and gave Brendan half a smile. "Can we listen to the phone call again?" she asked and pushed the speakerphone to Gregg.

He dialed a long series of numbers and Hank Johnson's voice boomed over the speaker. He railed against the answers he was getting, but Brendan's expression never changed. He'd dealt with dozens of irate investors. If he'd knowingly duped Mr. Johnson, he hid his guilt well. This voice was no different to him than the hundreds of others he'd heard.

Brendan talked over Gregg's recorded voice. "That can't be right," he said, referring to Mr. Johnson's argument about the timing. "You know we put the transactions into the system while we're on the phone. The system enters the time right then. There's no other way to do it. As soon as we get off, the phones give us another customer. He's got to be wrong."

"I don't think so," Sarah said. She pushed over a copy of the phone bill and a page showing the transaction in Mr. Johnson's account.

Brendan compared the two pages in disbelief. He'd heard Mr. Johnson say what had happened and now he saw the evidence, but he couldn't fathom how the discrepancy could get into the system.

"That's impossible," Brendan said.

"That's why we're here. This isn't supposed to happen."

"If you're looking for an explanation, you're asking the wrong guy."

Brendan wasn't coy enough to feign confusion. He didn't know any more about the problem than she did. She'd look elsewhere for the culprit.

Sarah stood up. "Let's keep this between us for now."

Brendan agreed, gave his boss a weak handshake and left without looking back. Her questions had shaken him. Both men were probably cursing her for turning an innocent problem into some devious plot to steal from customers, but neither of them could explain what had happened. Brendan was no thief and she owed him a visit later in the week to smooth things over. Gregg's bitter look told her that might not be enough. He closed the door and sat back down. She'd definitely tone down her next interview.

"We could have gone a bit easier."

"I didn't mean to upset him, but questions need to be asked."

"The guy's a star. The last thing I need is someone souring his attitude. There's no reason to accuse him of anything. He's a good kid. He answered the phone when Johnson called. He doesn't have anything more to do with your investigation than that."

Sarah raised her hands in submission.

"Message received. I'll go easier next time," she said.

"This is probably a simple mistake or a software bug."

Sarah was tired of hearing that. "I don't think it's a mistake."

"We're only human down here. We process thousands of transactions. Once in a while, we get it wrong."

"What if you didn't? Brendan's your best rep, right? He was the only one to touch the Johnson account in December. So what if he did everything right? The problem has to be upstairs."

Gregg seemed pleased with the idea if only to take the spotlight off Brendan. "There's only one person to go to with something like this, but I've already taken this problem to her once."

Chapter 22

Sarah followed Gregg to the elevator and up to the twenty-second floor. The morning had been a disaster. She came off immature and self-absorbed and now Gregg looked at her as dismissively as she looked at Stan. Reversing that impression would be a feat, but she vowed to give it her best. He was so much more than she first thought. The rugged looks camouflaged a depth she hadn't expected in a younger guy. Totally grounded and at ease with himself, he was as much a parent as he was a manager to the kids that worked for him. His maturity and intelligence were as attractive as anything she'd seen in him on her first day.

Gregg led the way in, weaved around the cubicles and ended up outside a dark office. He looked surprised to find the office empty at 10:30 A.M. It didn't look like she was coming in, but Gregg wasn't ready to leave. He asked an older man if he'd seen her. He hadn't.

They returned to the elevators and he explained that Erica was there night and day, six, sometimes seven days a week. Sarah asked if there was someone else who could help them and his expression immediately turned grim. "These guys don't care what happens downstairs, least of all Brad Foster."

"Isn't he in charge of IT?"

Gregg closed the lobby door before answering. "He's the biggest problem up here. Erica worked–"

"Did I hear my name?"

A woman stepped off the elevator smiling at Gregg. She was skinny and gorgeous, one of those women who could wear a boxy pantsuit and make it look sexy without trying. A line of drooling men probably followed her whenever she left the building. Gregg lit up and Sarah's hopes plunged. She wished the SlimFast had lived up to its name.

"Slacking again I see," he said.

"As usual."

Gregg made introductions and begged Erica's help with their problem. She led them back to her office with apologies for arriving late. The room was twice the size of Sarah's with the back wall made up entirely of windows. Sarah gazed over the southern part of the city and South Boston beyond. A slice of the harbor peeked out at the extreme left. Erica was barely visible behind stacks of paper and piles of manila folders. Greg stood, leaving the only chair not currently doubling as a shelf for Sarah. She checked her watch reflexively as she sat; not consciously reading the hands since she knew it was after ten thirty.

"I didn't realize you had it so good up here in IT." Her tone sounded nasty even to her.

Gregg looked as embarrassed as he did when she pressed Brendan for answers he didn't have. Crestfallen, she knew he was going to distance himself from her as soon as they left this office.

Erica was unfazed. "When you work ninety hours a week they don't mind if you come in late once in a while." She turned to Gregg with a wide grin. "Actually I just woke up an hour ago." She seemed proud.

"That's about a week's worth of sleep for you isn't it?"

"Do you have an idea about keeping me up at night?" The suggestion in her voice was unmistakable. Sarah would have given up hope, but Gregg ignored the implication and kept the focus on work.

"It's good for a few nights at least."

He launched into a recap of the Johnsons' problem. He reminded Erica of his argument with Brad and his visit to ask for her help. She shuffled through a few piles on the desktop, embarrassed she hadn't looked into the problem sooner then apologized for losing the documents he'd given her.

Erica's team had just implemented a system that tracked these transactions so this problem was her responsibility now. Gregg seemed relieved that she had official standing to help, but alarm bells started going off for Sarah. Erica fit the profile of a successful embezzler. She was responsible for the troubled system and she'd been asked to help and done nothing. She had longevity and influence within the company, something Sarah's instructors cited as critical. Gregg and his colleagues brought their problems directly to her, giving her a chance to see the dust she kicked up as she tramped around the company databases and took money from unsuspecting customers. She didn't look the part, but she had all the right qualifications.

There was an awkward pause with both Erica and Gregg looking at her, Gregg with his hand outstretched. She hadn't heard what was said, but assumed he wanted the letter. She handed him a copy and they shifted focus to it immediately.

"Sounds like he's got a legitimate gripe," Erica said when she was about halfway through.

"We paid him. Now we want to know what went wrong."

Gregg handed her the phone bill and she placed it on her keyboard with the letter. She stood up and walked around the desk. "I've got some time between projects, I'll start digging."

Sarah backed out toward the door.

Erica stopped a foot from Gregg and rested a hand above his elbow. "I can work every night this week but one. The company's buying me dinner if I recall."

"That's right. When should I pick you up?"

"I didn't realize you two were dating," Sarah spat from the doorway.

"It's not a date. The company is saying thanks for all the hours I put in on the fund services system. Gregg volunteered to be my escort because I'm chronically unattached and he's incredibly chivalrous."

"It could be a date," Gregg pleaded.

"We couldn't date. You're too sweet. We'd both want to get married and that would be a disaster."

Gregg froze. Devastated, hopeful or maybe just confused.

Sarah led the way into the hall, thanked Erica, and replayed the conversation in her head as they walked to the elevator.

When the doors closed they were alone.

"You didn't tell me you two were close."

"It's not what you think."

"Really. If I'd known there were going to be that many sparks I'd have worn safety glasses."

Gregg didn't answer. He watched the display flash '21.'

"If you two want to keep it quiet that's fine with me. All I care about is what happened to Mr. Johnson's money," she lied. "The whole thing does look suspicious, though. She's responsible for the system and it seems like everyone brings their problems to her. It doesn't look good from an internal audit perspective. If she was mucking around, no one would ever be the wiser."

Sarah stepped off the elevator and looked back.

Gregg was livid.

"If she was mucking around? She's in control of that system because she's the best programmer up there. She came from client services. She knows what we're up against. How can you fault her for being helpful?"

"I'm not accusing her of anything. It doesn't look good, that's all."

Gregg let go of the 'open' button and stomped off the elevator.

"You don't get it, do you? There is no one else. Those guys up there don't care what we need. If Brad knew how much she helped us, he'd make her life even more miserable."

"Those two don't get along?"

The story was getting deeper by the second.

"No one gets along with Brad unless they have something he wants."

Erica was fitting the profile better and better. She couldn't have been closer to these problems or have a better opportunity to cover them up. Gregg might do or say anything she asked. Sarah's day had been a personal disaster, but a professional boon.

Chapter 23

The bartender rushed off with the fresh twenty leaving Gregg to face his reflection over the array of bottles against the glass. A fresh haircut and a clean shave wrapped in his favorite royal blue shirt faced him meekly. He looked good save the timid eyes. His commanding presence had been beaten down by rejection after rejection. The eyes knew what they were headed for even if their master didn't. Two years ago they'd had this conversation and she'd turned him away. He'd been dropping hints that he'd ask again for weeks. So far all he'd done is stiffen her resolve, but when he wasn't pressing, she dropped hints of her own. She feigned innocence, but there was feeling behind her offhand comments. She wanted him close, but not too close, bouncing in the margin between friendship and romance. He was tired of bouncing. It was time to settle things. The two shots of tequila on the bar would give him the courage.

Gregg gulped the first shot. The fiery liquid burned its way down his throat and into his belly. The fumes lit up his nostrils until he stanched the heat with an even larger gulp of water. The bartender had taken pity and filled both shots to the rim. Did he know what Gregg was about to face? Had dozens of men sat here building up their courage before journeying across the street and up her stairs? The bartender had probably never seen her himself, but he'd surely seen the devastated results.

Gregg tipped the second shot, chased it down, and collected his change. Steadily out the door, he faced her apartment. The alcohol would kick in soon and help him blurt out what had to be said. Another drink or two at dinner and he'd be ready. She might not admit it, but the chemistry was there. Could he really give up if she turned him away again? He crossed the street wondering how he'd feel about all the lost time. Would he forgive himself? Would he lament years lost? Or was this the greatest pursuit of his life? Each step siphoned his resolve until he crested the stairs and faced her door. He rapped gently and the door swung open.

"Hey, look at you," Melanie beamed. She threw her arms around him, her fingers excited once they felt the fine threads of his shirt. She shifted a hand around to his chest and turned to Erica, "You've got to feel this."

Why couldn't Erica greet him with Melanie's enthusiasm? Why did she stand so coolly behind the kitchen counter with a hand on her hip and the other clutching a water glass? She made no move to come feel his shirt nor would she. She was forever pushing something between them; the counter here in the apartment, the table at dinner, her desk at work; anything to insulate herself from the spark. She foiled his every attempt to flick that fledgling spark into a vat of gasoline. If he could press his lips to hers just once the passion would roar out from behind those tranquil brown eyes.

However restrained she acted she couldn't hide the trouble she'd gone to. Her hair and makeup were freshly done and she was wearing a new skirt. It wasn't the little black dress he dreamed of, but seeing a hint of her bare legs over the counter was a thrill after years of baggy pants. In heels she nearly matched his height.

When Erica rounded the counter and came into the living room, she looked amused that Melanie still had both hands on Gregg's shirt. The ploy had drawn her closer, but she didn't look the least bit jealous.

Melanie rubbed unabashed.

"You better get over here," Melanie said, "before I drag him down the hall and show him how a real woman treats a hunk like this."

Erica smiled at the two of them. "I don't have exclusive rights."

"What's this dinner about then?" Gregg asked.

"Steve saying thank you. Was there more to it than that?"

"I thought so. Does that mean I'm not getting any action?" He was glad he said it in spite of the embarrassment he felt. The alcohol was working.

"Not from me," Erica shot back without hesitation.

Melanie still had her hand on his back. She leaned close, brushing his chest with hers as she stretched up toward his ear. Her sultry whisper was intended more for Erica than Gregg. "Come back after dinner. I'll make sure you don't go home hungry." She wouldn't betray Erica, but the longing in her eyes was unmistakable.

Erica sensed it, too. "Come on, Lover Boy," she said and linked her arm through his. She tugged him away from Melanie and toward the door.

Melanie gave a sly wink as they left. Progress.

In the taxi, Erica kept the conversation focused on work, her project and how Gregg's team had adapted to the new system. She clung to the technical and superficial, avoiding anything remotely personal. She wouldn't be dragged into a conversation about what was going on between them and even if he could force the subject, the ride wasn't long enough. He listened politely, biding his time even after they arrived at Mamma Maria.

The steady flow of couples entering and exiting the bar provided Erica with prompts to help keep the conversation light. Gregg did his best to exhaust every avenue of office conversation while they were in the bar. Erica couldn't have seemed more at ease.

A host summoned them to be seated and led them up a narrow stairway to the Piccolo Room on the second floor. The sole table, set for two, overlooked North Square. He handed them each a menu, the wine list to Gregg and departed, leaving them alone in the heart of the North End. The chatter from the bar was barely audible.

Alone in a setting women fawned over, Erica's eyes darted around the room as if she'd been kidnapped. "If I didn't know better, I'd think you were trying to start something," she said uneasily. Classic Erica: preemptively warning him not to say what was on his mind.

It wasn't going to work tonight.

"I've been trying to start this for years. It's time. Don't you think?"

"I don't know if I can handle the competition. You had Melanie hanging all over you tonight and Sarah all dreamy-eyed yesterday. The hunky-farmboy-in-the-city routine is really packing 'em in."

"You know what Melanie was doing. She sees the chemistry between us like everyone else. Why you choose to deny it I have no idea."

"What exactly am I denying?"

"That you're so crazy about me it scares you."

Erica reeled back as if she'd been slapped. She'd warned him not to try again. He expected a flat denial and a stern rejoinder for his audacity. He got neither. She didn't argue. She knew it was true. She refused to meet his eyes, searching the walls for the right words instead.

"It couldn't be more obvious," he prodded. "The only people at BFS not talking about us – is us. Why do you keep running from me?"

She took a long drink of water and set the glass down deliberately. "I'm not who you think I am."

The waiter took a step over the threshold and Gregg shooed him away with a solemn shake of his head.

"I see who you are. You'd make a fabulous kindergarten teacher. You help people until it hurts. I'm not sure who you think you are, but it's a no-brainer for the rest of us."

"Don't be so sure."

"I couldn't be more sure. I've known you five years and, trust me, I've been paying attention. Nothing's going to scare me away from you."

Erica waived the waiter in, opened her menu and asked for his recommendations. She was feeling pressured. Bombarded with uncomfortable emotions, she needed an escape, a calm minute to digest what he was saying. Chatting with the waiter was her only respite.

Gregg studied every nuance of her face as she ordered. There would be few interruptions in this cozy room. No way to evade the conversation without fleeing for the ladies room.

She settled on the lobster pasta.

Gregg hadn't read a single selection.

His eyes came upon the slow-roasted Sonoma rabbit by chance. He'd hunted rabbit on the farm, unsuccessfully. Erica seemed perturbed at the selection, but said nothing until the waiter left the room.

"You have no idea what you're setting yourself up for."

"I'm willing to take the risk."

She didn't deny the spark between them; didn't try to dissuade him with the usual office romance prohibition crap. She nodded, smiled and voila they were a couple. She never said so in plain terms and he didn't force her to, but there it was. His mind buzzed with celebratory images. He almost didn't hear her say that she never planned to marry. Never. No kids, no weddings, not a chance.

He looked across the table, deflated. The woman who represented the ideal mate in every possible way, refused to play a role that fit her so aptly. A shaky, "Why not?" was all he could manage.

"My parents weren't exactly June and Ward Cleaver."

In all their conversations she'd rarely mentioned her family. He'd talked about his constantly. He'd always thought it was the differing desires for their relationship. He strove to make it more personal, while she pushed hard in the other direction, never revealing too much.

"You never said anything."

"It's not something I talk about."

"Can we talk about it now? Whatever it is, it won't change anything between us."

She reached over and put her hand on his. "It's not a first date conversation. Let's give it some time before we get into the heavy stuff."

Chapter 24

The directors arrayed around the table in this post Sarbanes-Oxley world weren't as friendly as those of a few years ago. Gone were the days when Marty got a free pass for being a Finch. The old friends that had gotten him to the head of the table had been replaced by a bunch of outsiders with no stock. Some didn't even have experience in fund trading or banking. Worst of all was Bill Elliot, the man who faced him from the chairman's seat. He wasn't family. All he cared about was shareholder value, never mind that Marty's family controlled most of the shares. He encouraged the others to pry into operations, to poke around and see how things worked, to satisfy their curiosity. Financial statements weren't good enough for these bloodsuckers. They looked for trouble everywhere they went. They even questioned employees they met in the hall. When smart employees saw a board member roaming around unescorted, they ran for cover.

Marty didn't have anything to hide per se, but he'd spent the last forty years skating by. In a family of overachieving genius capitalists, Marty saw good-enough as a lofty goal. That's why they let Bill Elliot take control. He and the others constantly critiqued Marty's leadership. They attacked his policies and they were always building a case for his ouster. Mother said they were just keeping him honest.

Today Marty would showcase a shining example of his leadership. This presentation would stave off any action for months. A rare technology project with a positive ROI and a huge impact on operations, it was spearheaded by a dedicated employee that was easy on the eyes. Even the most bloodthirsty among them could appreciate that. If father were alive, he'd have been impressed.

Marty pressed the buzzer and Erica Fletcher walked in. The murmurs died away. All attention was on her as she attached her laptop to the projector and booted both machines. Marty left his seat as the display screen unfurled against the wall behind him. He pulled his chair out of the way and stood beside Erica.

"Gentlemen," Marty began, "today you will see the result of our years of investment in human resources. We have long selected the finest graduates and nurtured them through decades-long careers. This is but one example of how that effort is paying dividends." Marty extended an arm toward Erica. "It is my distinct pleasure to introduce Erica Fletcher. Erica was identified as a star early in her career. Just a few short years ago she was rising through the ranks in client services and we decided to move her into a more strategic position. We decided the information technology group could best utilize her talents."

"You decided," Brad interjected.

"Brilliantly, I might add."

Several throats cleared.

"She has excelled beyond even my expectations. Today she's at the forefront of systems technology. She's going to tell you about an effort she recently led that has enabled us to leapfrog our competitors. She has given us one of the most flexible and powerful investment management systems in the industry."

Brad glared down the table, but Marty continued his lavish praise undeterred. Erica's accomplishment validated his choice to move her into IT, a move he championed, a move he'd take full credit for.

"Erica is going to demonstrate our new fund services system. It has taken us from a rigid and archaic system, designed for any financial firm and given us one that is tailored to our specific needs. The people downstairs took to it with amazing speed. They became more productive almost from day one."

"Since when did you become a systems expert, Marty?" Bill Elliott asked from the chairman's seat. Bill was the first non-Finch chairman of BFS. He'd been on a quest to purge the remaining Finch cronies since taking the role. Removing Marty was item one on his agenda.

"The improvement will be apparent even to you. Erica will show us a system that looks and acts like a website you'd visit to buy a book or check which movies are playing at the local cinema. Managing our client interactions has become that simple. You can imagine what that will do to training costs for our new employees and the satisfaction of our existing ones. Customers will be delighted."

Members rustled in their seats eager to find flaw with Marty's success story. They'd find nothing today. He'd chosen this presentation for its safety. If they were looking to attack, they'd come away empty.

Brad broke in again. "Let's keep our feet on the ground here. The system's no cure-all, but the team has done an excellent job. Client services has been thrilled with the change. As you all know, a change like this involves a lot of disruption and I credit the *team* for the excellent work they've done to make the switchover as painless as possible. That's the biggest success in my eyes."

"Take it away please, Erica, and show us what everyone is raving about," Marty beamed.

Without much of an introduction, Erica flashed an image up on the screen. She explained how the client services staff documented customer calls and placed orders. The slow-moving screens were cumbersome and complex, her explanations convoluted. Soon the board members were whispering to each other.

"They've both lost it," a newer member said.

This wasn't the system Erica had shown Marty two days before. It took over a minute to find a customer's information and process a call. The members wondered how the staff entertained the customer long enough to wade through the screens. The murmuring grew steadily. Finally Erica threw up her hands and stepped back.

"Sucks, doesn't it?" She stood, smiling, waiting for a reaction.

Stunned, the members looked to each other for an explanation. They'd been duped. Brad was the only one who saw the charade coming. By the skeptical looks around the room, some of them still hadn't made the leap.

Erica flashed a new image on the screen that had a familiar feel to it. The boxes and buttons were intuitive. Marty could have given a meaningful demo in her place, but he'd never dare, not to this crowd.

She navigated quickly, finding customer information and simulating a transaction in the new system. Simple, fast, the comparison was striking. She had turned their eagerness to find fault against them. She tricked them into studying the old system so they could understand how well this new system performed. Clever. The earlier sneers and whispers turned to prods and smiles. They had felt the frustration of working on the old system and now they knew how brilliant her work was.

This presentation had impact.

Marty relaxed as the board members chattered about this accomplishment and what it meant for the fifty people on the nineteenth floor. What it meant for Marty was a board meeting with a tone entirely in his favor. In a few hours the directors would leave and they wouldn't be back until the next round of meetings in July. Three months bought with a quick call downstairs.

Three months and a bag full of credibility.

Chapter 25

Tap, steady, back, through...

Marty cajoled another ball into position on the strip of green artificial surface that stretched along the outside wall of his office. He took dead aim at the hole, doing his best to block out his current string of misses.

Tap, steady, back, through...

The ball rolled past the hole, half an inch wide right. It clicked into another ball and strayed toward the couch.

Tap, tap, tap. Tap, steady, back, through...

Five straight misses from six feet.

At least the round of board meetings had gone well. Erica's presentation ended the zingers about his competence. Bill stuck to the agenda, reviewed the quarterly financials and brought the meeting to a close. The outsiders flew home and Marty had the company to himself – as he should.

If only his putting problems could be solved with such a rational approach. A simple little motion, straight back and straight through with barely any force. In a family dominated by stuffy intellectuals Marty had always been the blue collar Finch. He loved football, baseball, any sport really, but by some warped twist of fate the only family sanctioned sport was golf. He swung well, he could chip and he was a wizard from the sand, but sooner or later he had to putt. That's when his game fell apart. Three putting from eight feet wasn't uncommon for Marty. The dozens of short putts he missed led to humiliating losses to his mother and sister. They played from the red tees, and they played twice as often as he did, but his last place finishes somehow validated his status within the family.

Tap, steady, back, through... "Shit!"

"I think you misread that one. You've got to watch the break on those five footers," Brad said as he strolled in without a knock.

The surface was level, checked every six months. The problem existed somewhere between his hands and the ball. More likely in his head.

"Ease up, Smart Guy. I married your sister not you. You I can get rid of with a stroke of my pen. No alimony. No heartbreak. No problem."

"What kind of shit was that in the board meeting today?"

"What are you talking about?"

"Bad enough you saddle me with some chick you plucked off the hotline, but you can't go praising her work to the board. I never said she was so spectacular. Did I?"

"You happen to be the only one of that opinion." Marty tapped another ball into position. He sent it rolling. It found the cup dead center and swirled to the bottom. "Knowing what your sister's told me, I can see why you two have a difficult time getting along."

"And why's that?"

"You hit on every attractive woman in the company. This one turned you down and you're pissed. Can't say I blame her."

"Give me a break, Marty. Technology is much more complicated than making nice on the phone. If you put the golf clubs away and walked around the office once in a while, you'd know that."

Marty stood upright and tapped his putter on the ground like a blunt sword. "Don't give me that bullshit. She's brighter than anyone on your team and she knows more about this business than you do. The whole place is buzzing over what she did. If we weren't related she'd have your job."

"She didn't do this alone. Far from it. She sucked up every resource on my team and screwed my budget for the next two years."

"I know she didn't do it alone. Bill approved your promotion to senior vice president. He also approved Erica's move to A.V.P."

"No way I'm moving her up."

"You're not serious. What do you have against her?"

"She screwed this thing. If I wasn't working day and night to help her, it would have crashed and burned."

"I find that hard to believe."

"I'm not promoting her."

"I won't force you to, but if you were thinking clearly, that's exactly what you'd do. Sleep on it."

"No need."

Bill was going to be surprised when Erica's promotion wasn't included in the announcement.

"I'm sure she'll do better on her next project."

"Not going to happen. She's not getting another one, not on my watch."

"What are you saying? You aren't going to unload her. Not now. I'd have an easier time explaining your departure."

"You want my support on the board, stop managing my people."

"Maybe you should open your eyes and try managing them yourself."

"I'll keep her around, but I'm not promoting her. She's going to support this system she's built. That's what she's good at and that'll keep her from running my team into the ground."

"You're making a huge mistake," Marty said, but Brad had already turned his back for the door. "Your promotion will be announced Monday."

He mumbled something inaudible on his way out.

Ungrateful prick.

Marty herded the balls back into the middle of the floor a good ten feet from the hole. Could his assessment be that far off? Was programming that tricky she couldn't pick it up? Surely her tenacity would translate to IT.

Tap, steady, back, through...

The ball rolled by, three inches wide.

Her presentation was ingenious, her project a marvel all around the office. How could Brad scoff at Marty's biggest boardroom coup? If Bill Elliot heard about this, Marty would be sunk.

Screwed his budget for two years, what bullshit!

Tap, steady, back, through...

Chapter 26

In the office early for no particular reason, Erica plunged into an inbox with over two hundred unread email messages. Most were trivia she'd ignored in the rush to finish her project. She culled through, deleting scattered congratulations and searching for something to latch onto. She'd spent the whole weekend pondering how her life had changed in a few short days. The project was a hit and the board was wowed by her presentation. Marty had hinted at a promotion. Things with Gregg had heated up, too and it seemed so natural she cursed herself for pushing him away for so long.

Her hands were full of energy, tapping, shuffling, but not finding anything to hold her attention more than a minute. Driven beyond distraction, she headed for nineteen. She'd ask Gregg how things were going and visit anyone who'd been out last week and hadn't used the system yet. That's how she rationalized it, but she really wanted to see how he'd handle seeing her in the office. Melanie had been thrilled at the news. Gregg had stayed past midnight on Thursday and Erica hadn't wanted him to leave even then. He was the one man who could make her break her promise to herself. She was plunging headlong into unexplored emotional territory and the jittery feeling was entirely new.

Out of the elevator and across the floor, Erica received a few words of encouragement here and there on her way to Gregg's office. He beamed adoringly at the sight of her entering his cube. This wasn't lust in his eyes; he didn't spring up to grab hold, he sat back and reveled in her arrival like a warm spring breeze. Her warm smile naturally returned his.

"Hey, what a surprise," he said.

"Thought I'd come down and check things out. Make sure no one's having trouble."

"You don't need a reason to visit. It's humble compared to yours, but you're always welcome."

Erica wished they'd started this two years ago.

"Heard about Brad's promotion. Is yours next?"

"What promotion?"

"You didn't see the email? He made S.V.P."

"When?"

"This morning."

The bastard! He wasn't above stealing credit, but how could he after she worked herself to exhaustion for eighteen straight months. She never saw this coming. He'd done everything but assault her to derail the project and now that it was a success he gets promoted. All he said in the boardroom was 'the team' did a great job. He never mentioned her and now she knew why. Whatever he said about her in private, it wasn't flattering.

She fumed all the way up to twenty-two then stood around the corner from his office trying to calm down. It was premature to blow up and make a scene. Her promotion could come next week or next month. She went in relaxed, hiding her distaste for the wretch behind the desk.

"Well Erica, you haven't visited in a while. How are things downstairs?" The snide expression might have meant things with Gregg.

"Everything's fine."

"Good. The board was pleased with our effort."

"I've heard. Congratulations on your promotion."

"Thanks. It's been in the works a long time. This last project pushed it over the hump."

"I guess that makes me the humpee."

Brad looked back to his monitor as if the conversation were over, a silent dismissal without a single word of thanks for eighteen months of sleepless nights. She stood motionless, waiting for a sign of humanity. It didn't come. Seconds passed awkwardly, neither of them spoke. She wasn't going to bow outside and let it drop.

"What's next for me?"

"What do you mean?"

"Do we have anything big coming up?"

"What you're doing now is very important."

"And what's that?"

"Supporting client services. That system of yours is going to need modifications. It's been a good week, but you can't expect it to be trouble free. Problems are going to come up. Who better to resolve them than you?"

"Ganesh for one."

"I'm moving Ganesh to the attribution project."

"Who's leading that?"

"Andy's got it. They kick-off the next phase in a couple days."

"You've got to be kidding."

"Andy's the best man for the job, pardon my phrasing."

"I brought this thing in on a shoestring. We've had less than a dozen bugs since Monday. Andy's been working for *me* the last year. How can you think he'd do a better job?"

"I've been preparing a formal review of your project management. It's not complete, but since you're here, why don't we discuss it now?" He was enjoying this. He was going to rip her performance when everyone else in the company was raving about what she'd done.

"What are you trying to do? You kept the staff so small it was practically impossible to finish on time. Then you took the credit for our success. What do you have against me?"

"It's nothing personal. I'm your boss whether you like it or not and there are some performance issues we need to discuss."

"What issues?" Erica screamed. She could hear people moving closer outside the door but didn't care. This was so wrong.

"Relax, Erica. If this conversation is going to be constructive you have to be willing to listen. Feedback is useless unless you're calm enough to process it."

"What planet are you from?"

"Fine, if you want to do this another time, I understand."

"No, I don't want to do this another time. If you have a problem with the way I handled this project, I'd like to hear it. Then I'll tell you what I think of you cutting my team in half two weeks before go-live. You're damn lucky I was here night after night bringing this thing in."

"I understand how you might feel that way, but you have to realize that we have other projects to deliver. Yours is not the only work that matters."

"That's bullshit and you know it."

"Erica, get control of yourself."

"I'm fine. It's you who's lost your mind."

Brad stood up behind his desk and pointed to the door. "Enough. Go back to your office and cool down. When you can act professionally you can start fielding questions from client services. If you don't like that, put your resume on Monster and find someone else to torment."

Erica walked to her office replaying the conversation in her mind. Her promotion was never an issue. Brad was against her from the beginning. He'd sabotaged her project. He'd made it impossible, hoping the project would fall apart. That's what he'd wanted all along: an excuse to fire her. When she pulled through, he had taken the credit. Now he was sticking her on support duty to try and make her quit. He even suggested it.

Why was he going to all this trouble to get rid of her? The other guys on the team followed Brad's orders blindly, but no one worked as hard as she did. No one came close. It wasn't discrimination. If anyone wanted women around, it was Brad. He ogled her relentlessly no matter what she wore.

She sat alone, angry and confused, wondering why she'd been singled out. It wasn't something she did. Whatever it was, it was Brad's problem. How it related to her, she had no idea.

Chapter 27

Nearly a week had passed since Sarah's meeting with Gregg and Erica and they hadn't returned a single email. Her phone queries were met with excuses and requests for more time. Three trips to his office produced scant conversation. He was polite but brief and his romantic interests were aimed in Erica's direction. She suspected that neither he nor Erica had researched Mr. Johnson's problem, nor would they. Sarah was growing more infuriated by the day. She wasn't sure which was worse: losing her chance with Gregg or watching the most important development of her career sit idle. Relying on the scam artist to dig up evidence of her own fraud was futile. It was time to find help elsewhere.

Stan was useless.

She couldn't go to IT. A leak there and her credibility with Herman would be shot. Gruff as he was, and annoyed as he'd be about her detour from his plan, Herman was the only choice. She arranged a meeting and made her third visit to the mahogany trimmed twenty-third floor.

Herman welcomed her warmly, but underneath the phony smile he discounted her input. She had no auditing experience and she hadn't been at BFS long enough to know anything he didn't. He'd change his mind once he heard what she had to say.

"How are things downstairs with Stan?"

She settled into one of the thick leather guest chairs. "Fine," she said.

Herman read through her noncommittal tone without missing a beat. "I'm surprised to hear you say that. I was expecting something more along the lines of – he's a lazy no good bum. Why'd you hire him?"

"Ok. Why did you hire him?"

"Believe it or not, Stan fits the job, my vision of the job, pretty well. He studied criminal justice and even enrolled in the Boston Police Academy."

"Failed cops make good auditors?"

"This one does. He wound up here because he has asthma. Flunked the physical. To him this is the backwater of law enforcement. He's got the right mindset even if he's a little short on motivation."

"A little short?"

"Better that than too gung-ho. That's something I'm far more worried about, particularly with you."

If her teeth weren't clenched, Sarah's jaw would have dropped open. Did he say he preferred Stan to her? She faced him dumbfounded. He couldn't be serious.

He softened his tone. "We deal with highly charged issues. Stan keeps his head and stays on plan. He might not be leading the charge at one hundred miles per hour, but don't underestimate him. He can sit with someone five minutes and know if he's got something or not."

"But he'll never find anything if he doesn't care about the work."

"Sarah, we're not cowboys and we're not policemen. We're here to help the operating units protect themselves. If we get too excited looking for bad guys, we slow everything down and we scare the heck out of people in the process. We're not out to hang offenders in the public square. Sometimes we decide to quietly part ways with an employee. That can be hard to swallow, but if that's our decision, you'll have to deal with it and keep your mouth shut. It's difficult to set someone free knowing he'll try to steal from another firm, but sometimes that's what we're asked to do."

"That's insanity."

"It's not ideal, that's for sure. It doesn't always happen that way, but when it does, you have to be able to let it go."

Herman stood up and took a step toward the door. "Don't worry about Stan. He's not a bad guy."

Sarah stayed rooted in her chair. "That's not why I came."

Surprise registered on Herman's face.

"I think I've found something," she said, minimizing her excited tone.

"In the payroll records?"

"No."

He hid his annoyance with a question about her progress on payroll. Completing the plan meant more to him than anything. As he said, he wasn't expecting to find criminals. He was working to earn his bonus. Sarah lied and told him she'd validated fifty employees. He relaxed.

"Exactly how did you come across this find of yours?"

"I was investigating that letter I showed you."

"Did you go back to January one?"

"Not yet. I was planning to but–"

"This is not the way we operate."

"I know. But I need to tell you what I've found."

"I don't need the Lone Ranger on my team. Remember our little conversation about Stan? Stan doesn't pull shit like this. He may be slow, but he's always moving toward the goal line."

"I know. I know, but I need your help." Sarah waited until Herman threw open his hands. "There's a real issue in that letter. The company paid off the client, but my research keeps running into roadblocks."

Herman sat back down and crossed his arms. "I'm listening."

She explained the timing of the order and how the customer lost over three thousand dollars. She told him how much Gregg had helped and how they'd run aground when they asked for technical help from Brad and Erica.

"You think there's a reason no one in IT will help you?"

"It looks bad. There's a discrepancy between the customer's phone bill and our records. It looks like the data's been doctored." Herman started fidgeting in his seat. "What if this isn't the only transaction? Someone could move the difference to another account and then get the money out. Where better to do that than from IT?"

"So we can't explain what happened and there's money to be gained." Herman rubbed his chin. "What have you done to investigate?"

"Gregg and I talked to," Sarah fished in her notes, "Brendan Purcell. He took the call. He's got an excellent record and," she paused for the right words, "he's a good kid. If I had to guess, I'd say he's not our man."

"Probably doesn't have the connections to pull this off. Not unless he's working with someone upstairs. Who else have you talked to?"

"Erica Fletcher. She's the go-to person for systems problems."

"I know Erica. Pretty popular around here. What did she say?"

"Not much. She said she'd look into it, but I haven't heard anything in over a week."

"So you want me to light a fire under her?"

"I'm not sure. I'm stuck and I've got no way around."

"You did the right thing. Systems people make me nervous. They can clean up after themselves in ways other people can't. I'm not ready to accuse anyone, but do you think she's hiding something or is she just busy?"

"I'm not sure. Gregg trusts her one hundred percent."

"But you don't?"

"I don't know. She seems friendly enough and supposedly she helps everyone down in client services, but I'm not getting anywhere."

"Back to my question. Is she busy or is she avoiding you?"

Sarah wanted to say she was stonewalling, but didn't want to speculate.

Herman went to personnel for Erica's file and left Sarah waiting. She wondered what she'd set in motion. Erica had the relationships, the access and the brains to do this, but was she the criminal type? Gregg trusted her completely, but he was in love. Was his judgment colored or was hers?

Herman returned and plopped the file on the low table between them.

"I got an update from HR. She's worked for four different bosses. If anyone knows this business from every angle, it's her. She received stellar reviews in her first three jobs, but for some reason things have changed with Brad Foster." Herman paused, thinking. "She's got access to customer data, she's smart and she knows just about everyone in the firm."

"So I'm not crazy?" Sarah asked. A fraud would explain the friction between her and Brad. Rules would need to be bent to cover up what she was doing. It also explained her reluctance to help.

"Let's not get ahead of ourselves."

Herman walked over to his phone and punched a few numbers. The ring played over the speaker and then a man's voice came on the line.

"Hey, Brad. I've got Sarah Burke on the line with me."

"Hello, Sarah."

Sarah's weak greeting was surely inaudible on the other end. Herman picked up the conversation. "Brad, we have a situation here involving one of your employees. I'd like you to spend some time with Sarah. Let her show you what she's got. Can you do that?"

"Something serious?"

"Can't tell. What's your schedule like?"

"This week's bad. I'm away most of next week. I could do early next Friday. Breakfast away from the office might work. If this is urgent, we could do something after hours."

Herman didn't give Sarah a chance to respond. "Let's keep this first meeting out of the office. Breakfast next Friday will be fine. Sarah will handle the details." Herman thanked him and hung up.

"Is it safe to bring another person from systems in on this?"

"Good thinking. It could be anyone up there, but I don't think we need to worry about the CEO's brother-in-law. Stealing from the company wouldn't go over well at family dinners. Don't treat him different than anyone else, but don't go throwing accusations around. It could be bad for both our careers."

Sarah felt foolish for the suggestion and the lecture made it worse. She left his office energized to get her investigation back on track. She'd catch up on that payroll project while she waited for Brad Foster to get back from his trip.

Chapter 28

The suitcase faced Brad from the bottom of the closet. Assembled after this insider trading opportunity plunged into a nightmare he couldn't escape; the case held enough clothes and enough money to get him somewhere he could melt away. He could live out his days comfortably in France. The problem was extradition. The moment he disappeared, information about the theft would surface and his face would be on the front page of every newspaper in the country. He'd seen the file complete with photos, time tables and other details. The file had kept him in line until now, but things were getting so hot that no one could protect him. Running had proved disastrous and going to jail terrified him. He sat, torn between sneaking off to the airport and going back to work to run the program.

His only other alternative was to call Marty and beg forgiveness. Marty would be furious. He'd call this a crime against the family. Unforgivable. Only the threat of negative press would keep him from prosecuting. Brad's sister would never speak to him again. That he could tolerate, but not what would happen if the authorities got the file. Before asking Marty for help, he'd need to have his partner under control and the file in hand. After being captured in the tunnel, he knew getting the file away from the boss and his goons wouldn't be easy.

The single CD on the bedspread reminded him of where he should be. This disc held his greatest technical achievement. The program siphoned money from small BFS clients in dribs and drabs and it had run undetected for three years. It had never left his BFS office before, but with Erica so close and internal audit bearing down, he couldn't imagine leaving the disc there no matter how good his hiding place was. He could never bring himself to stay late and run it again and that was going to be difficult news to deliver. He was woefully short of his six million dollar goal.

Frozen by fear with every alternative looking bleak, Brad cycled from the suitcase to the phone to the CD. The one constant was his ruthless partner. Disobedience wouldn't be taken well even after years of servitude. Brad remembered the night Stu Tinsley stumbled into the computer room. He'd gotten too close, asked tough questions and Brad flinched. He barked at Stu to mind his business and forget what he saw. Brad let it go, but the boss didn't settle for risks like Stu walking the halls.

Two days later, Brad asked the kid to help retrieve some records. The two went down into a dusty storage area in the bowels of an old warehouse. Stu recognized Brad's partner when he emerged from the shadows, but he never realized the trouble he was in. He answered flippantly. He pried and pried for information about what Brad was doing that night, never realizing his only hope was to run for his life and never look back. Seeing the gun sobered him a little, but he never believed he was in any danger. The first bullet changed that. Burning through his midsection, it would have been fatal without treatment. The kid was stupid enough to get angry at his executioner; cursing him for what he'd done, never realizing the bullet was meant to get his attention.

The first shot to the knee woke the kid up. It zipped through, missing the bone, and lodged in some boxes. The second met his knee cap, fragmented, and chewed up everything in there to gnarly rubble. Agony wracked his face. He begged. Swore he'd never tell. Promised he'd told no one. If he had they'd have met the same horrific fate. When the boss was satisfied he wasn't a threat, he put one in the kid's temple. They left him there. Dead for doing his job, wondering what his boss was up to, trying to lend a hand. He came down willingly and they left him there pooling blood on the concrete.

They left the warehouse together, but the body was never found.

Brad envisioned himself stuck in a prison cell for the next twenty years. His feet rooted themselves to the floor. He should have gone to the office, but he couldn't move. Refusing to follow orders was risking his life. Still he sat paralyzed for over an hour, his eyes cycling from the phone, to the CD then the bag.

The phone rang.

"If you're there, I guess you have my six million."

"I'm not going to make it."

"You don't make it, the shortfall comes from your share."

"Screw that. I do all the work. No way I'm giving up four million."

"People have to be paid, important people. If you value your share, get in there and get it."

"Impossible. I can't run this thing again"

"Don't turn into a coward on me, Foster."

"Coward? I've got the new internal auditor breathing down my neck. She's not a complete idiot like Stan."

"She's not a cop either. She's not staking out the building you dumb shit. She'll look at the access records. Keep pointing them at our friend."

"It's going to take a lot more than that."

"Let me worry about the details. Get going. There was a good swing today."

"What about Fletcher? She's there day and night. If she digs in the right place, we're going to jail."

"C'mon, Foster. Stop making excuses. You've been bashing her for two years. Don't tell me you can't keep her busy for a week."

"I assigned her support duty for the new system, nothing else."

"Are you that stupid?"

"I thought she'd quit."

"She didn't, did she?"

This guy thought he had everything figured. If he dealt with her for two weeks he'd know better. "What was I supposed to do?"

"Give her a new toy to play with. Keep her happy. In a few weeks Sarah will put it together. You two go to Marty together, wham Erica's gone. You make a quick exit and I hang around until the dust settles then retire."

"It's not that simple."

"It could have been if you weren't so stupid." The line went quiet for a moment. "This is going to work out well for you, Foster, even as stupid as you are. Make this run and make sure it looks like Fletcher was there. Help Sarah find what she's looking for. She'll do the rest."

"Are you nuts?"

"She's going to blame Erica. Don't you get it?"

"She'll start with Erica, but that's only going to hold water so long. The two of them are going to talk and she'll figure out Erica's innocent. There'll be a full-blown investigation and that sucker will be pointed right at us."

"The investigation will be brief. Now get my money."

Brad imagined leading Erica into another dusty warehouse. She'd be smarter than Stu. She wouldn't come easily and bruises wouldn't support the story very well, if they found her body, that is.

"How are we going to do it?" Brad asked.

"Worry about that when the time comes. For now, just get to work."

"She's a lot smarter than the last guy. Two of my team dying in three years is going to look suspicious."

"Listen, Chicken Shit. I can put you away a lot easier. You've seen the file. Don't make this harder than it needs to be. Try to disappear, try to rat me out, you know what'll happen."

Brad gave a longing look toward his bag.

"Get in there and get this done."

The line went dead.

The next week was going to be the most difficult of the ordeal. He didn't want to think about where Erica's body would end up or what part he'd have to play. He picked up the CD. One or two more runs. A few lies to the girl from internal audit and one last trip to France.

Brad imagined himself on a beach buying fru-fru drinks for a young woman in a dangerously small bikini. He did his best to hold onto that image as he headed back to work.

Chapter 29

A few minutes before eight, Erica walked into her office, clicked her computer on and sat. The routine collapsed when she touched down. Gone were the all-important missions that kept her running full-speed to meet impossible deadlines. Gone were the project plans with pages of excuses to defer social entanglements. The frenzy had vanished. She was left gazing at the awakening computer, wondering what was next.

Unaccustomed to such moments of introspection, her psyche seized the moment to ask why she pushed herself the way she did. Completely out of sync, she felt out of place and time in her own life. It was as if her consciousness had arrived long after her body, plopped down now into the middle of her life, suddenly self-aware for the first time. Could she have run this long, this hard in the wrong direction? She searched back through her past for the time she'd begun the chase. Her professional career was a marathon of overachievement with a supreme focus on learning more and producing more than anyone. She overwhelmed her competition with fanatical commitment. Back further still, high school was more of the same. She recalled grade school, a time when she spent most days transported into stories.

The feelings came flooding back, too. The torment from the other students felt fresh. The other first graders called her mother a killer. They said Erica would grow up to be a killer, too, and any boy dumb enough to be her boyfriend deserved what he got. Some kids were truly afraid of her, the others pretended to be.

Ashamed, Erica vowed never to become a victim like her mother. Surviving her father and the hazing after his death set Erica on a path to unequivocal self-sufficiency. That's when it all began. She pushed herself to the edge of physical endurance and mental toughness. Governance by an unrelenting will intensely sculpted mind and body, but left the whole of her emotional life untouched. Abandoned at an early age, her romantic desires lay unexamined, an unopened gift adorned with bright paper and ribbon, waiting. It wasn't clear what she was trying to achieve all these years or who she was trying to convince of her worth; the first graders, her mother, or herself.

Freed from her reputation by time and circumstance, Erica led people naturally. She learned at an inhuman pace and put forth incredible effort to reach her goals. This was how she came to work for Brad, to pour out two years of her life and propel him to a promotion he didn't deserve. She would have accepted her role with grace if he hadn't betrayed her so purposefully; more so if he'd been the first.

Wasn't she the model employee?

Few worked as hard as she did, but here she sat with an assignment that signaled it was time to move on again. She'd known Brad wanted her out from the beginning. Still, her resume lay half-drafted at home.

She fumed through the walls at Brad.

Her mother would say she'd misplaced her anger for her father. She refused to take orders from any man and that doomed her to a succession of disappointments. She needed to learn to go along, to talk through issues instead of bottling them up. Then she would succeed. Erica agreed that she managed-down well and managed-up poorly. She needed control.

Melanie saw a great opportunity to heat things up with Farm Boy. "Take a vacation. Get naked," she said. After all she'd put into this company, a shift into the slow lane was in order, but Erica wasn't looking to slow down. It was time to get even with Brad.

Gregg appeared in the doorway carrying two dozen bursting red roses and Erica knew precisely what had to be done. The answer had been sitting on her desk for weeks.

"Hello, stranger," he said as he strode around the desk, all smiles. He set the etched glass vase on the desk and kissed her cheek.

"Great way to keep the office romance low key."

"You get flowers all the time. I just deliver."

"Marking your territory?"

"No need. I did an email blast last night, handed out flyers in front of the building this morning, and I'm running a full page ad in the Globe on Sunday. The flowers are an excuse to visit."

"You picked a bad day." Erica caught him up on her conversation with Brad and her suspicion that he'd taken credit for her work and ruined her reputation with the board. He had turned her promotion into a demotion, giving her the choice to support client services or quit. Brad would prefer the latter.

Gregg's expression sagged as the details rolled out. His empathy for her situation shouldn't have been a surprise, but this wasn't what Erica had come to expect from relationships. Gregg had been intent on her for over four years. He listened and he knew innately what she thought and felt. She couldn't stop babbling, burdening him as she was and yet he couldn't have been more tuned in. He was interested. Not just in her looks or her financial success, all of her. She had the urge to get up and throw her arms around him, but resisted.

Gregg brightened after a lull in the conversation. "Why don't we get away from here? We could spend a few days on the farm. It's quiet this time of year and my folks would love to meet you."

"Really? Why me?"

"What's not to like? Brains, beauty, and I hear their son has totally flipped for you."

"What happened to taking it slow?"

"This is taking it slow. My first thought was the Caribbean. You in a bikini and me in surfer shorts for two weeks or so. It would be a lot more fun than the farm, but I didn't imagine you'd go for it."

"You imagined right."

"Think about the farm. Getting away from all this concrete will do you good. I could show you a few trees and some animals that don't live on crumbs in the park, you know, nature."

"I'll give it some thought."

Gregg ventured a step toward Erica's side of the desk. She looked down her nose toward the open door. He faltered a step, but came around and kissed her anyway.

She watched the hall long after he'd gone.

The rest of the day offered few distractions. Erica dug into an old problem that promised to show how unfit a leader Brad was. He'd angrily rejected Gregg's request for help and soon everyone would know just how wrong he had been.

Hours passed quickly. She set up some new equipment and reloaded the December data. She had the system working by six-thirty. It felt odd, but she packed up and left the problem unsolved for the next morning.

She didn't notice the thick man in the dark suit on the corner. He appeared heavyset under the straight-cut suit, though closer inspection would have revealed bulging muscles. He watched as Erica weaved out among the concrete planters that guarded the building. He talked into his phone, shifting his feet as her sneakers bounced across the street and headed off through the park.

He followed from a full block's distance, limiting himself to a hurried walk even though he couldn't match her pace. He'd try to keep her in sight, but he knew where she was going.

Chapter 30

Erica shoved the door closed.

Melanie curiously poked her head around the corner. She held three tank tops, none warm enough for the late spring weather.

"What's the occasion?" Melanie asked.

"What do you mean?"

"What are you doing home? It's not even seven."

"Good thing you weren't throwing a wild party. I'd have to get lost." Melanie knew better than to bring her college friends here. She'd done it once and Erica was clear she wasn't letting her apartment turn into a college hangout with beer cans piled high and food stains on every rug. Melanie had been the perfect house guest since.

They'd grown surprisingly close given the twelve year age difference and the late hours Erica kept. Erica's influence mellowed Melanie a bit and Melanie lightened the mood whenever she saw the chance.

"Something up at work? Gregg spending too much time in your office?"

"He brought me roses today."

"The boy's in love. You would be, too, if you'd stop pushing him away for five seconds."

"Someone's got to keep a cool head."

"Yeah, don't go running off and doing something rash like having sex."

"He kissed me twice in the office today."

"You have a real office, with walls I mean?"

"So?"

"Don't be such a prude. Shut the door and grab those tight little buns."

"All I need is my boss to walk in and find us making out in the middle of the day."

"Erica, this is two thousand six. People are having sex in public. A kiss or two at work isn't going to kill you. Don't think your boss hasn't banged chicks right on his desk, or yours."

"Gross. I can see whose side you're on. I suppose you think I should go to the farm with him this weekend." The way Gregg and Melanie conspired, she'd probably known about the invitation for weeks.

"He asked?" She waited for a nod. "Absolutely. Go! Spend some quality time. Meet the parents. Who knows what could happen."

"If I listened to you, I'd be married in six months."

Melanie questioned why marrying Gregg was a bad idea. Erica argued the evils of marriage to Melanie's recounting of Gregg's boundless virtues. Neither budged. Erica changed into her running clothes and started out toward the river. Melanie headed for the shower to prepare for a critique group that featured more drinking and flirting than journalism.

. . .

Caleb Priestly watched Erica trot down the stairs and lift her leg to the rail for a stretch. She rested her head on her knee and grabbed the sole of her sneaker with both hands, something Caleb couldn't do. She stretched the other hamstring likewise and then hopped down to the sidewalk. With one hand on the rail, she lifted the opposite foot and grabbed the toe of her sneaker. She stretched one quad then the other.

She didn't act squirrelly like a target who was mixed up in something dangerous. She was a solid citizen from a nice neighborhood. She gazed off into the distance preoccupied with her thoughts. She didn't react to the men who checked out her tight spandex pants as they walked by. She had no idea she was being followed and that would make tonight's work simple. If he was careless then things would change.

She jogged off down the block and disappeared around the corner. Caleb timed two minutes on his watch before leaving the car. He should have tuned in to the microphones in the apartment, but there was nothing to hear. He followed her here and he'd seen her take off. Better to get it done quickly before she came back.

Traffic on Clarendon was thick with cars pulling off Sturrow headed toward Newbury or Boylston, but on the Marlborough side, traffic was light. He palmed the pick and tension wrench and slipped across the middle of the block without drawing any attention. No one was within half a block of the building as he trotted up the stairs and checked the lobby. He worked the tension wrench into the keyhole then raked the pins once, twice. A few of them caught. He worked the pick carefully now, click, click, click and the lock turned. He pocketed the pick and wrench as he would his key and headed inside.

Two hundred two was at the top of the stairs. He'd never been inside, but he'd seen it on the monitor the rare days she went home while he was tailing her. The lock was newer than the one outside, but there was no one in the hall to watch him pick it. He could take a full minute and it wouldn't matter. If someone came he'd feign key trouble and knock. He counted thirty-four before the handle turned. The door stuck on the threshold and he shoved it open. He quickly shut it and donned thin leather gloves.

Caleb needed a hiding place she could reach, but one that she wouldn't discover between now and when the cops came looking. He wished he'd brought some packing tape to slap the envelope to the back of a bureau or bookcase and get out, but the boss had insisted he use things from the apartment to plant the stash.

The desk drawers held nothing useful. He checked his watch: four and a half minutes since she'd turned the corner. Plenty of time. He rifled the kitchen drawers until he found the typical junk drawer everyone seemed have. It held paper clips, a dish filled with loose change, staples, and take-out menus. He clutched a roll of masking tape and turned toward the desk. He'd be gone in another forty seconds.

The shower stopped.

He'd heard it running, but assumed it was in the next apartment. Someone was here, it could be the boyfriend. If he'd heard the commotion in the kitchen drawers, he'd come looking. Caleb wheeled around. No doors except the one he came in and the closet next to it. He stalked across the kitchen and back into the living room. The place was sparse, nowhere for a two hundred twenty pound man to hide.

A towel ruffled briskly.

Caleb crammed himself under the desk, his knees jammed up under his chin. With the high-backed leather chair pulled up close, he was nearly invisible from most of the apartment.

The bathroom door opened. Moist steps, bare feet on linoleum. Closer. Across the kitchen and into the living room. Legs came into view, shapely legs, naked up to a light pink robe that looked damp. The roommate. How could he forget the damn roommate? Water dripped on the carpet. The feet turned toward the front windows and then the kitchen. If she knew he was lurking this close she'd scream her head off and he'd have to whack her. He should have listened to the microphones. Luckily, she walked over to the door and chained it.

She hesitated, looped through the kitchen and closed the junk drawer. Then, seeming satisfied she was safe, walked back to the bathroom. Her search took less than a minute. The blow dryer started immediately.

There was a recess beneath the top drawer, high enough so her legs wouldn't hit it when she worked and low enough so it couldn't be seen except from underneath. Suddenly less picky about his hiding spot, he pulled the large envelope from his jacket, careful not to disturb any of her prints that might still be on it. He fastened it to the underside of the desk with long strips of tape. Her prints were on the blue plastic holder inside.

Standing again, he eased into the kitchen and returned the tape exactly where it had been.

Quickly to the door, he removed the chain, eased outside and pulled it shut with a thump. Rattling downstairs, he palmed the last doorknob with his glove already removed. He pocketed the gloves on the landing and strolled down the steps casually as if he were heading out to dinner. He melted across the street and drove away.

. . .

The constant thumping of sneakers on concrete put Erica at ease. People spread out all along the river, but no one could pester her while she kept moving. This was her time to feel strong and put the world in perspective. Three miles passed too quickly for her to organize her thoughts on this day. A few blocks past her apartment she turned and walked back to cool down. Inside and up the stairs, she unlocked the inner door and gave it a shove with her shoulder. The chain caught and it jerked to a stop.

"C'mon, Melanie, let me in."

Light footsteps approached. Melanie peeked fearfully through the gap in the door, her eyes timid, ready to run at the slightest provocation.

Melanie unchained the door.

When Erica stepped through, Melanie shut it tight and re-chained it.

"What's going on, Mel? You ok?"

She asked if she looked that shaken-up and Erica indicated the chain. Neither of them secured it with any frequency.

"Someone was in here while you were gone."

Erica's eyes darted around the room. The windows were intact, the kitchen neat, the desk undisturbed.

"Did you see someone?"

"No, but I heard him rustling around the kitchen."

"The kitchen?"

"Maybe he was looking for a knife. I'm positive I heard silverware rattling. I came out, looked around and everything looked fine. I chained the door thinking I was imagining it and went back to drying my hair."

She paused. Something was coming. Erica couldn't imagine what.

"The door slammed shut and I ran back out. I don't know what I was thinking. I should have locked myself in the bathroom and called 911. All I had on was my robe. Who knows what would have happened if I caught him inside. He could have killed me."

"Was it someone else's door?"

"The chain was swinging. He had to be inside to unchain it."

"God, Mel. I locked the door, I know I did."

Erica gave her a solid hug. They stood together a long moment. Neither said anything, both wondered why someone had chosen this apartment to sneak into. Nothing had been taken. There wasn't time. It had to be a random thing. If someone had chosen them, it was because two women made an easy target. They would've had a rude wake-up call if Erica had been home.

She remembered the two men who cornered her in the alley behind the apartment late one night. They'd maneuvered her between the buildings where no passerby could see and sneered their obscene intentions. The accomplice, wobbling a bit from booze, hung back to block her way out. The leader moved in from the other side knife in hand. He never asked for money. He leered instead, closing to a few feet and gesturing with the knife toward parts of her anatomy he yearned to explore. One such jab came close enough for Erica to clamp down on his wrist, break his forearm and disarm him. Confused, he howled in pain and hunched over to protect his arm. She drove her palm through his nose then cracked down sideways against his knee. The man crumpled in a quivering bloody heap. His partner slinked away down the opposite end of the alley.

Melanie pulled back.

"Did you check if anything was missing?" Erica asked.

She hadn't. She still clutched the phone. She was probably too scared to do anything but huddle in the living room and wait for help. Erica left her there and checked her room. There were sixty-eight dollars in her purse and the checkbook was in its usual hiding place at the back of her underwear drawer. She didn't own any jewelry worth stealing, but what she had was in and around the inlaid wooden box on her dresser.

Melanie watched from the hall. "Gregg should be here any minute."

"Why?"

"My mom didn't answer, so I called him. He was running for his car before I hung up."

"Great." Erica hustled to shower off three miles of sweat and get presentable. She heard voices in the kitchen before she finished toweling off. Her jeans and white tank top were a bit too form fitting. The boy didn't need encouragement, so she detoured into the bedroom and slipped on a white button-down with thin pink stripes.

Gregg and Melanie were on the couch with their backs to Erica as she approached. He stood up as she reached them and met her eyes with a look of grave concern. "Are you ok?" he asked.

He reached out for her hand and she let him hold it a second before sitting down next to Melanie. "Fine. Nothing's missing." She left only a sliver of the couch to her left, expecting him to shift over to the low chair facing them.

He squeezed in, their thighs pressing together. The two women shifted like dominoes, wobbled by his choice of seats. "Has anything like this happened before?" he asked.

"Nothing. It's a great neighborhood."

"You need to call the cops."

"Not a chance," Erica blurted. She'd hated cops since the night they pried her away from her mother. It was over a year before mother came home; a year Erica spent as an orphan. She'd learned to take care of herself since then and she knew most cops were decent, but she'd never call one unless she was bleeding to death and out of options.

Gregg looked confused by the venomous reaction. Cops were different back home on the farm for sure. "You need to call," he said. "What if this guy breaks in somewhere else?"

"This is Boston. There are break-ins every day. What are the cops going to do besides ask annoying questions and rifle through our stuff? That's if they even show up."

"You should still call."

Erica massaged the muscle above his knee and turned to face him squarely. "It'll be fine. We've got you to take care of us. Nothing to worry about." Gregg was strong, especially through the shoulders, but Erica wasn't sure which of them would be more useful in a brawl. She was fifty pounds lighter, but ten years of karate had to account for something.

Erica kissed him gently and eased back into her space on the couch. There'd be no sending him home tonight, but there'd be no calls to the Boston Police either.

The three of them sat in relative silence for over an hour. Melanie couldn't shake the jitters. She asked Gregg to stay and he was overjoyed. He'd brought an overnight bag and, ever the gentlemen, he'd left it in the car so he wouldn't seem presumptuous. He went outside to fetch it, probably dancing all the way down the stairs.

While he was gone Melanie admitted she was spooked. She was glad Gregg was staying, but with the semester almost gone, she was thinking about going home to her parents. Erica would miss her. She'd been an ideal roommate, though how much of her good nature had to do with Erica paying her room and board, Erica would never know. She was a mature twenty-two, forced to cope with the realities of life when her father was laid-off and she nearly had to drop out. Erica had been forced to grow up much sooner.

She'd be sad to see her go in the morning.

Gregg tried to lighten the mood when he got back. He suggested an early trip to the farm, a long weekend to meet his family and see how the rural folks live. Oddly, a weekend with his parents seemed more inviting than a weekend alone in Boston.

Chapter 31

Gregg spent the early morning hours watching the red numbers on the desk clock and listening to sporadic comings and goings outside. He'd lived five years in the city and still hadn't grown used to the constant commotion of cars and voices at all hours of the night. The insect and animal noises around the farm were different, life affirming sounds of one partner calling for another. Here the noises were sharp, chaotic, dangerous; drunken revelers returning home or men like the one who let himself in yesterday.

Gregg hadn't slept more than an hour at a stretch when Melanie perched on the opposite chair clutching a cup of coffee. Warm in his sweatpants and the blankets Erica had laid out, he surveyed Melanie without getting up. Her hands shook and she leaned close like she wanted to lie down next to him so he could wrap his arms around her and keep her safe. She acted like this was her first brush with harm. Odd she'd chosen journalism as a profession. If she couldn't handle a break-in, how would she report the sorts of things that qualified as news? Being the victim had far more impact and maybe the encounter would bring a more humane perspective to her reporting.

Erica showed no ill-effects from the break-in when she came down the hall an hour later. She hadn't been inside when it happened and she wasn't as vulnerable as Melanie. Still, she seemed genuinely glad to have him in the apartment and that was a relief. He'd worried that staying the night might be a strain that would push them further apart, not that things could move any slower.

She snuggled herself midway on the couch, forcing him to roll to his side to make room. She had left no doubt about where he'd sleep last night, so her coziness was a complete surprise. Melanie was the one who'd asked him to stay, but Erica was glad he was here. Melanie had said she had feelings under there. He hoped they were starting to break free.

After breakfast Melanie announced she was going home and wouldn't come back until graduation. Embarrassed by Erica's generosity and ashamed to leave her alone when she might need help, Melanie wanted to stay, but she was too frightened. She gushed thanks to Erica and credited her for receiving her bachelor's degree on time. Gregg wondered if Erica had been giving her more than a free room these last few months.

Gregg called the office and took the rest of the week off. He lugged a few boxes down for Melanie and by the time the car was loaded, Erica had agreed to spend a long weekend at the farm. She packed for three days, a long time away on very short notice. She'd lost her zest for work. He wished her feelings for him had dimmed her dedication, but he knew better. Something had affected her deeply. The odds were on the break-in or her problems with Brad.

Her Cross Country only had fourteen hundred miles. She rarely had a chance to drive it in the city and he was glad to let her break it in on the trip to the farm. He guided her down the highway and through a series of turns that all looked the same to anyone who didn't live here.

The first of his father's corn fields came into view and he pointed out the long flat row that stretched over a mile, interrupted only by the pond he'd fished in as a boy and the cranberry bogs on the far end. They rounded the corner and climbed a steep hill past the cow barn. She slowed down expecting the driveway and he motioned her to keep going. He pointed out the fields on both sides of the road and she looked back in disbelief that they could still be circling his father's property. The apple trees on the left were surrounded by piles of brush from the late-winter trimming. She finally turned in past the stand of pine trees, down the long dirt drive and up alongside the massive red corrugated barn. The surprise registered on her face as she looked out over the corn fields below and the roads they'd traveled. They gazed over brown fields, the crimson rectangular bogs and the tall stands of pine trees where the Turner's property blended into the forest. The bright green fairways of the golf course peeked out of the trees in one corner of the sprawling landscape. She'd lived in the city her entire life and she'd probably never had a yard of her own. Three square miles was unfathomable to her.

"This whole place is yours?"

"My dad's," he corrected.

"You don't even have neighbors."

"We do. They're just a bit further apart than you're used to." Gregg indicated the Miller's house on the opposite side of the field. Erica squinted, but the asphalt shingles were hard to make out among the pines. His brother's house was closer, a hundred yards down the main road, though he didn't qualify as a neighbor. She turned in circles, taking in the vastness of the farm.

Gregg hoisted the bags from the trunk and led her across the dirt parking lot toward the modest ranch he'd grown up in. Gregg's father, Frank, stood on the back of a pickup and pushed against the huge new heater as Gregg's brothers guided and pulled from either side. He led Erica over and made introductions. Frank explained what they were doing. Everyone was polite in front of Erica. His brothers would have plenty of comments later.

He led her through the unlocked front door. Mom had all she could do to stay in the kitchen until they walked the length of the hall. She wore a pale dress covered with a white apron that featured an apple pie with a piece missing on the front. She'd dressed up for Erica.

She left the wooden spoon in the pot she was stirring, came over and threw her arms around him. After he kissed her cheek, he turned and introduced Erica.

"Hi, Mrs. Turner." Erica began to extend a hand and looked baffled when mom hugged and kissed her like a long lost daughter. He should have warned her about that. He'd never seen Erica hug anyone except him.

Mom held Erica at arms length and looked her up and down. "It's nice to finally meet you. Gregg's told us so much about you."

"Really." Erica fired an accusatory look.

"Why don't you help me finish up? We can get acquainted. I'm sure Frank and the boys could use Gregg's help outside."

Erica flashed a 'don't you dare leave me' look.

"I should at least be here to defend myself."

"Nonsense." Mom made a sweeping motion to shoo him from the kitchen. He made a quick appeal to Erica, who gave him a look that said, 'I'm trapped and you're going to pay.'

Nonetheless, Gregg picked up the bags and carried them to two neighboring rooms at the end of the hall. He could hear his mother's constant chatter and he walked out dreading what she would say. She was a sweet woman with an innocent directness. She used it like a battering ram to get at what she wanted to know. Erica was a closed book. He hoped his mother would figure that out and have the good sense to back off.

Outside, Gregg pulled on a pair of leather gloves and hopped up on the tailgate. He caught a conspiratorial look between his brothers as he joined them in the bed of the truck.

"Hey, does your boyfriend let you drive?" Tom asked.

Gregg ignored him, grabbed hold of the frame and grunted as they all pulled together.

"Gregg, man, you've gone soft from city living. Maybe you should go help mom in the kitchen," quipped his youngest brother Rick.

Gregg didn't argue. He missed the farm. His brothers had married women who played the farmer's wife perfectly. They cooked, cleaned and raised children while their husbands worked themselves to the brink from planting to harvest. Erica would never fit that mold. She was tough, independent, educated, and not the slightest bit marriage-minded. This bothered Gregg far more than any worn-out one-liner his brothers could throw at him.

The men jerkily rocked the machine off the truck and onto the tractor. When they jumped down and got ready to move it inside, Tom began again, "You know, Gregg–"

Frank cut him off and offered some support for his eldest son. "That's enough boys. When either of you makes as much money as Erica or Gregg with those fancy city jobs, you come talk to me. I thank God your mother stuck to home. She would have been impossible to live with otherwise. Cut your brother some slack."

The conversation ended.

The brothers uttered only a few directional adjustments to Frank as he maneuvered the tractor into the back corner of the barn. They didn't make even one rude gesture as they guided the heater into place. They were busy hatching new jabs for later.

As soon as it was aligned, they abandoned the machine and went inside. Getting it hooked up was a job for another day.

Chapter 32

Erica found herself alone with Gregg's mom. He hadn't said two words about his family on the ride down, instead talking about the farm and what happened there this time of year. She stood in his childhood home wondering what he did here as a kid. Everything about this place was different from what she'd known and she had no idea what his family would expect of her. Mrs. Turner divided her attention between four pots on the stovetop and a roast turkey cooling on the counter, while she sputtered a constant stream of questions that Erica wasn't ready to answer.

There was a cozy table in the corner that overlooked the expansive brown field. "Can I help you set the table, Mrs. Turner?"

"Please, Dear, call me Sue." She showed Erica into the dining room to a cabinet stacked with dishes and a drawer filled with silverware.

Erica grabbed four forks, knives and spoons and followed Sue back into the kitchen.

Sue began stirring gravy, but stopped when she saw Erica headed for the breakfast nook. "Not there, Dear. We'll eat in the dining room."

Erica turned back to the room they had left. "Which places shall I set?"

"All of them."

Erica counted. "All ten?"

Erica's mother was her only living family. Mother had a boyfriend who'd asked to marry her twice. With his two children the marriage would bring her entire family to five. Dinner for ten on Wednesday was quite unexpected.

"The whole family's coming," Sue said. "Gregg has two brothers, Tom and Rick. Tom's wife, Dianne, is driving over now. Rick lives next door with his wife, Claudia, and their two boys, Matthew and Justin."

"Wow, you have a big family." Erica repeated the names to herself as she placed silverware around the table.

Sue peeked in from the kitchen. "Not so big, just two grandchildren. My sister has seven. On Memorial Day we have a cookout and all of Gregg's aunts, uncles and cousins come. There were over ninety people last year."

"How do you remember all those names?"

"Remember? We're never apart long enough to forget. In a family this big there's always something to celebrate. We see each other pretty often. Don't worry, you'll learn them easy enough."

Erica stared at the first place setting, wondering how Sue turned a three day visit into a lifetime commitment. Or was it Gregg?

Sue appeared behind her and reached for a fork. "Let me help you, Dear. Forks go on the left, knives and spoons on the right. Like this." Sue picked up a napkin, creased it diagonally and set the fork on top.

Erica blushed. Proper table setting wasn't something she'd learned from her mother. She wished she'd taken the initiative to learn on her own. She had a queasy feeling about her first impression, but Sue changed the subject to Gregg's future as an excellent husband and father. Erica forgot her place-setting weakness and moved on to larger worries.

The men burst in the front door. They headed for the kitchen sink where they washed one after another and passed the towel from man to man before hovering around the sliced turkey on the counter. They took turns distracting Mrs. Turner while the others sampled her cooking. She knew what was happening, but feigned ignorance. Erica watched, relieved to be free of the homey chat with Mrs. Turner. She had no inclination for cooking or mothering and she gladly tuned in when Mr. Turner started talking about planting time.

The screen door slammed behind Matthew and Justin as they ran full speed into the kitchen.

"Boys!" shouted Frank.

Sneakers squealed as the boys skidded to a halt in the middle of the kitchen floor. "This is not a racetrack. There are twelve hundred acres outside. You can go out there and run yourself silly until the fields are planted. Inside, we walk."

Rick glared at his children.

"Yes, Sir," they mumbled.

Frank motioned them to come to him. Erica turned slowly toward the dining room, not wanting to see them get spanked. From the corner of her eye, she saw the boys give their grandfather a tight squeeze.

Sue herded a reflective Erica and the rest of the family toward the table. Frank came in last carrying a grandson under each arm. When he set them down, they climbed into seats on either side of Sue. Gregg and Tom sat at the opposite end, on either side of Frank while the women and Rick clustered in the middle. As Frank said grace, Erica bowed her head and spied the faces around the table. Frank and Sue were firmly in control, yet their children and grandchildren adored them. It didn't take a special occasion to bring them here. The atmosphere was so foreign she lost track of Frank's prayer.

When grace was said, Frank passed heavy platters filled with turkey, ham and vegetables one by one to Gregg and on down the table. As Erica passed the platters to Claudia, she noticed how young she looked, thirty or thirty-two. She hadn't spent much time with children, but figured Matthew to be at least eight.

"You must be proud of the boys. They act so grown up," Erica said.

"They grow up fast. I can't believe Matthew's ten and Justin's nine."

Erica nodded as she passed a dish of mashed potatoes. Babies at twenty-two? Dianne looked about twenty-five. No doubt children were in her immediate future. Was Erica a spinster in this room, single at thirty-four?

"They don't behave this well at home. Grandpa keeps them in line."

"I noticed."

Sue chimed in from her end, "Don't let his bark fool you. He's a big teddy bear."

"I'll keep that in mind," Erica said.

CJ West

Dianne looked up from her plate. "Gregg tells us you're almost finished with your master's."

Erica nodded. "Finally. All the work is done. I graduate next week."

Sue looked down the table at her husband. "That's terrific! I don't think we know another woman with a master's degree."

Frank tore off a large chunk of bread. "I don't think we know a man with a master's degree, except Dr. Colby and maybe one of the teachers down at the school. Computer Science, isn't it Erica?"

"That's right." Erica had an odd feeling about the Turners. She'd only been dating Gregg a week and they knew so much about her. "Is there anything Gregg didn't tell you?" she asked.

"Gregg doesn't talk much. We can barely get a word out of him."

Erica wondered how much Boston had changed him. The Gregg she knew could charm anyone. He was a strong manager and mentor, far from the shy kid Sue described. "He's told you plenty about me."

"We've never seen him so taken with a woman before," Sue said.

"Can't say as I blame him," Frank added.

Erica blushed for the second time in an hour.

Gregg avoided her eyes.

"So what embarrassing childhood stories can you tell me? Is there anything I need to know before things go too far?"

Gregg's eyes dropped to his plate.

Rick and Tom straightened in their chairs, eager for a laugh at their brother's expense.

Frank started them off with a story everyone but Erica had heard at least twenty times. "Gregg is quite a golfer. You see those two trophies there behind Sue?" Frank pointed proudly at two matching gold men golfing atop glittering, sixteen-inch platforms. "Gregg and I won the local four-ball together. It's the biggest tournament our course has – mind you we don't have much time to practice in summer. Three years ago, we came to the last hole of the championship match tied. I lost my ball so it was all up to Gregg. He hit two huge shots. The second one landed on the green."

130

Rick gestured impatiently. "Yeah, yeah. He hit the green in two and made an eagle putt to win the tournament. I think the putt gets longer every year. How long was it again? Forty feet?"

Frank glared at Rick. "You know it was thirty feet and I'm sure Erica is glad to hear the story even if you aren't."

Tom raised a finger. "I think she'd like to hear about the yellow jackets in the orchard." Everyone smiled.

Erica waited to see who would tell the story.

Sue spoke up first. "When Gregg was a teenager, he stepped on a hornets' nest while he was picking apples. Hornets flew out of the ground and right up his pants. I guess they got him pretty good. He stormed off to the barn and poured gasoline down the hole. Lord knows how much because he still won't say. When he lit the nest, the ground exploded. He killed the hornets and two apple trees. It burned so bright I could see it from the house. If the grass was any longer, or the tractor was any further away, he would have burned half the orchard."

"It wasn't that bad," Gregg protested.

"Erica Dear, I have pictures. He burned a black circle in the grass five times the size of this room," Sue beamed.

"Can we talk about something else," Gregg pleaded.

"That was a great story," Erica said, rubbing her hand above his knee.

Matthew and Justin pushed their plates forward and asked if they could go see the new batch of chicks. With permission, they excused themselves and headed outside.

Frank called after them, "It's getting cold, don't keep those young ones away from the light too long."

The children disappeared with another slam of the screen door.

Sue looked down the table. "Erica Dear, why don't you tell us about your family?"

"There's not much to tell. It's just my mother and me."

"What about your father?" Everyone's attention focused on Erica.

"He died when I was four," she said stiffly.

Forks clinked down with a collective gasp.

Claudia put a hand on Erica's elbow. "I'm so sorry, Erica. What happened?"

"I don't like to talk about it," Erica snapped.

The room went quiet. Gregg reached under the table and held Erica's hand as if that could somehow protect her from the past.

"It must have been hard growing up without a father," Sue pressed.

No one was eating now. All eyes were on Erica, not with the accusatory glares she'd seen from hundreds of kids in school, but with a budding compassion for her loss so many years ago. She wondered how the expressions would change if they knew she was better off without him. Even Gregg had no idea. After the horrors in grade school, she'd never told a soul again. "Really, I'd rather not talk about it, if you don't mind."

"It was a long time ago. Almost thirty years, isn't it?" Sue asked.

Stomachs tightened around the table, wincing in sympathy. Erica gave a slight nod and focused on her mashed potatoes. Being singled out as the only vegetarian in a house full of farmers with a turkey and a ham in the center of the table would be bad, but she'd rather have that conversation than the one Sue was driving toward.

Sue shifted in her seat. Her head buzzed with questions that needed to be answered. The others fidgeted. They knew she wasn't going to let it go.

"Was he sick?" she asked.

Gregg squeezed her hand, an apology of sorts for his mother. The table fell silent. Erica couldn't answer. Memories of her father's life and death still haunted her dreams. It was something she needed to forget. She stood up, her lips quivering as she addressed Sue. "Will you excuse me? I need some fresh air."

Erica walked to the front porch, looked at the wicker chairs and then at her car parked on the hillside. She could be home in an hour if she didn't get lost. Gregg could return her bags when he came back to the city. If he knew what she was hiding, he wouldn't blame her for leaving. He had to know it was something awful. Sooner or later he'd ask the same questions and he deserved the truth. She felt her pockets and looked down at her empty hands. Her keys were inside. She had to go back in no matter how uncomfortable it was, but not yet.

She wondered what they were saying about her as she gazed into the darkness. The night sky was murkier here. There were no lights for miles. Crickets chirped and frogs peeped in the stillness. The glow from the house only extended a few dozen yards, but the moon threw a surprising amount of light around the fields and outbuildings. She could see well enough to navigate the farm, but she couldn't imagine leaving the porch unless it was for her car. A thousand hungry creatures could be hiding in the shadows.

Gregg came outside and stood close to Erica. "Sorry about that. I should have warned you about my mother. Sometimes she doesn't know when to stop, but she doesn't mean any harm."

"Your whole family's sweet."

"Let's take a walk."

"You sure you still want to?"

He turned her head toward him and raised her chin until they looked directly into each other's eyes. "Nothing could change my mind about you. Nothing. Whatever happened is in the past. Tell me, don't tell me, that's up to you."

They walked away from the house and into the shadows at the edge of the farm. As her eyes adjusted to the dim light, Gregg rambled through the family history she should have quizzed him about in the car. She relaxed until a pack of coyotes howled in the distance. The chilling sound had her clinging to him for the next two hours. They walked side by side in the cool night air and Gregg rattled off stories about every building and tree they passed.

Tom and Rick drove off with their families. Gregg didn't call out. He stood with Erica in the grassy field and watched the tail lights fade into the night. When she was too cold even in his sweatshirt, they walked back to the house and settled into separate rooms for the night.

Chapter 33

It seemed like only a few minutes later Erica woke up to a burst of loud noises outside her window. It sounded like the men had gotten up early to stack metal plates, dropping them on top of each other from two feet high. At six o'clock the sun had already brightened the shades. She lay back, aching for sleep, but the crowing roosters and the growing light prodded her awake. The metallic noises kept booming. Soon she gave up, showered and went to the kitchen. Sue cooked French toast, scrambled eggs and bacon simultaneously on the stovetop. Frank waited at the table, his attention focused out the window. Gregg was nowhere in sight.

Sue gave a hearty smile and indicated a fresh pot of coffee.

"I'm sorry about last night. I didn't mean to upset you, Sweetheart."

Erica found a mug and filled it. "It's not your fault. You'd think after all these years, it would get easier, but it doesn't."

Frank watched a corner where the brown field met the trees. He was intent, but if there was something going on out there, Erica couldn't tell. How could Gregg sleep through all the noise?

"If you ever need someone to listen, I'm always here."

"Thanks," Erica muttered. "Dinner was great if I didn't mention it."

"You're welcome anytime. Did you sleep well?"

Erica had dreaded facing Sue and Frank after running away from the conversation at dinner. Alone with them she should have been uneasy, but she felt as if she belonged here. She'd never been in a more accepting, affirming place. No wonder Gregg came home every weekend.

"I didn't sleep long for a woman on vacation," Erica said. "What's all that noise?"

"The boys are shooting crows."

"Do they have to do it so early?" She asked, taking a seat next to Frank. If he was watching them, she still couldn't tell.

"Daybreak's the best time. They lay out rotten apples and hide in the trees between fields. The crows fly in for the apples, but they're tricky. One move and they vanish." Frank imitated a darting bird with the outstretched fingers of both hands. "The boys make a competition of it. On a good day they'll get three or four each."

"They shoot them for fun?" She must have looked horrified because Frank snapped to attention.

"No, no," he said. "The crows raise heck with the corn. I'd shoot them all if I could. They're in the fields as soon as we plant – digging up seeds. Then when the corn's grown, they go from one plant to another, eating a little here and a little there. They turn piles and piles of corn into very expensive chicken feed. Not like the deer. They pull off an ear and eat the whole thing. I'd rather they didn't, but I can tolerate them."

Sue smiled toward her husband. "He tolerates 'em because I like seeing them in the fall after the corn's been cut."

An affectionate look passed between them. Sue had more control on the farm than Erica believed possible.

"What about all the ducks out there?" Erica asked. A hundred gray and black birds had settled into the lower part of the field away from the noisy shotguns. She hoped they weren't next in line for target practice.

"Those are Canadian geese. They only eat what drops on the ground and they leave a lot of fertilizer behind. The boys shoot one once in a while and we eat it, but they're a little tough. I prefer the chickens and turkeys we raise," Frank said.

"How many chickens do you have?"

"We keep sixty or seventy most of the time. We don't sell them. It's more of a hobby and a comfort knowing where your dinner came from. I hatch quite a few chicks this time of year because I have time to tend the incubator. You ought to have Gregg take you on a proper tour. He'll let you hold a few. They're cute – fuzzy little buggers."

Would she see tonight's dinner in one of the pens around the farm?

Before she could ask, the boys tromped in from the back porch, shotguns in hand, breeches open, the muzzles pointed constantly toward the floor. They were all decked out in green camouflage from their hats to their boots. Rick and Tom lugged the guns to Frank and Sue's room.

The brothers squeezed in around the table. Gregg nudged Erica over until she nearly touched elbows with Frank. The boys rehashed the morning's events for their father's entertainment. Gregg dropped five birds, his proudest shot from directly underneath. The bird fell to earth with a thud ten feet from him. Rick dropped three birds and Tom only two. Frank was riveted as the three brothers mimicked the twists and dives the birds used to avoid them. When they were through, Gregg goaded them that today's result was typical; it took both of them to do the work he did in a day. Frank agreed when it came to shooting or golf. Erica wasn't sure if she was proud or disturbed by his success.

Gregg and Erica spent a quiet day together touring the farm and the town where he grew up. Everything was small scale; the single elementary school that served the whole town, the two convenience stores too distant to be convenient. Just getting to the grocery store took twenty minutes. Every road was humped and the residents compensated by driving down the center, that way they were on top. It was odd at first, but they rarely saw another car. What they did see was trees. Everywhere they went trees blocked them in. Now and again they passed a corn field or a hay field that stretched impossibly long, bigger than she could have imagined.

When the sun started sinking in the afternoon, they settled into a clump of trees that looked down over a long brown field. This was Gregg's favorite spot as a boy, far enough from the house to be secluded, but not a long walk.

Gregg sat with his back to a sturdy pine and Erica reclined against the solid muscles of his chest. "What do you think of the farm?" he asked.

"I've never seen any place so big and your family's so nice," she said, rubbing his arm. "You can't help but be at peace here."

"Could you live here?"

"It's too far from Boston." She felt him sigh. "If I didn't have to work, I'd live in a place like that." She pointed to the hilltop. "I bet there's a great view over the trees. And I like the way the long grass swishes in the wind. The house wouldn't have to be big, but it would have a barn and horses." Erica imagined a house in the empty field and what she'd do with a horse. She'd always pictured herself living alone in a city apartment. No apartment building would be erected here. This was a place for a family. There had never been children in her future, but they were a big part of Gregg's.

"My dad's been saving this spot for me since I was ten."

"It's beautiful,"

He could start building anytime. Owning the land meant he could build it piece by piece as time and money allowed. He might not know anything about construction, but if he grew up on the farm he had to be comfortable with tools. Adding herself to this picture brought a sickening feeling. Things would go wrong inside the new house and his parents would hear them arguing.

"Do you really want to live a hundred yards from your parents? More importantly, would your wife?"

Everyone in his family seemed eager to be together. Would he ever understand what her childhood was like? Would he be afraid of her if he knew that her mother had killed her father when she was four? She might never get a better moment than this to explain, but she couldn't get started. It sounded horrible even to her. He didn't pry into her thoughts, rubbing the tiny muscles near her spine instead.

"I guess I'll have to ask my future wife."

"What?"

"I'll ask her if she wants to live a hundred yards from my parents."

"Tell me what she says."

"I think you already know."

"You're getting way too confident. I'm still trying to get over you killing birds so they don't eat the corn."

They sat snuggled into growing shadows and watched the birds fly here and there to pluck seeds from the field. Erica brightened as he held her close and the sun dipped lower.

"What happens when we go back to Boston? I don't like the thought of you in that apartment alone. What if that guy comes back?"

"I'm a big girl. Ten years of Karate, remember? If he comes back, he'll be in more trouble than he knows."

"I'd rather you stayed with me."

"I'm not Claudia or Dianne."

"That doesn't mean I won't worry. A break-in isn't a joke."

Erica let herself nuzzle into his shoulder, turning her face up toward his. "You're adorably overprotective."

He protested again so she kissed him there in the cool shade of the pine. His safety concerns were replaced by desires she wouldn't quench out here in the open. Need welled in the depth of their kisses, bodies molded together. In all the time he'd been pursuing her, she'd never imagined this moment. The desire sprang up on its own, consuming her thoughts until they were just two intertwined bodies exploring each other.

Back in Boston they could have spent the evening in bed. She wished he'd ask to pack up and go. She craved him. Not the desire to go through the motions and satisfy her man; to do what needed to be done. She rubbed her hands over his solid chest, pressed herself against him, hot with desire to feel his skin against hers.

Gregg didn't know how to react. He was shocked by the change. Every time she eased the intensity of her kiss, he drew back, satisfied. Each time she drove back into him she felt his delight as he surged to meet her.

When they finally left the tree, Erica was shivering from the cold and plotting ways to casually sneak into his room.

Chapter 34

Brad reclined across the aisle, his feet straddling the open cabinet in front of him. His chair pressed against the cabinet behind, his head resting on the sheet metal, his eyes closed. The cold room demanded late hours with only spurts of activity between the long cycles when the computer labored and the operator waited. At 10:30 P.M. this posture was common. Marty would expect a bit more formality from his newly-minted senior vice president brother-in-law. He'd be furious if he knew about the program Brad was running in his computer room.

The numbers on the screen didn't matter anymore. There weren't enough transactions for this last run to make up the gap. He'd be at least two and a half million short and his mind spun with potential consequences. Would the boss take the shortfall from his share? Could he, if Brad was the one delivering the money? It sounded like a huge sum, but Brad didn't need the two and a half to rebuild his little house in the French countryside and retire in style. His biggest problem was ending this thing and leaving BFS without arousing suspicion.

He needed a plausible reason to leave Boston. His first plan was to get married, but that had fallen flat. In a year of looking he'd had a few hot encounters, but nothing that would qualify as a relationship. No woman would pick up and move with him to France. He hunted for jobs in other cities, but nothing had panned out there either. He was stuck between an inept brother-in-law, a maniacal power-hungry partner and an employee with a grudge.

Brad wanted out. He didn't want to return from this next trip, but the boss wouldn't let go until they were in the clear for good. He wanted certainty, a closed investigation and someone else doing time in their place. Ludicrous. Stupid as throwing rocks at a sleeping bear, but it wasn't Brad's call. He'd do what he was told and help pin this on Erica. The call from Sarah Burke showed promise, but it smacked of a prolonged investigation and a nasty legal battle. The truth would come out in a courtroom. Brad would face Erica's lawyer from the witness stand. She'd understand the crime once the charges were spelled out and she'd have years to research and prove her case. She'd know he was guilty, but knowing and proving were two different things. How long could he stand the intense scrutiny?

The distinctive click and flash broke the steady hum of computers. Brad jumped out of his seat without pausing to breathe or even open his eyes. Scrambling to the end of the row and around the corner, he left the CD he'd used to steal over a hundred and seventy-five million dollars right in the server. The program was still busily changing customer transactions as Brad ran, ready to battle his way out of the server room and on to the Canadian border. He took two hard strides across the tile floor then stumbled awkwardly to a stop when he saw Herman behind the camera.

"Priceless." The camera flashed again. "You pussy. Where the Hell are you going?"

Brad faced him dumbfounded, his heart racing, gasping, unable to catch his breath. He felt exposed standing in view of the hall. The photos proved nothing, but Herman didn't need them. Why torment him this way? Herman had to be covering himself. If someone found them together, he'd show the pictures. Brad would go to jail and Herman would get a raise.

"It's a miracle you haven't been caught. Is that all it takes for you to cut and run? Someone walks in and you bolt? Grow some backbone."

"Screw you. I'm risking my ass here and across the pond. All you do is hide behind the phone. Without me you've got squat."

"Simmer down, Bradley. Let's get our disc and cover our tracks before someone finds us and I'm forced to turn you in."

The prick would do it.

Back at the server, the program finished. Brad put the files back to normal and removed the CD well before the regular backup started at midnight. As he did this he wondered why Herman picked this last run for his first late-night visit to the computer room. He seemed to know everything Brad did day or night. He didn't need to come here.

The two men walked into the tiny security room, Brad watching every corner for trouble, Herman as calm as if he were ordering lunch in the company cafeteria.

"Well, this is it. How much of my six million did you get?" Herman asked as Brad made the changes on the building access computer.

"I'm about two million short, but I was interrupted before I checked the final numbers. I guess we'll see."

"Interrupted? Looked to me like you were sleeping. Don't worry. It's not a big hit. We can handle it."

Brad wondered if he meant they'd share the shortfall. Herman tucked the camera into his breast pocket and Brad was reminded of the dusty storage area the night Herman killed Stu Tinsley. Herman blocked the only door. He could pull a gun and end this in seconds or he could wait until morning and show his pictures to the police or the SEC. Not likely. He still needed Brad to deliver the money, but a similar line of thinking earned Stu Tinsley four bullets.

Brad stared at the computer a few moments after he'd finished removing the record of Herman's computer room visit. When Sarah saw these records, she'd go full speed collecting evidence against Erica. Brad would come through this rich for doing the heavy lifting and keeping quiet. He stepped away from the computer and Herman's easy eyes made him believe it was true.

"I think we have a problem with the girl," Herman said.

"Erica or Sarah?"

"Erica, Dumb Ass. You pissed her off then assigned her the only job that leads straight to us. She's been gone two days. I'm worried she's off with the feds building a case."

"She's hasn't figured this thing out in two days."

"What if she's been working it for the last two months? We have no idea how close she is."

"Relax. She's pissed over my promotion. That's why she went away. She hasn't had time to breathe never mind do any research. My worry is making the charges stick. We don't have a problem until we accuse her. When we do, we'll have to lay out the scam. That's when we're vulnerable, not before."

"Think about it, Brad. She works ninety hours a week for over a year then suddenly takes off. Why? Where'd she go?"

"She didn't say."

"Aren't you her boss?"

"She's got fifteen weeks unused vacation and we're not exactly the best of friends. I couldn't stop her. And you know what? I'm glad to have her out of here. I've got the run of the place. She's taking a few days off. That's it."

Herman turned his nose up at the CD in Brad's hand. "Get rid of that thing. Break it into tiny pieces then check her office and find out how much time we have."

"The place would be swarming with cops if she knew. She's curious and she knows something's wrong, but she doesn't have any idea how big it is."

"Get in there and find out what she knows. Buy us another week."

"You're the auditor. Why don't you go in there and steal her notes. Get your ass in the line of fire for a change. See how you like it."

"If I go in there, I'm coming down hard on someone. I'm not ready to do that yet. You're her boss. Get in there and do what I'm paying you to do." Herman slipped out into the hall without waiting for a response.

It was eleven, but Brad didn't dare come out of the closet behind him. He timed three minutes on his watch, long enough for anyone who'd seen Herman leave to forget which door he'd come from.

Quickly to Erica's office, he flipped through her files. If someone came by he'd fudge something about a problem in client services. Doubtful anyone was still working at 11:12 P.M.

The folder he was looking for was blank on the outside. He would have passed it by if it wasn't on top of the stack. He immediately recognized the letter inside. He'd shredded this same letter and the phone bill twice already. The first time shocked Turner in front of ten people. The second time he'd taken the documents from Erica's office after she'd gone. Turner resurrected the documents twice and twice he snuck them to Erica. Brad had turned them both into enemies, but it couldn't be helped. Erica had to be controlled and there wasn't a better option to deal with Turner that day in client services. Brad's name was scribbled several times in the margins. They were committed to proving he was involved. Sooner or later they would.

Herman was right: she was getting close. The problem was stated a dozen times in her handwriting. She just hadn't made the leap to the answer. A dozen explanations were hypothesized, most of them scored out repeatedly as if to blot out distracting thoughts. One hypothesis appeared to be under investigation and it wasn't far from the truth. She'd made a list of people who could directly access the database and change the time manually. She was thinking along the right lines, just not on the right scale. Changing transactions by hand would be fraught with errors. It would be an easy way to make ten thousand here and there, but it was no way to make two hundred million.

Brad ran the folder and its contents through the shredder outside Marty's office. The waste was incinerated twice a week. By the time Erica reconstructed her file and started over, she'd be the center of the investigation. He wasn't eager for that nightmare to begin, but he'd be glad when he had it all behind him. Soon he'd have nothing to hide, nothing that anyone in this country could find.

His final problem was Herman's file. He needed to find a solution to that problem soon.

Chapter 35

The Arizona sun was so strong at 8:00 A.M. that Tobey could almost hear the sidewalk sizzle outside. His nose didn't register the smell of urine in the corners of the narrow stairwell as he waddled down the concrete steps past scores of residents who'd sleep until noon. A dozen women earned their living in the midnight hours cramped in their little rooms. Others idled the nights away, drinking, commiserating and using darkness to steal enough to get by. Tobey would be sleeping, too, if his orders weren't so specific. The simple job afforded him a roof over his head and he wasn't going to be thrown out in the blazing sun over something as trivial as getting up before eight o'clock. He kept the alcohol to a minimum this time of the month and made sure he arrived every day before eight-thirty.

Even the lobby was unmanned this early as he walked through and emerged into the fierce morning sun.

"Tobey. Where you goin' this early?"

"Down to central. Get some day work," Tobey said even before turning around. The voice belonged to the one man he didn't want to see. Larry had taught him to survive in the park. They shared good fortune and protected each other from the kids that roamed around after dark looking for trouble. When he landed this job, he bought Larry a bottle of Chivas Regal. That turned out to be a big mistake when he learned the rules. Larry knew he'd come into money and he hounded Tobey for handouts constantly. Tobey helped when he could, but he couldn't give Larry the thing he needed most: a roof.

He turned to see Larry's weathered face down on the sidewalk. He hadn't picked this spot by chance. He'd flopped here to protest being abandoned. Tobey had no choice. He had to leave him here and he wished he could tell him why.

Larry sat up with great effort. "Gonna be ninety-five today. You're too old to work in this sun."

Tobey had come here to escape the elements. He survived the first winter easily, but hadn't considered how brutal the summer sun would be. An Arizona summer was as unforgiving as any northern winter.

"I'm too old to sleep outside. I got to work."

Larry pushed himself higher and flattened the soles of his worn out shoes against the concrete as if he'd get up and come along. He didn't need an invitation, but he waited for something. An apology maybe.

"I gotta go. Catch you later."

Larry grunted as Tobey jaywalked to the opposite corner and headed down the next block. Two years of merciless sun had baked Larry's face to a grisly leathery texture. Tobey felt sorry for him, but couldn't risk winding up back in the park. He hurried around the next corner and went inside the postal center. The counters didn't open until nine so there wasn't anyone inside to see him open the box.

The key turned and he found two envelopes. The first had the familiar blue BFS logo. The address printed on the check showed through the cellophane window. The larger envelope looked familiar as well. He clutched them in his fist and hustled to the ATM. There he opened the check and carefully copied the numbers onto the deposit envelope.

He withdrew three hundred dollars when he was finished. Normally that amount had to last an entire month, but the second envelope would have instructions for another job, one that meant a hot shower and another handful of cash. He didn't bother to read the message. He pocketed his receipts and headed back to his apartment.

. . .

145

Three days later Tobey followed the same routine, but this time he walked three blocks north to meet Carlos.

This place was swank. He buzzed once and the door clicked open. He took the elevator to five and hiked to the end of the hall. The door swung open before he could knock. Carlos welcomed him in.

"Right on time," Carlos said as he shut the door and chained it.

The .45 holstered under Carlos' shoulder didn't bother him. He had a job to do and Carlos was here to make sure things went smoothly. As long as he did what he was told, he needn't fear Carlos or the gun. He delivered the receipts to the table and flashed the unopened envelope.

"The check cleared. It's bank day," Carlos said.

Tobey nodded and headed off to the shower stocked with shampoo, soap and even an unopened package of razors. The clean fiberglass shower reminded him of his life before the accident when he had his own place. He had pride back then, a real job, a decent life. When it collapsed he'd lived minute by minute for almost a year, drinking himself into a stupor most days. Luckily, Carlos stumbled over him in the park before he wasted away. Now he was coming back. Carlos put him up in that rat infested place full of drunks and prostitutes, but at least he was indoors. If he kept it up better days were coming.

Freshly showered and shaved, he put on the white shirt and suit that Carlos only let him wear to the bank. There was a new tie on the doorknob, blue with a sandy beach and a fleet of tiny sailboats. He tied the tie, stepped out into the living room and waited for Carlos to look him over.

Carlos tugged on the tie and smelled his breath. He hadn't had much the night before and he'd brushed his teeth this morning. Carlos couldn't tell.

"Remember, the wiring instructions are prepared by your accountant. Let the manager fill out the forms. Sign them and get back here with the paperwork they give you. Don't leave without it. No paperwork, no green."

"You got it, Boss."

Carlos handed him the letter and Tobey strolled down the hall looking like a man with a million bucks.

146

Chapter 36

Stan palmed the plastic button and his Coke thunked and rattled its way down through the machine and poked out the bottom. As he came up with the can, a hand clamped down on his shoulder. The familiar voice boomed across the empty lunch room as if he were talking to someone sixty feet away. "Stanley J. Nye. Way you been man? You gone corporate on me?"

Stan turned to meet Sean's beefy shoulders at eye height, his thumb still squeezing Stan's clavicle. Sean's mailroom duties required him to roam the office continually. He enjoyed talking about the latest movies and classic cop dramas almost as much as Stan. When they crossed paths they'd drift into a vacant office or conference room and chat away a half hour. They hadn't had such a chat in two weeks. Stan had been too busy to notice. Sean looked slighted. He seemed to know their chats were a thing of the past.

"Herman's working me to death," Stan said.

"No wonder. That partner of yours is a pit bull. Showed Herman how real employees supposed to work."

"Herman thinks I'm it."

"What about Pit Bull? She taken a bite outta you yet?"

Stan forced a laugh.

"That way, huh. Tryin' to impress her? Never works, yo. Woman's gotta have respect, yo."

Stan had worked more than ever lately. He'd changed since Sarah brought her big eyes, long straight hair and curves to the team. He'd done dumber things to impress a girl, but he usually knew going in. This change snuck up on him, but Sean saw it clearly. It could have been Herman that Stan was trying to impress. He'd latched on to Sarah's enthusiasm from day one. Odd, he'd never complained about Stan's meager output. He'd never pushed Stan to do anything and it had been too easy to fall into the rut of chatting with Sean every day. There were others, too, a circle of BFS underachievers he idled with all around the office. They'd find new distractions to moderate the drudgery, but Stan couldn't get back the time he'd wasted for the last eight years. He needed to get upstairs and start making amends.

"Sean, Dude. I have a job. Sometimes I've gotta do it."

"You done more lately than the last three years. Every time I come by you're click, click, clickin'."

"Big plan this year."

Sean leaned in. "You told me you could make that shit up. No one cares you said. They care now? Miss Pit Bull watchin'? Or you watchin' her?"

Stan stepped around Sean's wire cart.

"Click, click, click," he said as Stan made his way for the elevator.

Funny Sean remembered what he'd said about fudging audits. He'd done it more than once. Nobody cared. Herman wanted his plan attained and didn't care how. They weren't catching criminals, not like the police out in the world. Even if they caught someone, they were powerless to do anything without the cops or the SEC.

Stan slipped off the elevator wondering what sort of embezzler could be lurking around BFS. Most of the executives had worked for Marty's father. He treated them like family and they were untouchable even to him. They wouldn't steal and ruin a good thing, but how vigilantly did they watch their employees? That was Stan's responsibility and he'd done a lousy job.

He paused outside Sarah's doorway before walking in.

She instinctively covered her work, extending her forearm over a few sheets of notes and a manila folder. The label was too small for Stan to read. She held the arm out before her, stiff and unmoving, and smiled up in a pathetic attempt to look casual in spite of her awkward posture.

"What are you trying so hard to hide?" He walked closer leaning to one side and then the other.

She didn't budge. She flipped the pile over, pages down, blank folder on top. "It's personal."

"Like you have a personal life. I know you think I'm an idiot, but come on. I *am* your partner and I've been busting my hump so you can go off chasing bad guys."

"I appreciate that. When I have something I'll let you know."

"Let's get real. I've been doing this a long time."

"Pretending to, anyway."

"You think you can glide in here and uncover a conspiracy in two weeks? It doesn't work like that."

"And what makes you so sure you know what I'm after?"

"It's obvious. You're looking to hang someone and make a name for yourself. That cowboy crap might work in consulting, but this isn't a six month project. You're going to be working with these people two, three, four years down the road. If you last that long."

She flushed, pressing her lips together to hide her reaction. The consulting thing hit a nerve.

"What do you want, Stan?"

"Not a solitary thing. I'm here to help."

"Help who? Me?"

"You're brand new to this. I know you think I'm lazy. Maybe you're right, but you need my help."

A powerful hiss, escaped her lips. "I'll manage."

Stan picked up the picture of all eight Burke's and hopped up on her desk. His choice of seat drove her nuts. "This business is about people. You read them as well as I read Chinese."

Stan motioned for the folder.

She didn't move, but the snobbish air was gone. She nodded toward the door and Stan gladly went over and closed it. She relaxed in her chair, but didn't turn the folder over. When Stan resumed his seat, he could have snatched it. He considered moving the stapler to tweak her instead.

"I think I've found something."

Stan gestured with his hands wide.

"I've found a discrepancy in an order that no one can explain. The problem cost the customer three thousand dollars. Gregg Turner asked IT for help three times and got nowhere."

"It's probably just a record keeping thing. Don't start throwing accusations around until you're sure it's not."

"Herman thinks it's more than a record keeping thing."

Bitch!

She felt his anger and backtracked. "I asked his advice and he set up a meeting with Brad Foster."

"Makes sense. Brad's a scum and he's got access to everything. When are you two going to rake him over the coals?"

Sarah thought a long moment and admitted, "I'm meeting him alone."

"What's the point of that?" he asked. Aware of the insult, he started to apologize, but she didn't look offended.

"It's preliminary."

"You think it's someone else, huh?"

Sarah clammed up. What did she think she was hiding? He didn't need a degree in criminal justice to know she'd be searching IT for her perp. She'd probably been hiding the name from the moment he'd walked in.

"So you're looking on the programming team for someone smart enough to fudge records. Someone with strong relationships around the office. That rules out a lot of people up there."

Her tense expression would crack if he hit the right name. Brad was Stan's choice. He was arrogant, territorial and he managed by fear. Strange, she wasn't interested in him as a suspect.

She offered nothing.

"So if I'm right, you're taking a hard look at Erica."

Sarah held back a gasp.

She had a lot to learn. She was going after the one IT person who was above suspicion and she did such a lousy job hiding her reaction, she'd told him who it was.

"You've got to be kidding," he said. "We're talking about embezzlement here! Erica Fletcher's no criminal."

After a long pause, Sarah finally broke. "She's right in the middle of it. She manages the system with the suspicious transactions and guess who everyone runs to when they have a problem?"

"Not a chance."

"I don't care what you think, Stan. I'm not asking for your help. Just keep quiet. If this gets back to her and she runs, it's your head."

"I'm not that stupid."

"You'll change your tune when she's in cuffs."

"My money's on Brad."

"Brad's got no part in this. His family owns this company."

"Fine. Do what you want. When Erica's found guilty, I'll buy you dinner, you choose the restaurant. If it's Brad, I choose the place and you pay."

"I don't date guys from the office."

"So, I've heard."

Sarah ignored the barb. "Gregg and I brought this problem to her. We told her how critical it was and she sat on it for two weeks. Tell me she's not hiding something."

"Ever think she might be busy?"

"Everything points to her."

"You couldn't have picked a less likely cheat."

Sarah sat and stared. The conversation was over and now she was concocting some crazy scenario that he'd partnered with Erica to defraud the company. He'd had a lot of influence over the last eight years and a lot of responsibility he hadn't lived up to. Sarah didn't invite him to help and she wasn't going to. He left, knowing the keys in his pocket would get him a look at that file after she'd gone.

Chapter 37

Carlos rolled a sinewy string of drool off his tongue and let it drop in the center of the gray sharpening stone. The knife scratched tight circles, spreading the lubrication while he kept his eyes on the street from his fifth floor window. Soon, the drunk tottered into view in a suit worth more than all his worldly possessions combined. Carlos had followed him dozens of times on the trip to the bank and back. He always walked straight to the bank as instructed, but often stopped for a few nips in a little store a block and a half into the return trip. He looked sober plodding up the block, but unenthusiastic for someone about to receive over three months' income. Carlos wouldn't care if he were wasted today.

Carlos dialed the cell.

"Yeah," a gruff voice answered.

"He's on his way back."

"Hold on." Keys clicked on the other end of the line.

"We've got it. Take out the trash."

Carlos pulled the blade across his jeans, wiping the saliva from one side of the blade then the other. He was about to click off when the voice shot back. "No fancy stuff. You're not carving a turkey. Use the tools I gave you and make it look like he offed himself."

He closed the phone and played his thumb over the razor sharp edge he'd honed for the last hour. He sheathed it regretfully and dumped a thousand dollars in twenties on the table.

The bum shuffled to the door five minutes later. He let him knock twice before letting him in.

"Everything all set?" he asked.

Tobey's eyes landed on the money and he drifted toward the table, ignoring the question and leaving the door half open behind him.

Carlos closed it and grabbed him by the shoulder. "You been drinking?"

"No, Sir," Tobey said, straightening up and facing Carlos for the first time. "Things went fine. Same as always."

"Good. The transfer went through. You can have your money as soon as you get out of that suit."

Tobey turned for the bedroom. He'd performed the routine dozens of times before. He closed the door and Carlos listened as he wriggled out of the jacket and tossed it on the bed.

Carlos screwed the silencer onto the end of the .45. He'd have enjoyed taking a swipe at beheading him with the katana he kept in his bag. The bum was so slow the sword would hit him before he could move, but the boss wanted this one permanently unsolved. Not that anyone cared about this loser, but the gruesome methods Carlos enjoyed tended to attract attention. "Raise a clamor," the boss had said, "and go to the slammer." The boss was freaky about forensics. Gloves were a must and ignoring instructions, no matter how trivial, would put you on someone else's task list.

Carlos pulled on his gloves and waited by the door with the gun ready. When he heard the water running, he slipped in. The old guy was leaning in toward the mirror with his hands on either side of the sink, supporting his tired body after the ten block walk. He was a good four inches taller than Carlos and fifty pounds heavier.

He never saw Carlos in the reflection.

His heel on tile brought the old man around, shooting upright, startled that he was no longer alone. Before he could turn, Carlos drilled a hardened fist into his kidney and dropped him to his knees, smacking his forehead on the sink on the way down. The impact rang solid, snapped his head back and he hovered an instant before collapsing the rest of the way to the floor.

Carlos needed an explanation for the bruises. He could have stood him up and done it there, but who knew where the bullet would end up if it ricocheted off his skull.

He yanked him out from under the sink and rolled him headfirst into the tub. If he shot himself here, he might fall and hit his head as he'd done on the sink. Tobey didn't resist and he didn't react when his knees and elbows whacked the fiberglass. The sink had knocked the fight out of him. He looked up glassy eyed as Carlos leveled the .45 a few inches from his temple. There was no fear in his eyes as the hammer dropped. He hadn't had time to understand what was coming. Maybe Carlos was doing him a favor. His head jolted with the entry, deforming and oozing its contents down toward the drain.

Now the work began.

He pocketed the silencer, pressed Tobey's fingers onto the grip and barrel, leaving at least four good prints, some overlapping others, and let the arm slump naturally down by his side. He tucked the gun into the hand where it came to rest. He drew the shower curtain around the tub to keep the smell in. The toiletries he stuffed into a bag in the main room. He piled the crumpled suit in on top and whisked through the drawers with gloved hands to make sure the old guy hadn't gotten smart and left something behind. Finding nothing, he deadbolted the door and collected the bag.

He'd already wiped the room clean and he hadn't touched anything he wasn't taking with him since. Now with the bag by the window, he threaded forty-pound fishing line between the panes, passing three feet of it outside before winding it around the lock and tying a loop inside. With the window carefully open and the line protruding out, he passed his bag out to the fire escape and hung a pot full of pansies on the loop.

Halfway out the window he noticed the thousand on the table. He hurried inside for it and climbed back out. He pulled the window shut then steadily pulled the line until the lock turned into place. Next, he wound the line around his gloved hand and jerked, snapping it somewhere between the panes, leaving no clue that someone had been inside with Tobey when he'd met his demise.

Chapter 38

Carolyn Fletcher was a killer; not a deranged lunatic who killed for a thrill or an inner city thug who killed to take what she wanted from the meek. She'd killed only one man, her husband Dale, and then only to escape a life of physical and emotional abuse that was impossible to bear. Still, this one act defined who she was and who she could never be again. That moment forever changed her relationship with the one person that had mattered above all others, the one person she would give her life to protect.

Intermingled in a flash of hatred and fury, she'd seen a glimmer of a new life for her and her young daughter, Erica. She picked up her husband's golf club and swung mightily. She earned her freedom, but it came with problems she didn't anticipate. Single parenthood was harsh. As much as she tried, she couldn't stop the children from taunting Erica that her mother was a murderer and that she'd grow into one, too. Ostracism made Erica strong, but it also pushed the tiny family apart. Carolyn had her own regrets to cope with as well. During her pregnancy in high school, Carolyn had felt the isolation Erica must have felt in grammar school. The pregnancy trapped her into a relationship that degenerated into a life of abuse. In darker moments, she unconsciously blamed Erica, just like Erica blamed her for the way the kids treated her at school.

Carolyn deserved the blame for both mistakes.

She whisked the vacuum around the living room carpet too fast to remove the deep down dirt, just as a clean house and a home cooked meal were insufficient to repair the gulf between mother and daughter. Busy as she was, Erica made few trips to the apartment, precious few that didn't coincide with a holiday or another special occasion. Today's last minute visit was disconcerting. She hoped it was just another protest about her impending marriage and becoming a step-sister to a ten year old, but she worried it was something more serious.

Ten minutes later the vacuum was tucked in a closet and the lasagna nearly baked when Carolyn answered the door. Erica walked in with a foreign air about her. She wore new jeans and a knit top, surprisingly casual for a Monday after work. She moved with an ease that had been missing since childhood. She stepped in, placed her hands lightly on Carolyn's waist and rested her head against her shoulder a second before pulling back.

Carolyn ignored Erica's disapproving glance at her tank top and snug jeans. She dressed younger than her own daughter, who was so modest she swam with a T-shirt over her bathing suit. Erica seemed to be fighting the stigma of her mother's teenage pregnancy, a fight Carolyn had long since given up. If a fifty-two year old woman could turn a few heads, she had every right.

Carolyn closed the door and invited Erica inside. "I was surprised by your call. Everything ok?"

"Great. I had a mini vacation. I needed some time away from work. You know, I forgot how nice it is to sleep in. I can't remember the last time I had five days off in a row."

"Fighting with your boss?" Erica had been raging against authoritative men since her father died. The school psychologist expected her to become a pleaser like her mother, but her will was far stronger than anyone suspected. She made a hard turn in the opposite direction and dedicated herself to self-sufficiency. She excelled academically, financially, and physically to the point of obsession. Carolyn worried that the tight lid she kept on her emotions and her never-ending struggle for control would leave her bitter and alone. So far, experience proved her right.

"How could I not fight with him? He's a sadistic dictator, who also happens to be clueless *and* he has it in for me."

"That's my girl, go along to get along."

"It's not my fault he's a tool."

"What about all those college professors you had such a hard time with? Were they tools too?"

Erica steamed. The relaxed expression was replaced by a more typically tense look. Carolyn felt a bit guilty, but she had a responsibility to steer her daughter toward happiness. The battle with her father was long won. If she'd just live and let live, things would come much easier. Rather than apologize, Carolyn led Erica to the table, set out the salad and cut the lasagna.

Erica told of her problems with Brad. How he'd taken away her teammates until it was impossible for her to finish her project and how she'd worked day and night to succeed in spite of him. When she told how Brad had gotten the promotion she worked so hard for, Carolyn couldn't help but share her daughter's heartbreak.

Erica didn't ask about Ted or the wedding plans and Carolyn didn't bring it up. She'd be glad enough if Erica would put aside her vendetta against marriage for a few hours and come to the ceremony.

Carolyn crunched into her salad and asked what Erica had been doing with her time off.

Erica lit up as she described her trip to the farm. It was the first time she'd gone away with a man. A farm seemed the least likely of all places for a girl who'd lived her whole life in the city, but her time with the Turners had an impact. The relaxed look was back as she related her tours around the fields, the town and her fishing trip with Gregg.

Carolyn wondered if Erica had found the man who could change her mind about marriage. The smile on her face said it was possible.

Chapter 39

The passengers pressed back into their seats as the jet charged down the runway and rose in time for a glimpse of the setting sun before turning east over the ocean. Brad focused on a clump of blonde hair several rows ahead remembering the sexy smile she'd flashed as he boarded. She was the hottest woman on the plane. He'd watched her every movement as she swished down the aisle, stretched to store her carry-on in the overhead compartment, and especially when she bent to find a book in her leather bag.

The head of light hair bobbed over the seat as the plane climbed into the sky. When it leveled off her eyes settled into a worn paperback without one glance to the rear. For several minutes he awaited any sign a liaison might be possible during the weekend. He considered walking up the aisle, but when she failed to turn and meet his gaze even once, he stared gloomily out the window and mentally reviewed his preparations.

The 'laundry trips' were fairly routine except for the night crossing in the Cessna. Every detail he considered prepared him to survive those few hours. He had plenty of fuel in the underground tanks. When the weekend was over, he'd have enough left for an emergency flight if he needed to get out of the country quickly. He'd checked the weather reports before leaving Boston and no storms were expected in the area for several days. He'd make one more check before takeoff to be sure.

Years earlier, he'd cruised headlong into a storm that lurked for him in the mountains. After hugging the valley floor under clear skies, he'd circled a tall peak and flown straight into thick black clouds that were nearly invisible in the dark. The whipping winds had battered the tiny plane almost swallowing it whole. He'd made it through shaken but intact. After that he'd never flown without a recent weather report. Navigating the mountains and evading the authorities were dangerous enough.

He'd survive this trip and in a few weeks it would be over. As much as he hated Herman, his plot was true genius. Only Stu Tinsley came close to discovering them and the only thing that made him suspicious was Brad's overreaction to his innocent questions. Next week, they'd tell the executives how the scheme operated and the firm would be thrown into chaos. Marty would fight back to preserve his place in the company his ancestors built. They'd blame Erica and she'd be thrown in jail without a word printed in the media. Marty would compensate some of the victims then force Brad to resign. His sister, Sharon, might never talk to him again and he'd be unemployable in the investment industry. That was the best case scenario. If Herman sent the envelope things would get much worse.

Trusting Herman was the biggest mistake Brad had ever made. He was so slick and persuasive that Brad never questioned his motives. Herman told him about three companies that were in trouble with the SEC. Brad shorted them and made a killing never realizing that Herman was calmly gathering evidence he'd use to control him later. Brad went along as his conversations were recorded and his stock trading activities monitored. Rather than tip his hand, Herman nudged him forward until Brad had made an illicit fortune that guaranteed his cooperation. Herman persuaded him to take part in a larger scam without resorting to his leverage. Brad followed willingly until the day he realized he had no way out.

That day had come almost two years earlier. Brad had flown into Switzerland illegally and was sitting in his Cessna at the edge of a clearing. When the sun rose, he got out of the plane to head into town. As soon as his feet touched the ground, a rifle appeared in the bushes and a border guard named Evan emerged behind it. Only then did Brad realize how helpless he was. He had no link to Herman except a bank account number. Luckily, Evan was alone when he saw the plane. Luckier still, Brad was carrying enough cash to buy his freedom.

He realized too late that he'd been duped. When he got back home, a case was waiting on his kitchen table. The evidence inside had been doctored to indict Brad without any link to Herman. From that day forward he was completely under Herman's control. Herman could easily send him to jail, but he needed Brad to run the program. He promised to frame Erica if Brad followed orders. When she took the fall, the scam would end and he'd be free. She'd settle into a nine-by-nine cell and he'd settle into a new place with a good woman.

Movement in the aisle caught his attention.

His eyes settled on the flight attendant's hemline as the lights in the cabin blinked off. She scurried back and forth comforting weary passengers, retrieving empty beverage containers, and delivering pillows and blankets throughout the cabin. He gave a sly smile as she shuttled to the makeshift kitchen. She'd be back.

Several sleepless hours later, Brad disembarked alone scanning the crowd for anyone who might be watching. He looped around the terminal making stops in the restroom and two gift shops. He circled back on himself four or five times until he was certain no one was following. He didn't recognize either of Herman's goons in the crowd and no one else in the terminal seemed interested in him. He dropped his overnight bag in front of a payphone. Keeping the arrangements secret was one of the few things Brad and Herman agreed on. Two years had passed and only Marcus, because of his position at the bank, knew how the scheme worked. Brad had added his own helper to make traveling easier, but he only knew that Brad slipped into Italy, went to the bank and slipped out again. He hoped Herman's goons knew just as little.

He removed a small leather notebook from his bag, slipped some change into the phone and dialed. A husky voice answered.

"Cousin Vinny?" Brad asked.

"Si."

"It's Jean-Claude. Everything ready?" Brad asked.

"Si, everything's fine."

"Good. See you at the usual time."

"Ciao." Vincent hung up. He'd known for weeks that Jean-Claude was coming. The last-minute confirmation assured he'd be waiting.

Brad rushed to the rental counter, eager to get south of town and away from the traffic. He watched tourists tote heavy bags as they stopped to decipher signs. People waited in every available seat and lined the walls in the gate areas. Tourists milled shoulder to shoulder through the wide passageways. He admired the stylish French women as they rushed by, casually glancing at his physique, so powerful and manly compared to the puny Frenchmen they were accustomed to. He strutted down the center of the terminal invigorated by their admiration.

The woman behind the rental counter recognized him as he approached. She clicked rapidly on the keyboard, retrieving his reservation without asking his name. Natalie stood tall and slender behind her computer screen. Wisps of long dark hair gently fluttered in the air currents of the terminal as she hurried through her work.

"Bon Jour, Natalie. How've you been?"

"Fine, Mr. Foster."

"I'll be in the city Saturday. Can I buy you a glass of wine?"

"Not this time." Natalie smiled, but spoke abruptly.

"How about dinner then? You could show me around the city."

"My boyfriend is very jealous. He would not approve."

"I won't tell if you won't."

Natalie walked to the far wall and retrieved two keys.

"What can it hurt? It's only one dinner."

She avoided eye contact as long as possible. "There you go, Mr. Foster, your car is in stall one twenty-seven. Just sign here."

She held the contract for him. He signed it and she handed him his copy and the keys. "Have a nice trip."

"Thank you, Natalie."

Brad hadn't expected Natalie to agree, but he was compelled to try on every visit. He left the counter, rushed to his car, and drove aggressively through the city streets, darting and turning, choosing his path with the familiarity of a local. The engine shrieked as the car raced around a young girl in a slow moving sedan, leaving the last obstacle to the open countryside in the rearview mirror. Further and further from the city, the traffic thinned. He alternately slowed and raced ahead, allowing cars to pass and accelerating to watch if those that didn't matched his pace. None of the other drivers seemed interested in him or where he was going.

He pushed the car ahead. He needed rest before the night's work.

The hills approached and faded as he floated past endless waves of grapevines stretching for the sun. He did his best to focus on the road, but thirty hours without sleep, two of them staring at the painted lines, weighed down his eyelids. The engine slowed as his body relaxed at the controls. The wheel gently vibrated to the hum of the tires. His hazy view of the road flickered and faded to black. His head drooped forward until it nearly touched the small black steering wheel.

Tires churned over the gravel shoulder shaking Brad to life. His eyes widened at the scene ahead. His heart leaped in his chest, the rush of energy shocking every muscle to action. He wrenched the wheel left. A wooden fence flashed into view as the car swerved out of control. He jerked the wheel back. The car hopped and skipped, responding to the frantic gyrations of the steering wheel. Momentum hurled the car over the gritty surface, wheels scrambling to align themselves with the direction of the road which seemed to be ever-changing. He slammed the brakes to the floor, throwing the car into a final skid. Long streaks of warm black rubber swerved sideways to a stop. The car straddled the centerline facing the grassy field beyond the fence. Brad's pulse thundered. He panted, cursing his carelessness, and thanking God for good luck and fast reflexes.

For the next thirty minutes he drove with a keen thankful-to-be-alive focus on the road. He rolled up a long driveway to a house screened from the road by thick groupings of evergreens. The dilapidated structure was dwarfed by trees that had grown up beside it and a large barn that stood at its back. The house itself was worthless if not for the secluded location. It was far from the nearest town and far enough from the road that Brad had to strain to watch for passing traffic. When he was satisfied no one had followed, he pulled open the wide doors and parked the rental alongside the garage's permanent resident. He removed a canvas cover to reveal a boxy looking sedan, generously tarnished with dents and scratches. He draped the cover over the rental car, casting a cloud of fine powder into the air. Brad Foster and his sporty rental were about to disappear.

He hopped onto the cracked vinyl seat and turned over the ignition. The machine reluctantly groaned to life, spewing exhaust into the garage. Together with the powdery mist it created an atmosphere that was uninhabitable. Brad left the car to shake off its slumber and trailed through the house checking the doors and opening every window. The house was laden with even more chemicals than the garage, poisoning the air and coating the floorboards with powdery dust. The chemicals were harsh enough to repel any living thing, including Brad. The fumes assailed his eyes and nose as he opened window after window to let in breathable air.

The house creaked and moaned with every step as he searched for anything out of place. There were no footprints in the powdery residue, not two-legged ones anyway. He pinched the long thin tails of the most recent trespassers and flung their tiny carcasses through an open window. Satisfied the upstairs was safe, he trotted downstairs and out to the garage where he killed the engine and then headed down to the cellar.

The loose dirt crunched as he made his way along the stone foundation toward the switch. A loud clack brought the buzz of electricity and light, exposing tools, scraps of building supplies and other relics piled throughout the small, damp room. A few turns and a click of another switch brought the ancient water pump to life filling the musty air with its rumbling, rattling labor.

Brad walked the narrow path between the piles of clutter and kneeled before an old trunk. Careful not to disturb the cobwebs and dust at its sides, he opened the lid and removed some old clothes. He placed them carefully on the path among the footprints he made with each walk to the water pump. It was the only part of the room that had been disturbed in the last thirty years and he wanted it to continue looking that way.

He lifted out the bottom of the trunk to reveal the dirt floor below and then scraped away the dirt until he struck plywood. Underneath the wood he found a metal surface with a shiny black dial. A proud grin crossed his lips as he marveled at his ingenuity. Buying the house was clever, but hiding everything so well was brilliant. Even if Herman found the house, the contents would be safe.

He removed the notebook from his bag, dialed the numbers and opened the lid to a large metal container buried beneath the cellar floor. The space was neatly packed with all the tools he'd need, including a black .45, which shimmered as he inspected it. He released the clip, checked its contents and slid it back in. He pulled the action back and let it slam forward. The mechanism moved stiffly, having never been fired. Its clip was always loaded when he stored it away. He checked the weapon every time he picked it up, knowing one day it would be the key to his survival.

He holstered the gun and placed it and three spare clips into his bag along with a smooth wallet he removed from the safe.

He stored his own wallet for the duration of his visit.

"Hello, Mr. Jean-Claude Verrier. Nice to see you again," he said to himself as he neatly replaced the items in the trunk. He left the room looking exactly as it had for the last three decades and walked upstairs to prepare for breakfast or lunch, he wasn't sure which.

Chapter 40

Brad fumbled for the alarm clock and silenced it. A rush of cool afternoon air hit when he left the blanket and hurried to pull on his clothes. Still longing for the warm bed, he strapped the holster to his chest and donned a light jacket. The wallet on the nightstand held a shiny identification card with his picture. The name Jean-Claude Verrier was printed boldly along with the address of the rickety house. He pocketed the wallet. For the next day and a half, he would become Jean-Claude Verrier. He stuffed his travel bag inside a battered, oversized briefcase and headed across the back yard to the barn.

Inside, he gathered two heavy ropes that dangled from the rafters and heaved downward with all his weight. The ropes looped through two overhead pulleys and attached to a huge canvas. As it rose, it exposed the huge hole Brad had chain-sawed out of the rear wall. The two-by-six supports he'd added years earlier were now bending under the weight of the roof. There was ample clearance to taxi in and out, but the supports looked as if they'd give way soon.

As the canvas was raised, light flowed in and illuminated the most modern machines on the farm. A shiny tractor sat hitched to a Cessna Skyhawk SP. The plane would have shined too, if not for the do-it-yourself paint job. A patchwork of green and black blotches camouflaged the plane when viewed from above. The bottom was painted a solid pale gray to blend with the sky when viewed from below. The registration numbers had been painted over and the transponder removed to create Jean-Claude's version of a spy plane. It was decidedly low-tech, but the plane had carried him across the border undetected several times.

Jean-Claude was an excellent pilot, though not a licensed one. He'd only existed for two years, sporadically at that, venturing out of the shiny metal box to pay his taxes and move money out of Italy. Brad Foster received his pilot's license at twenty-three and did anything he could to defray the cost of flying. He flew traffic reporters around the city, gave flying lessons, and flew himself on business trips when the company would reimburse him. Herman bought this plane, but Brad took little joy in flying it. These tension-packed trips were about stealth. When it was over he'd buy a faster plane and fly for the sheer joy of it.

Fueled and checked out, he towed the craft to the head of the runway. The sun would set soon. The hitch popped from the plane and he drove the tractor back inside and unfurled the canvas cover. He ran to the plane, conserving the last precious minutes of sunlight. The plane taxied across the long field that was once thick with vegetables, spun around and shot down the makeshift runway. It quickly leveled just above the treetops, flying as low as possible through the valley.

Anyone near the route would be alarmed by the low-flying plane and some might call the authorities, but by the time anyone responded, he'd be in Italy. Immediate threats would come from the air. He scoured the horizon for other planes and listened as the air traffic controllers instructed airborne pilots. The setting sun at his back hid him from anyone flying overhead en route to Lyon. The small craft was invisible to instruments as it skimmed seventy feet above the treetops. Even so, he avoided the path of any plane below ten thousand feet.

Jean-Claude descended to sixty feet above a long meadow exploding with purple flowers that bloomed in the warm May sun. He took no notice of the magnificent scenery as he buzzed low over the heads of a few straggling hikers. Headlights snaked their way through the mountain roads illuminating trees along the rocky slopes. Wary of the tall peaks and the planes above, he hardly noticed the darkness blotting out the scenery below until he began struggling to find the landing area.

A jagged slope descended toward a tiny village. He followed down into the valley and circled until he found a familiar pattern of lights. He climbed high to make his approach, cut the engine, and silently glided the Cessna toward the dark field. Vincent wouldn't hear the engine from his house two miles away. Odd he hadn't figured out how Jean-Claude made his way across after so many trips. There were other ways, all terrain vehicles and trains. He could sneak across in the trunk of a car, but apparently, Vincent wasn't curious enough or smart enough to figure it out. Maybe he didn't want to upset the arrangement. Jean-Claude would rather land on his farm and save the two-mile hike, but there was no need to tell Vincent now. Better to limit him to chauffeuring.

Jean-Claude switched on the landing lights as he descended to the level of the grassy field. A moment later the craft touched down, bumping and hopping over the uneven terrain, rolling to a stop tucked in a corner of the field. The dark shapes at the edge of the clearing gave no hint of trouble. The only structure in sight was an old shack, shadowy and still, that seemed to stoop more and more with each visit. When he was convinced it was safe, Jean-Claude jumped down from the plane with his briefcase in one hand and a machete in the other. He chopped two dozen saplings and piled them against the front of the plane until he was satisfied it would go unnoticed for the day.

He stored the machete and headed off into the trees.

The rocky slope was dense with waist-high bushes that rustled and cracked with every movement. Any creature within six hundred yards heard his labored climb up to the dirt road that led to Vincent's farm. Passage on the packed earth of the road was quieter and he moved along in near silence.

A burst of rustling leaves startled Jean-Claude, freezing him as he listened to the sounds of the forest. He raised the .45 and swept the terrain ahead, ready to shoot anything that moved in his path. The deafening sound would frighten off any creature he'd encounter. The two-mile trek in the dark woods unnerved him. Crossing with a strong light had been easier until he realized it exposed his every move. Darkness concealed him, so he adjusted to walking by moonlight, calming the anxious voices in his head with assurances he didn't really believe. For a thousand bucks he could have bought night-vision goggles online. He had no idea why he hadn't.

Jean-Claude holstered the gun and moved on down the road. If he stepped on a snake, it would wrap itself around his leg biting his calves over and over with sharp fangs. The leather sneakers offered no protection.

Fifty yards down the road, he heard a loud rustling in the trees. Something heavy dashed downhill away from him, directly toward the farm. He pictured himself bumping into a bear and feeling its claws swipe him off his feet. The animal's crushing weight would pin him, squeezing the breath from his lungs as the enormous front teeth gnawed his flesh. The image froze him and again he drew the .45.

Before he made another step, he whispered, "Mr. Bear, I suggest you pick on someone who's not carrying a semi-automatic handgun."

He moved on with the gun leveled in front of him, a steady trickle of sweat dropping from his forehead to sting his eyes as he maneuvered through the darkness.

The road paralleled the path of the animal he'd spooked. He walked along hesitantly, attuned to every sound in the trees ahead. Every step brought him closer to the mauling he anticipated, but the animal didn't show itself. Several times a falling branch or a scurrying in the leaves immobilized him with fear. He told himself these little explosions of ruckus were squirrels or rabbits, but he didn't think these animals nocturnal. He pushed along nervously silent, dreading his next encounter.

A discarded tire at the roadside marked his approach to Vincent's farm. He left the road and descended a tree covered slope. Progress was noisy, alerting any creature nearby to his approach and at the same time deafening him to their movements. He stopped every several yards to listen for anyone or anything attracted by the breaking branches and rustling leaves.

Snap. A breaking twig echoed in the stillness fifty yards away.

Jean-Claude's head whipped toward the sound.

A light flickered twice.

Jean-Claude whistled out a low note followed by a shrill ending and repeated his call two more times.

The light flickered three more times, signaling him to come forward.

Jean-Claude dragged his feet through the tangled underbrush toward the small circle of light. The commotion of branches and leaves underfoot didn't concern him anymore. He was almost out. The short, thin figure waiting for him waggled the light as he pushed the last few yards to the narrow path. Vincent shook his hand and lit the way as they hiked along the edges of the fields that sloped down toward his home.

The moonlight cast a glow on rows of seedlings dancing in the light breeze. With Vincent beside him and a wide field of view to assure him no animals were nearby, Jean-Claude relaxed for the first time in hours.

"Vinny, what would I ever do without you?" Jean-Claude asked.

"You could cross over in a car like everyone else."

"Sounds easy."

"Yes, and there are lights," Vincent chuckled, knowing how nervous the dark woods made Jean-Claude. Vincent worked this land season after season. He was at home here. Nothing in the forest bothered him unless it ventured into his fields to graze.

"Driving would ease your nerves," Vincent said. "But I'm not complaining. This work's easier than farming."

Brad looked back at the woods and wondered about the animal he'd heard running this way. He hoped it would move on before his return hike the next morning. That would be his final crossing.

Vincent was glad for the company this time of year. The isolated farm made an ideal layover point, but Vincent had months of pent up conversation to let loose. He endlessly recounted the happenings on the farm since Jean-Claude's last visit. The chatter continued into the stone farmhouse and didn't stop when Jean-Claude stretched out on the couch to get some sleep. The accented English rambled on into his dreams.

Chapter 41

Jean-Claude's eyes popped open as Vincent emerged from the kitchen, paced across the tiny living area and disappeared into the hall, only to step out of the kitchen again a moment later. Vincent had been circling all morning, peering out over the fields that surrounded the tiny house as if he expected an army to assemble among the vegetables and attack.

"Relax. You're making me nervous," Jean-Claude barked.

"Better to be prepared, no?"

"I hiked here in the middle of the night. No one knows I'm here."

"Marcus knows. There must be others."

"We've got nothing worth stealing." Jean-Claude kicked the empty briefcase under the coffee table. "When that's full, we'll both worry."

"Si, Si." Vincent collapsed into a reclining chair, pretending not to watch the long dirt driveway.

The hours before the trek to town stretched Vincent's nerves and Jean-Claude's tolerance, until the two men buckled into the glistening Mercedes parked out front. The contrast between the pristine automobile and the ancient stone building couldn't have been more glaring. The sagging roofline and peeling paint were neglected, but Vincent bought himself plush leather seats and satellite radio.

Jean-Claude turned a bewildered eye to Vincent's dark profile. "How can you afford this car?"

"You afford it for me."

Vincent's cut was enough for a few payments, but not a new car. Did he think this was going to go on forever? Jean-Claude couldn't tell him this was the last trip. Vincent would discover it for himself soon enough. He'd have to find another way to earn his payments or he'd be forced to sell the car. Vincent drove on unencumbered by the guilt Jean-Claude suffered in the passenger's seat. He was enthralled by the performance of his new car as he raced it up to speed and banked hard through tight turns. He slowed at the edge of town and they turned off the main road and wound down densely packed streets. They squeezed between a row of cars on one side and trash cans and debris that spilled off the opposite curb careful not to scratch the paint. They rolled to a stop beyond a small alley. The clogged back street would slow their exit, but Jean-Claude avoided showing himself in town as much as possible.

They stalked down the alley on foot skirting cardboard boxes and trashcans between the low stone buildings. Jean-Claude stopped a few paces from the wide sidewalk and scanned the faces in the park across the street. A group of mothers sat with several children toddling around. Beyond them, the fountain bustled with neatly dressed people enjoying an early lunch. Several older men read the paper and tossed crumbs to the birds jostling for position at their feet. None of them looked threatening.

Jean-Claude led Vincent out onto sidewalk and briskly toward the bank. The people rushing past took no notice of them, but up ahead on the street-side bench, one man watched their approach with interest. He was thin and young, a man who should be working on Thursday afternoon. Maybe he was.

The holster rubbed against Jean-Claude's arm as he walked. Closer now, the man on the bench leaned back casually to disguise his interest. Jean-Claude considered walking past the bank. He slowed, but as he did, Vincent strode ahead completely unaware of the threat Jean-Claude sensed.

"Vinny," Jean-Claude blurted in a low whisper.

Vincent didn't slow. He stopped only to pull open the door to the bank and by then, he was a full five yards ahead.

The man on the bench sneered menacingly. This was the man from the airport tunnel. The skinny guy who'd grabbed his hands while his buddy banged him up. Herman had sent him. Maybe Herman knew about the deal with Marcus. Maybe he knew all along and he'd waited until now to get even. The big guy who threw the punches could be idling the car, ready to speed away from the hit.

Jean-Claude cut in front of Vincent and headed inside behind the protection of the bank's brick walls.

The lobby of Banca di Turino was small by American standards. It mainly serviced the farmers and other small businesses in the mountain villages. The lone guard faced the patrons with his back to the wall, where the open lobby afforded him an excellent view, but nowhere to hide during a shootout. Jean-Claude noticed his grey hair and the glasses in his shirt pocket. He wondered how fast the old man could pull the gun and whether he could hit anything once he did.

Ahead and to the right, three cameras captured activity at the teller windows and the vault entrance. Jean-Claude had arrived precisely on time, but the manager's door was closed. He veered left to avoid being filmed and settled in a seat with his back to the tellers, the cameras, and the line of customers. Several paintings reflected bits of the lobby behind him. His eyes shifted back and forth, watching the manager's door to his right and the guard to his left.

Marcus had never kept him waiting. Three minutes in the lobby seemed endless as images of running police played over and over in his mind. When he subdued thoughts of arrest, he imagined the big guy and his partner rigging explosives under Vincent's car. Vincent would turn the ignition and a loud click would sound. The flames would rip up through the seats sending body parts flying, blood spattering and thousands of torn green bills fluttering through the alley.

Jean-Claude shook himself back into the moment.

Vincent sat opposite watching the patrons transact their business, his face in full view of the cameras. The nervousness from the farmhouse was replaced by a cheery fascination with the other customers. He hummed an unfamiliar tune and tapped a rhythm on his chair.

When the Manager's door creaked open, Vincent slapped his hands on the arms of his chair and rose. Jean-Claude stayed fast, watching the man in the manager's doorway from the corner of his eye. The big guy from the tunnel was talking to Marcus. They shook hands heartily and the big guy walked behind Jean-Claude, across the lobby, and out the front door. Vincent stutter stepped toward the manager's office, glancing back at Jean-Claude often enough for anyone to know they were together.

Marcus, the bank's manager, turned sideways to step through the doorway. His massive round torso brushed the frame on both sides as he passed, his swollen arms hung limp, resting against his sides. He breathed heavily as he met Vincent and Jean-Claude with a broad smile.

"Ciao, gentlemen," he said. He gave a reverent nod and labored back into his office. He side-stepped around his desk and squeezed into his chair, his thighs pushing the arms several inches further apart than they were designed to go. Jean-Claude sat across the desk, and Vincent stood beside the window watching the lobby.

"What was that about?"

"An acquaintance of yours I believe, checking our progress."

"I trust you didn't overestimate our good fortune."

"I may have overlooked two million for you and a small sum for my services."

Jean-Claude hadn't trusted Marcus since he suggested skimming from the account. Marcus took an extra cut, but Jean-Claude always suspected he'd be looking for more. He wouldn't be above blackmail if he learned Jean-Claude worked for BFS. Hopefully, the goon hadn't given him any clues.

"Let's start with the balance."

Jean-Claude scribbled the account number, checked it with his notebook, and slid the slip of paper across the worn desk. Marcus clicked on his computer terminal, wrote a number below Jean-Claude's, and passed it back. 36,475,058.

"Dollars, correct?" Jean-Claude asked.

Marcus nodded.

"Excellent. Wire ten million to this account number in the United States." Jean-Claude carefully copied the number and handed it across.

"This is unusual."

"A surprise for a dear friend who's helping us."

"Quite generous compared to my meager stipend."

"Not the type of help you'd want to give."

Marcus banged each key as he entered the transfer information into his terminal. His face soured, jealously longing after the huge sum he saw passing through his hands. Certainly he felt the risks he took were worth more, but that was between him and Herman.

When he was done, he turned the computer screen toward Jean-Claude.

Jean-Claude verified the numbers and nodded his approval.

Marcus reclaimed the screen and Jean-Claude sat back, while the machine delivered the money to an unsuspecting recipient. Vincent turned a coin in his fingers and peered through the thick glass into the lobby.

"Ok, what's next?" Marcus asked.

"My two million in cash. Make it tight. Last time it barely fit in the case. I'll take the rest in two checks – seventy-thirty."

"How much do you want to leave?"

"Ten thousand." Jean-Claude would have taken it all, but that would signal Marcus that he was losing his most profitable client. Better if he learned the news when Jean-Claude was safely out of the country. Marcus could keep the extra ten thousand.

Marcus made some calculations and disappeared through the heavy door at the rear of his office. When he did, Jean-Claude rose to watch the lobby. Several customers had left the bank. Vincent walked to the bookshelf and examined the photos displayed on top.

"Can you believe his family is this big?" Vincent asked.

The round happy faces all had thick dark hair. All were enormous. He wondered if Vincent referred to their numbers or their size. "Who cares? I just want to get my money and get out of here," Jean-Claude said.

For all his earlier nervousness, Vincent seemed inattentive.

Marcus returned ten minutes later pushing a small cart piled with tightly bound stacks of hundred dollar bills wrapped in plastic. Jean-Claude packed his briefcase to capacity. The two million made the case as heavy as he could manage on the long trip back through the woods. He tucked the two checks deep inside his front pants pocket where they'd be safe.

Marcus was a risk. He knew the account numbers here and the ones in the states that the money came from. If he ever discovered Jean-Claude's real name, blackmail was a definite possibility. If he told Herman about the millions they'd siphoned off, Jean-Claude would turn up dead in Boston. Marcus could do a lot of damage. Jean-Claude would be much better off if he disappeared. There was no one to stop him from shooting Marcus right here except the feeble guard in the lobby.

Marcus was so fat he could barely move. A quick clean shot would kill him in his chair before he could lift his flabby arms. Jean-Claude could swing the door open and fire off six or seven shots at the guard before he could draw his gun. He wasn't sure he could he hit him across the lobby, but the street was a greater risk. The alarm would be blaring when he stepped outside and he could get nabbed by a passing cop. He eyed Marcus as he buckled the briefcase then glanced at Vincent. Vincent would be too stunned to help. He'd probably wet himself when the first shot went off.

Jean-Claude shoved a stack of bills to Marcus, twenty thousand dollars for his silence. Marcus swept the stack into his top drawer, unaware how close he'd come to a sudden, violent death.

"Don't lose those checks now. They're hard to replace," Marcus joked, reveling in Jean-Claude's nervousness.

"I haven't lost one yet."

The huge man stood up behind his desk. "Take my advice: spende il denaro velocemente," he said in an eerie voice.

Jean-Claude's Italian was poor, but he knew sarcasm when he heard it. He squeezed the meaty hand and shook it deliberately. "Thanks. That goes double for you."

The words had no effect on Marcus, but Jean-Claude didn't care. He was halfway home. He walked through the lobby and out onto the street, swinging the forty pound case back and forth to make it appear lighter than when he entered. The men weren't on the bench across the street nor were they around the fountain or the lawn. He scanned for their faces in every window and car. Nothing. Halfway down the alley, he left Vincent alone with the briefcase and doubled back. No one moved in their direction.

He trotted to the car and craned his neck underneath before they got in. Nothing suspicious had been added. Vincent looked at him as if he were crazy, but he didn't explain. He told Vincent to get them out of town anywhere but toward the farm. They meandered through open country roads where no one could follow without being seen. Jean-Claude had never been this afraid for his life. He'd worried endlessly about going to prison, but after today he was as expendable as Marcus. These men would kill him with precision and dump his body without a second thought. The handgun was little comfort against professionals.

A dozen miles from the bank he remembered what Marcus had said. "Vinny, what is velociminty?"

"Velocemente means fast or quick. He said spend the money quickly. Does he know something?"

Jean-Claude wondered what Marcus had said to Herman's henchman back at the bank. He doubted the two were scheming against him. Marcus was a bit player in this scam. If anyone should have been worried it was Marcus. "He's just a greedy, fat man taking everything he can get his hands on. He's nobody," Jean-Claude said, almost believing it himself.

"He doesn't think he's nobody. He was cocky, like he knew something was going to happen and he wished he could watch."

Jean-Claude was taken aback by Vincent's insight. It was no coincidence that the thugs from Boston appeared for this last withdrawal. This would be the most dangerous trip. Jean-Claude searched the fields in silence wondering if he'd make it back to Boston.

"I don't think he liked the transfer," Vincent said.

"Next time, he'll ask for more money."

Marcus might not wait that long.

They made a wide arc around the town and back to the farm, intently surveying every car and face they passed.

Back at the farm, it was Jean-Claude's turn to pace. He spent the afternoon and most of the night traveling from window to window, waiting and watching. The fields were dark again and although he was anxious to get started, he needed some light to navigate through the mountains. The sun would rise soon, followed a few hours later by hikers and campers and other tree huggers who'd see him fly overhead. He collected his briefcase and overnight bag, thanked Vincent for his help, and started for the door. Vincent stirred, patted the thick envelope in his jacket and smiled as Jean-Claude quietly opened the back door and hiked across the open field. He climbed up the slope and settled into a thick stand of trees to observe the woods before climbing the rest of the way to the old dirt road.

The minutes passed slowly as he listened to the rush of leaves under each bird and squirrel stirred by the coming dawn. He rose to leave, then froze, hunched-over, half-standing. Two figures were barely visible in the pre-dawn light as they trotted across the field and spread out. Jean-Claude's chest sank as he watched one of the men stop just inches from the outer wall, duck under the windows and sneak toward the front of the house. The other man moved toward the back door.

Jean-Claude unbuckled his holster and raised the .45. The bead drifted on and off the dark outline at the back of the house. The man was big and muscular, like the man in Marcus' office earlier. Across the field, he was entirely blocked out when viewed through the sight on top of the barrel. Jean-Claude couldn't hit him at this range; he might not even hit the house. The shot would give away his position, but it would give Vincent a few seconds warning. He eased the weapon down. Vincent would have to get out of this himself.

Jean-Claude climbed for higher ground as the men entered the house. He squeezed between two large rocks that would provide excellent cover no matter which angle they chose to attack from.

CJ West

The man at the back door burst inside. If Vincent was still half asleep and tiredly watching the driveway he'd have no chance.

A sharp crack echoed from the house.

Vincent wasn't holding a gun. He'd be face down on the floor with a pool of blood gathering where his face met the wooden planks.

Jean-Claude lay wedged into the rocks afraid to move, waiting for the assault and wondering why the assassins had come so far for him. He pulled himself higher over the rough surface for a better view. He watched with his face pressed against the rock as the men emerged from the back of the house and stood together on the grass. One of them talked into a palm-sized phone and tucked something into his jacket. Jean-Claude guessed it was the envelope he'd given Vincent hours earlier.

The silhouettes lacked detail in the faint morning light, but one was much broader than the other. They couldn't have followed them from the bank. Marcus must have told them where Vincent lived. Jean-Claude wished he'd shot him when he had the chance. His heart thundered as he forced himself to lay still and quiet, watching the men and planning tactics to defend himself.

The first man folded his phone and the two of them retreated back around the house and disappeared. The engine of the Mercedes started, barely a whisper across the field. A faint cloud of dust rose as they sped away. They weren't even going to look for him.

Chapter 42

Bob Hicks followed Erica into the elevator and the two parted to opposite sides of the car as the doors closed. His eyes trailed the fringes of her skirt and on down to her heels. She hadn't worn a skirt to work since her original interview sixteen years ago. She certainly hadn't chosen this outfit for Bob's benefit, yet she didn't give him the sneer he normally would have earned for such obvious gawking. After watching her parents' marriage disintegrate Erica had never sought a man's attention. At thirty-four she realized for the first time that a turning head wasn't something to be feared. It was actually affirming, especially from a good looking twenty-something. Her visit to the Turners' had changed her. She wondered how long it would take Gregg to notice.

Bob walked off the elevator with his head over his shoulder. He narrowly missed one of the columns in the lobby and Erica chuckled as the doors closed. She wanted to follow him and visit Gregg, but she didn't want to add to the rumors that had been swirling around them for years. They were going to kick into high gear as more people saw them together, but it didn't matter anymore. They were a couple. They should have been years ago. A delighted reflection faced her from the shiny panel.

She strode to her office two hours later than usual, looking and feeling like a new woman. Not one person noticed. Heads were down and fingers were poised on keyboards in every cubicle she passed. Brad was still on vacation for another day, but tight deadlines pervaded.

Forty-two emails waited in neat ranks, payment due for three days off. A dozen voicemails begged a quick response. She was going to suffocate under a never-ending string of questions from people desperate for help with whatever minor technical glitch was bogging them down. She longed for the pressure to create, the pressure to deliver the impossible, but Brad would never let her feel that pressure again. Not here.

Her hard-driving approach had caused problems with bosses before, but it was different with Brad. She'd worked her heart out, kept her mouth shut and still Brad had fought her from day one. Surely her mother was wrong. Whatever his reasons for antagonizing her, it wasn't her fault. Not this time.

Gregg's problem was the biggest challenge that faced her.

Both Gregg and Sarah were convinced it was serious. A dozen people had seen Brad shred Gregg's documents, but only Brad knew why he acted the way he did. Being Marty's brother-in-law put him beyond the reaches of HR. He could do what he liked. What would Marty do if he knew how much damage Brad had caused around his company? Maybe telling him would change things. Not likely. Going to Marty would only push the conflict between them to the next level. One of them would have to go and the odds said it would be her. She hated the work Brad was giving her so much that she was willing to take the risk. Ousting Brad was her new mission.

She shuffled through one pile of folders then another. Her research was gone. It had been the last thing she worked on before leaving with Gregg for the weekend. She knew she'd left it on top of the stack, but spun to search the filing cabinet anyway. Years of project reports and notes on various technologies crammed the drawers. The folder wasn't among them and it wasn't on her desktop where she'd left it. Only Gregg and Sarah cared about this problem and neither of them would take her research without asking.

Brad's reaction to this problem had been over the top. She'd never told him she was working on it, but if he'd taken the folder, it wasn't petty trickery. Mr. Johnson's ire, Brad's raving assault on Gregg, and the contradictions within the data added up to something more than any of them knew. Sarah had good reason to be excited. It was no accident that her notes had disappeared a second time. This was no software bug. Brad was hiding something – something huge. This was her chance to repay him for years of torment.

She picked up the phone to call Sarah. She was abrupt and gung-ho, but Sarah wouldn't come into her office and take her work. She might have the authority, but she wouldn't have the guts, not after a few weeks on the job. Erica dialed Gregg's extension, but hung up before it connected. She hopped off her chair and headed downstairs to feed the rumor mill.

Standing outside Gregg's cube, Jane Wheeler gave Erica a smile that said she'd heard the news and she approved wholeheartedly. Erica turned and tapped a short fingernail against the aluminum trim of Gregg's cubicle. She examined her fingertip while she waited, resolved to let her nails grow to a more elegant length, maybe even paint them. Gregg didn't seem to mind them as they were. All smiles, he finished his call quickly, his eyes surprised by her outfit.

She stepped in when he took off his headset, landed her hands softly at his waist and angled her lips up to meet his. She caressed his soft lips long enough that work in Jane's cubicle came to a stop. Gregg slowed to pull away twice before she finished. When they faced each other from inches away, Gregg gushed over the change.

She eased her fingertips up toward his pecks and withdrew a foot away. He stood stiffly at his chair, his head barely visible above the cubicle wall, his body awaiting her command.

"This is a nice surprise," he said.

"I was going to call, but I couldn't resist sneaking down for a visit."

"No need to sneak." He indicated the chair next to his and tilted his head in Jane's direction. She rolled her chair forward out of sight.

Erica didn't have to look to know she was watching. She pulled herself up on the desktop and waited for him to settle back in his chair, tense about how much or little he should be looking at the leg draped off his desk.

She dangled her black heel toward the knee of his khakis. "Relax, will you?" She leaned in toward him. "I came to chat about that problem you brought me a couple weeks back. Remember the Johnsons?"

"You kidding? I have shredder nightmares."

"I made some good progress last week, but I can't find the file. You didn't borrow it, did you?"

He looked offended. "I wouldn't. You didn't lose it twice?"

"Definitely not."

The protective look he had the night of the break-in was back.

"You think Sarah would take it without asking?"

"Doubt it." Gregg's eyes darkened. He sensed it, too. There was more to this than a computer glitch, but with so many ears on the other side of the cubicle wall, he couldn't say so.

After a long silence she leaned in close as if she were about to kiss him goodbye. "It's not a mistake," she whispered.

"What?"

"It's not a bug."

"Can you prove it?"

"No. But it makes sense, doesn't it? Brendan's too sharp to enter the transaction two hours late. Johnson knows when he called. The phone records prove it. Someone's mucking with the data and I think we both know who it is."

"You can't believe that."

"Who else could it be?"

"He doesn't need money. His family's got more than God."

"Not his family, his sister's family. Who knows what he's got?"

"No way he blows a sweet gig like this for a few thousand bucks."

"He got a few thousand from Hank Johnson. We're talking millions."

Gregg's eyes widened, disbelieving, locked on hers. He shook his head a few times, fighting the logic, but eventually it overtook him. "What if you're right? Are you safe up there?"

Erica's proof was gone and even if she had ironclad evidence, the decision was Marty's. He couldn't fire his own brother-in-law, never mind prosecute. It would be easier to shoot the messenger. She needed to rebuild her case and when she brought it, she'd better not face him alone.

"We need help," she said.

"Sarah?"

"She thinks I'm the devil. Mostly because she has the hots for you."
He smirked.

"I'd rather start smaller."

"Who then?"

"Stan Nye."

"C'mon. The guy's an idiot."

"Maybe. But he's on the IA team and you know where he stands."

"You want me to go up there with you? It might take both of us to wake him up."

"Not yet. I'm going to re-create my work from last week. I want something that will light a fire under him."

"No one can light a fire under Stan Nye, not even you."

"We'll see."

Chapter 43

Jean-Claude skimmed the Cessna dangerously close to the treetops with the rising sun at his back. A group of early hikers scattered from a clearing as if the plane was about to crash land in their midst. Backs turned, scampering away, none of them could identify the plane or its destination. Inside, Jean-Claude wondered why Herman had sent the men to kill Vincent. He knew almost nothing and he'd worked cheap. Whatever Herman's reason, it was one less person who knew about the scam; one less potential blackmailer in their past. He hoped Herman wasn't thinking the same way about him.

Jean-Claude circled low around the base of the last peak and followed the widest swath of treetops back to the farmhouse. He skirted the edge of a lake and aligned himself directly downwind from the makeshift runway. When he reached it, he descended below the trees and landed without rising or circling to make his approach. He touched down and his momentum carried him to the entrance of the barn where he quickly retrieved the tractor and towed the plane inside. In minutes, the canvas cover descended and hid the plane from view. To anyone trying to follow the craft, it had silently vanished mid-flight.

Jean-Claude lugged the heavy case into the second floor bedroom. Vincent's murder still disturbed him, but he told himself he was better off. He wondered about the opportunity he'd missed with Marcus. He couldn't imagine Marcus would ever find him, but a hint of doubt would have him checking the shadows for the rotund banker for years to come. Herman's goons were a more immediate threat. They knew where he lived and they'd already proven they could slip inside without him knowing. He could come home any day to find them waiting. If he really wanted to be safe, he needed to get rid of Herman, but could he look a man in the eye and launch a bullet through him?

He debated with himself as he stood in the closet and removed one of the trim boards. He stuffed the money from the briefcase into a hole just below the ceiling. Stack by stack the little packets fell between the wallboards and landed on dozens of others, completely hidden, safe for years to come. The two million he'd skimmed on each trip had filled six gaps between the wall studs. This was his reward for taking all the risk. Herman would never know.

He went down to the cellar and stored Jean-Claude's papers. He'd never had even a brush with the law as Jean-Claude. If he ran into trouble in the states, he could quietly retire here in anonymity. He removed a dense box of .45 cartridges and two sets of credentials from the safe. One driver's license and passport identified him as Brad Perry, the other set belonged to Brad Foster. When everything was in order, he killed the power and dowsed the house with enough chemicals to kill the mice and insects for the next fifty years. No creature was going to make a nest of his retirement fund. As long as the house didn't burn, the money would be there when he came back, no matter how long it took.

Brad pulled the tarp from the rented BMW and switched cars, covering the dented old Fiat in the garage.

Back by the barn, he prepared a test for himself. He set a bucket on a stump and backed up a comfortable distance, where he presumed he wouldn't see the eyes of the man he was about to shoot. Brad lifted the gun, imagining Herman's face on the pail and fired. He couldn't see a hole from sixty feet away. Walking halfway up he could see the smooth, plastic surface was intact. The bucket was more than twice the size of a man's head and he'd missed completely.

He stepped back for another shot, a little closer than the first. He steadied and fired again. Three shots sailed by and burrowed into the grassy

185

runway. Brad walked closer, now only twenty feet from the bucket. He fired and the bucket jumped immediately, a triangular black hole poked in one corner. The bucket tipped over and rolled a few feet behind the stump. Encouraged, he fired again; a direct hit, punching a hole through the center. He fired rapidly, punching another hole, missing, and finally smashing half of the bucket away before the empty gun refused to fire. He replaced the clip with a full one and emptied it faster than before, barely waiting for the barrel to come level before firing. There was power in the loud steady reports. He wished he'd started practicing sooner.

He walked to the car and slowly pressed fresh bullets into the clips and stored the gun and ammunition under the seat of the Fiat. He locked the garage and hoped no one would discover it before he returned.

The BMW was a pleasure to drive after the rusty Fiat and the trip to meet the tour bus passed too quickly. He hung a camera around his neck to make the purpose of his trip self evident. He opened his wallet and removed everything except eight hundred in cash and the documents that identified him as Brad Perry. The border guard had sold him this passport and he'd used it to enter Switzerland nearly a dozen times. In all his trips to France, there was never a record of Brad Foster leaving the country until he returned home.

Brad purchased his ticket and climbed aboard the bus, choosing a window seat halfway back. A motley crowd filled the seats around him. A young couple, newlyweds judging by the shine of their rings and their faces, sat across the aisle. Teenage children in the seats ahead, chatted continuously with their parents in high-speed French that Brad couldn't understand. Several older couples shuffled on board and finally Brad found what he was looking for. A young man, neatly dressed in blue jeans and a royal blue dress shirt, limped down the aisle looking dejected for an American on vacation. Brad nodded to the seat beside him and the man sat down. He would be Brad's best friend until two minutes after they were through security.

Brad raised his hand as the young guy sat. "Hi, I'm Brad Perry."

"I'm Charlie, Charlie Marston."

"What are you doing out here by yourself? It's no bustling tourist stop."

"My father just bought a share in a local vineyard. We're out here getting to know our new partners."

"You moving here for good?"

"No, we have a winery back home. That's where I'll end up. My dad likes to tinker with small vineyards. He drags us along for company."

"Sounds interesting. Not your run-of-the-mill job."

"Winemaking's more like a mill than you think."

The bus wound its way out onto the main road and steamed along. "Which vineyard?"

Charlie pointed to a side road that led past Brad's rundown house. "It's about fifteen miles up on the mountain side."

"The one with the huge stone barn with a spruce tree on one side?"

"It's a hemlock. Pretty far off the beaten path for an American. You have a vacation place here or something?"

"I bought an old place a few years back."

"Cool. Maybe we can meet for a drink."

"When I said old, I mean really old. Not a place you'd want to visit. It was an old vegetable farm that went bust, a shack really. I'm going to knock it down eventually. I just haven't gotten up the energy yet."

"Let me know. Might be fun. I could use an excuse to get away from the vineyard for a few days."

Charlie's soft hands, neat hair and clean shaven face looked more at home in an office than a construction site. "You don't look like the type for demolition work."

"I don't mind real work. I'd do it just for the change of scenery. Trust me. I've had winemaking rammed down my throat since I was ten. Anything different would be a pleasure."

Charlie and Brad talked all the way to Geneva. Charlie invited any reprieve from the tedium of his father's business and Brad promised to visit the vineyard and sample some of last year's wines. When the passports were checked and the men walked off the bus, Brad's mind returned to business. He'd never see the young American again.

CJ West

Brad walked into a café, chose a window seat, and watched every face that passed. The café was nearly empty and the people on the street moved about with no apparent interest in him. It seemed the goons from the day before hadn't followed him here.

When the appointed time came, he paid his check, crossed the street and walked into a huge marble lobby. The richness of this place was a striking contrast to the farmer's bank. Brad imagined the ill-gotten wealth of several dictators stored somewhere beneath the marble floors.

A man in a dark suit walked briskly to Brad and guided him across the lobby and into a small room. A serious-looking guard locked them inside. The transactions were completed in minutes and Brad relaxed for the first time in two days. He left the room with nothing to do but idle around until the return bus trip. The forty-five million in this bank was more than he could imagine spending, never mind the twenty in cash stuffed in the walls of his dilapidated place in France. Once he was free of Herman and Erica, life would be grand.

He browsed the shops and imagined the things he'd do to keep himself entertained for the next twenty-five years.

188

Chapter 44

Sarah arrived at the restaurant at quarter to seven, sat on the couch and watched dozens of guests make their way into and out of Avenue One for breakfast. She'd waited over a week for this meeting and she was anxious to get started even at this early hour. Her typed questions lay in the folder on her lap, ready for the biggest meeting of her career. Herman's call had set it up. He'd gotten Brad to meet her here where she'd have his full attention. She'd make progress on her investigation today, the first steps forward since Erica Fletcher stalled it weeks ago.

Brad strode in from Avenue de Lafayette looking pale and tired for someone just back from vacation. He flagged down a hostess who led them to an isolated table. Brad sat with his back to a solid divider.

The waitress whisked in, filled their coffee cups and rushed off.

Brad didn't waste time with pleasantries. "What's this about?"

"I wanted to talk about mutual fund transactions and security."

"No, no, no. I didn't come here to chit chat about IT. Herman asked me here because something's wrong. I want to know what it is."

"We're concerned about some mutual fund transactions that may have been altered."

He leaned in sternly "Let's skip the hypotheticals. Tell me what you've found and I'll try to help. I'm not going to play guessing games this early."

Sarah's face reddened. She'd heard about Brad's Neanderthal behavior and came in expecting to outmaneuver him. Thirty seconds into the meeting she was cornered. She shouldn't tell him what she suspected, but if she didn't, she might as well get up and walk out.

"I told you. We're worried about mutual fund transactions. We think someone's making unauthorized changes. I need to know how."

The statement deflated Brad's cocky attitude a bit. He crossed his arms and stared. It had to be a blow. It was his job to prevent this sort of breach and the accusation couldn't be welcome. Whatever he was thinking, he didn't respond.

"If I told you I *knew* someone was getting in, what would you do?" Sarah asked. "Where would you start?"

He took off into a detailed discussion of the measures they'd taken to prevent data theft. His ego was stinging for sure. She listened politely as he bemoaned the access every young CSR had down on the nineteenth floor. No one could get in from the outside according to him. The SQL and web servers were locked down and audited by an outside security firm every six months. They'd never had a blip on those reports. He had no doubt the breach was coming from inside. He boiled it down to two possibilities: someone from nineteen making changes through the system or someone getting into the computer room and going around the system. He believed the problem was on nineteen.

"I'm not looking for some kid down in client services."

"How do you know?"

"It's bigger than that. Someone's making changes, but leaving no trace in the system."

Brad looked perplexed. "How do you know they're making changes if there's no evidence?"

"Customer complaints."

He asked how many and when she admitted it was a single complaint he turned away in disgust. When he turned back, he growled through his teeth keeping his voice low enough so no one else could hear. "You didn't bring me here for one complaint."

Herman had thought the evidence compelling. She should have expected Brad's reluctance, but she was blinded by dreams of a huge raise and promotion for her discovery. She'd assumed his cooperation and now she'd have to earn it. She sat back, sobered, glad to see the waitress appear to take their orders.

Brad feigned a pleasant attitude for the waitress giving Sarah a brief reprieve to collect her thoughts. She'd expected a defensive, apologetic man who felt guilty about failing his brother's company. There was nothing apologetic about Brad.

As soon as the waitress walked away he piped up, "Ok, enough dancing around. It's time you tell me what you've got."

Her power in this conversation had evaporated. She wished she'd brought Herman along. She felt exposed, forced to tell more than she should. Brad was responsible for IT and the CEO's brother-in-law. Telling him should have been as natural as telling Herman, but something was holding her back. She didn't like it, but she was out of options.

"Someone is altering trades, but it's not someone downstairs. I think it's someone in IT."

Brad locked eyes with her. "Ok. Let me say this really slow so you can understand. You think someone's changing data. I get that. What are they doing with it?"

"I think you got it right when you said someone was bypassing the system and going straight to the database. There's no audit trail, but records have definitely been changed."

He slammed his hands on the table.

Startled, Sarah jumped an inch off her chair.

He deliberately annunciated every syllable. "Changed how?"

She'd never been frightened of a co-worker before, but she believed Brad might just jump over the table and attack her. She forced a deep breath.

He must have seen how scared she was because he pushed back from the table and forced a calm voice. "What do these changes look like?"

Sarah told him about the Johnsons' account problem. He took a copy of the statement and circled the transaction on the 29th. He seemed annoyed at being asked to research a single customer complaint. If he wasn't a senior vice president she would have guessed he was a bit unstable.

She worried that he wouldn't take the problem seriously, but didn't dare press him any further. He ruled out an Internet hack. He told her that the database could only be accessed directly from the computer room. No one in their right mind would sit in front of all those windows and steal from customer accounts. He was stuck on the idea that someone downstairs was responsible. Sarah was convinced he was wrong and told him so.

"Do you have any idea how complex this system is?" he mocked. "Tricking a system this complicated would take years of work. The chances of getting it exactly right are miniscule. Think about the money we spend on security, auditing, and all the work they do downstairs to prove the numbers. We have enough problems trying to process transactions honestly. If someone was messing with the data it would show up all over the reports."

She pointed to the statement in his hands. "We can't let this go. Can't you at least find out who accessed the database on the twenty-ninth?"

"Dozens of people access the databases. I can't question everyone."

"The Johnsons' transaction was pushed after the three o'clock deadline. It would have to have been done after three forty-five on the twenty-eighth and probably before close of business on the twenty-ninth. Doesn't it make sense to start there?"

He wasn't thrilled, but he agreed and halfheartedly stuck the account statement in his planner. She finished her toast and watched Brad sip his coffee until the waitress came with the check. Brad handed the waitress his credit card and watched her go.

"I need to ask you one more thing," she said.

He nodded sternly, his agreement to cooperate still fragile. She almost couldn't get the words out and she hoped what she was about to ask wouldn't send him into a tirade.

"A few weeks ago Gregg Turner came to you with a problem."

Brad grinned immediately.

"He says you threw his documents in the shredder."

Brad said nothing as the waitress delivered the bill and disappeared. He signed the slip and folded it into the leather holder.

"I'm sure Gregg's making it out worse than it was. He's been here long enough to know we have a system for handling problems. He's supposed to log a ticket upstairs, but he thinks just because I'm on nineteen, he can interrupt whatever I'm doing. I was in a bad mood and I let him have it."

"So you put him in his place."

"Something like that. Not my most shining moment, but Gregg knows better. I'm surprised he mentioned it."

Sarah followed Brad out into the street, but as soon as he hit the sidewalk, he turned toward the financial district and picked up his pace. He didn't want to be seen with her. It was best, though she would have felt better if he'd said something before hurrying off.

He was going to start digging. He was responsible for those systems. If someone was defrauding the company he'd be standing next to Stan and Herman when the heat came down. Brad wouldn't lose his job, but he'd get his wings clipped for sure. With that much incentive, he was bound to deliver better results than Erica had.

Satisfied with her morning's progress, Sarah let Brad get two full blocks ahead before following. She detoured down Summer Street and then along Washington, browsing in the windows as she went, thinking about the day Brad would deliver her proof. Marty would congratulate her then. After a few short months she'd break the biggest scam in BFS history.

Sarah was about to make it big time.

Chapter 45

Stan clicked on the cartoon Darth Vader to begin a round of movie trivia. Before Sarah arrived on the scene Stan had played contests on several websites each day in addition to his chats with Sean. He never worried about the company tracking the sites he visited. He lobbied to be in charge of Internet traffic monitoring a year earlier, but the company decided it was an invasion of privacy. Stan was smart enough to stay away from anything that could get him in real trouble. The movie sites were a huge time waster, but they were harmless. Strange, he felt guilty for playing even though he hadn't played once the previous week.

He aced the first five Star Wars questions, easy stuff, characters, vehicles, planets. Question six was tougher. It asked him to organize a list of four characters in the order they appeared in episode two. Stan stared at the names, struggling to remember scenes he saw years earlier.

Movement at the door caught his attention.

He instinctively minimized his browser window.

Erica Fletcher breezed into his office, closed the door behind her, and stopped two feet into the room.

"A lot of my dreams start like this," Stan said.

"All G-rated I hope."

"Mostly. How about yours?"

"Sorry. None of my dreams take place in your office."

"Bummer." Hotties like Erica had dreams, but Stan would never be privy to them. An occasional visit would have to suffice. "What's got you sneaking into my office and driving me mad?"

She chose a chair directly across the desk. "I've got a problem."

In his years at BFS few people sought his help. His work ethic wasn't a secret among the veterans and the mystique of internal audit warded off the junior staffers. Things had changed in the last few weeks. Sarah's tactics made people nervous and they came to Stan for reassurance with questions like, 'Does she really think I'm a crook' and 'Do I have to answer a question like that?' He assumed Erica could fend for herself.

"Does this have something to do with Sarah?"

Erica looked confused. "Not exactly."

"Let me take this in." Stan dramatically pressed his hands to his chest. "You're coming to me for help. I should bake you a pie for a proper welcome. I don't think you've ever…" The annoyed look said she wanted to get to the point. He apologized and asked what was on her mind.

She leaned in and began in a whisper even though the door was closed. "I have a situation. I think it's serious and I'm not sure where to go." She went on to describe her meeting with Gregg and Sarah and the problem with the Johnson account and the disappearing notes.

He asked why she didn't go back to Sarah curious whether it was her string-'em-up mentality or her interest in Gregg that drove them apart.

"She sees me as the enemy."

Stan knew why.

Sarah was on to something big. If Erica was working the same problem from a different angle, she was Stan's way in on the bust; his opportunity to salvage his reputation before Sarah destroyed it in her first month on the job. Stan put himself at her service.

"Someone's doctoring files."

Stan gasped a lung full of excitement and one full of embarrassment. If this was truly a theft, he'd let it go undetected for years. "Can you prove it?"

She told him about the customer's proof and how when she was getting close to an answer, her notes had disappeared from her office a second time.

The money in this one case wasn't huge, but when she told him about Brad putting the documents in the shredder he knew she was on to something. He'd heard about the shredding fiasco, but assumed it was Brad showing off for a girl. He never imagined Brad Foster would get caught up in something like this. He had everything to lose, but who better to grab files from Erica's office?

Stan couldn't believe his luck. "You think Brad's involved?"

Her grim nod said she believed it, but wasn't ready to get her hopes up.

"How cool would that be? Busting the biggest ass in this place. The boss' brother for God's sake. Where do we start?"

"From the beginning. All my research is gone. I could work through it again, but that would take days. I was hoping we could start from the other end. Figure out who's on systems they shouldn't be," she said.

"If it's Brad, he can get in any system any time he wants."

"It could be anyone up there."

Stan reminded her about the shredder incident, strange behavior even for Brad. He could easily sneak into her office and if he got caught, he could say he was checking on her work. She told Stan how often Brad was in the office late. He didn't write code anymore and he didn't directly manage projects, so what was he doing? They agreed managing thirty-seven people couldn't keep him that busy. Brad wouldn't be their only suspect, but he was top on the list.

Could a senior vice president be fool enough to steal from customers? Stan had never taken that threat seriously and right now it seemed to be his biggest failing. Sarah and Erica believed it was happening. They couldn't both be so committed and dead wrong. It was Stan's laziness that made it possible. He could feel his face reddening; his subconscious knew it was true and his face grew red hot with embarrassment. He needed to make it right and he needed to do it fast.

"Any links to Brad other than his hysteria downstairs?" he asked.

"I don't have a link to anyone. Anything that resembles proof keeps disappearing, but I have a pretty good idea how it's being done. Someone is adding transactions to the database at night. Sometime between market close and market open, hundreds, maybe thousands, of records are getting added. I stumbled on it because when you look at the records unsorted, they line up in the order they were added to the database. There were bunches with times around 3:30 P.M., but they were entered after transactions that were stamped with later times."

"So you *know* someone's messing with the data!"

"Looks that way."

"You said the transactions were entered together?"

She agreed.

"Do you know when? Can you point to one specific time?"

"It happened on three or four days that I know of. I'd have to dig, but I could find the transactions again. I can't say exactly when they were added, but I can give you the day and a ballpark time."

"Good. I'll get a security report from upstairs. It'll show who was on the systems when those transactions were entered."

"You ask for a security report and Brad will know in ten minutes."

"What then?"

"This type of change has to be made from the computer room. If we knew who went in and out, we'd have a place to start. We won't be able to convict anyone, but at least we'll know who we're after."

Stan fished in his desk and waved his master key at Erica. "Let's go. Time's a wasting."

"We can't go in there now. The whole group will see us. We need solid proof before we let anyone know what we're doing."

"Good point. I'll meet you up there around six."

"Better make it seven-thirty. Developers work late, especially Brad."

Stan couldn't believe he was agreeing to stay until seven-thirty, but he was spending time with Erica Fletcher. This job was looking up.

Chapter 46

The folded piece of paper lay hidden underneath Erica's keyboard as she waited for her teammates to head home. The hastily gathered list of dates would tie one of them to the suspicious transactions in the trading database. Friendly faces passed her door and she assured herself none of them could be the culprit. Down on twenty-one, Stan was anxious to get started. He'd called four times and it wasn't even seven o'clock. He accepted her delays, but she worried he'd lose patience and appear outside her door with a dozen people still in the cubicles. Fortunately, Brad wouldn't be one of them. She hadn't seen him in an hour.

The calls were an unwelcome surprise. She'd counted on Stan's apathy. All she wanted from him was to open the doors and get out of the way while she investigated. His laziness was corporate legend, but something was different tonight. It could be a hurry to get home, but his phone voice sparked with excitement. He knew the background and he'd drawn his conclusion quickly; the same conclusion Erica was afraid to admit. Stan had been working on this before she'd arrived in his office. She hoped he'd been discreet. An accusation against Brad Foster would throw the office into turmoil. Stan was primed to go after Brad looking for kudos, but he might get something entirely different. Erica wanted to see Brad punished, but she knew the kind of scrutiny her argument would receive. She'd chosen Stan for his patience and now she hoped she could rein him in long enough to gather her evidence.

Now that Stan knew, the consequences of the truth being out were unavoidable. Maybe she hadn't believed it herself until she said it, but Stan's excitement left little doubt. Brad's world was headed for collapse. Getting caught stealing from the family firm would mean ostracism. The Finches might cover it up to avoid the scandal, they might not. Prosecution meant losing everything, his job, his freedom, his family. A man would do extraordinary things to escape that fate. Knowing she spent most of her waking hours within a dozen strides of his office gave Erica a chill.

She sat alone pondering the days to come.

The noise in the hall dulled and the office began to close in on her. Brad had snuck in here twice to take her files. He knew she was getting close to catching him and he was desperate to stop her. She didn't wait for Stan to call again. She got up and headed for the printer. At the door she turned back and printed an old memo in case anyone saw her. She explored rows of empty cubicles and dark offices. Brad's was vacant as was the computer room. She doubled back to her desk and dialed Stan.

He was upstairs in less than two minutes. He slipped his key into the security room lock pausing only long enough for Erica to catch the door before descending on the keyboard. He clicked confidently to the first date Erica gave him and scanned the entries after six o'clock. Erica could barely keep up. He narrowed the list to people who entered the computer room. He spun around to face her, a single name on the list behind him. Entering at 9:50 P.M. was Erica Fletcher, IT. The door opened again from the inside at 10:56 P.M., presumably her exit. He checked the other dates and found the same result. According to the system only Erica entered the computer room on the nights in question.

The search was a bust. She had no proof and she risked losing her only ally. Stan gazed through her. She hoped he was bright enough to know a guilty woman wouldn't lead him to the evidence. None of the dates stuck out in her mind. She spent so much time in the office, likely as not she'd been in the building on those nights. Whoever framed her had chosen his victim well. With a nearly blank social calendar, she'd be hard pressed to find an alibi. The security guards and cabbies knew her well, but they wouldn't remember specific times she'd left. The only person she saw often at night was Brad and he wouldn't volunteer to help.

"This doesn't look good," Stan said rousing her.

"You know—"

"It's not me you need to convince," Stan said raising his hands. "Any of these dates mean anything to you?"

"Not a thing."

"Bummer." Stan hunted around the room for something. He opened a wooden closet door. Inside was a small screen, a VCR and a stack of ten VHS tapes. The screen views rotated through three shots: the computer room, the lobby on twenty-three, and the hallway outside. In eight years Erica had never noticed the cameras and no one ever mentioned them.

Stan pulled the tapes and scanned the labels. The tiny numbers aligned in neat columns of blue and black ink. Erica recognized Brad's handwriting when Stan displayed three tapes in a line for her.

The dates looked random at first.

After a minute the pattern was clear. The tapes were changed each day and the dates recorded. At the end of the week, the tapes were put aside and another set was used. The rotation showed a steady progression of dates from tape to tape, Monday to Friday. Stan held his finger on a day where the progression was interrupted. It was the first date on Erica's list, a Wednesday a few weeks ago. This tape hadn't been used with its mates the previous cycles. Someone had swapped it in. How Stan deduced this in ten seconds, she wouldn't know.

Erica watched Stan with newfound respect as he browsed for the next date on the list and found another break in the pattern. Someone was replacing tapes in the rotation on a fairly regular basis. They both knew why.

"You don't have a VCR in your office, do you?"

"Of course not."

"I know where we can find one."

Stan put everything back, logged out of the security PC and led Erica out into the hall.

"Where are we going?" she whispered.

"To find those tapes."

It was darker now. For all his bravado, Stan didn't turn on the lights. The security lighting was enough for them to follow the hall to Brad's office. All Brad's desk drawers were locked. Undeterred, Stan checked the wooden file cabinets arrayed around the room and found a half dozen VHS tapes neatly aligned at the bottom of one drawer. These tapes had been in and out of the rotation, too. Odd, but not proof.

Stan scooped up the tapes and headed out.

"Where now?'

"HR. They have a VCR for training. Let's see what's on these."

Stan moved through the building like he owned it. His access could get him anywhere and he wasn't shy about using it. Going to Stan was a better decision than she'd imagined.

They wheeled the cart out of a cramped closet at the back of HR. Stan plugged in the TV and VCR and popped in a tape.

It played black and white checkerboard static.

It should have shown the last views from the security cameras. Stan tuned in the TV. Poor as the reception was, he recorded a bit of local news. It played back fine. The tapes had been erased, all six of them.

"Could we restore these?"

"Not a chance," Erica said.

"Too bad. Your boss is hiding something, but it's going to be damn hard to prove. Will the server access records help?"

"Probably not. He could use a generic administrative account. If he did, there's no way to prove who logged in."

If Brad could fake her identity for the card reader, could he fake her network credentials, too? He'd done a good job framing her, but there had to be something more, something that linked to him. She had to prove she'd been somewhere else at least one of those nights. The blank security tapes were useless. She'd have to find another way.

Stan tapped her shoulder. "He's pointed this right at you. No one else could do it. We both know that, but if Sarah sees those records, there'll be no changing her mind."

Stan scratched his chin and stared toward the city skyline. He absently unplugged the equipment, organized the cart and returned it to the closet.

Erica watched helplessly.

"Not exactly what I was hoping for," he said. "But it could've been worse. We could have told Herman. At least now we've got some time."

The words were a huge relief.

She had to prove she wasn't the one in the computer room and she had to do it quietly. Once Brad knew she was trying to discredit him, he'd bring Herman and Sarah to Marty's office, all three proclaiming her guilt in unison. She needed some way to prove she'd been at home one of those nights. She wished she'd slowed down more often. The last year was a blur. She wished she'd kept her eyes open.

They agreed to strategize overnight and get back together in the morning. They split up at the elevator. Stan went home hours later than usual. Erica detoured up to twenty-two to return an armload of blank video tapes.

Chapter 47

Flabbergasted at the sight before him, Brad stopped short and held back a gasp. He ducked into the corner cubicle so silently she didn't notice. Years of skulking around these halls at night had taught him to move with stealth and tonight the habit paid dividends. He crouched low, leaned a single eye into the hall and watched her lower the security tapes into the drawer. If she was putting them back, she knew they'd been erased. He'd tell Marty the erasure was thorough security practice and he'd believe it, but she knew better. She'd finally figured it out. Time for her to go.

She didn't stop with the tapes. She went methodically drawer to drawer, skimming files and browsing through stacks of CDs. She knew what she was looking for. She pulled books off the shelf, fanned the pages and put them back exactly as they'd been. When she'd finished every unlocked drawer and shelf, she came to where he'd expected her to search first: his locked desk. She checked behind pictures, under his keyboard, and under the phone, carefully putting everything back where she found it. Finally she lifted the paperclip tray and found the spare key.

She opened each drawer and searched more thoroughly here.

He glared as she picked up a CD and inserted it into his computer; only a blank to her, but so much more valuable with her prints on it. She rifled dozens of personnel files, stopping on one in particular, probably her own. She tried all the CDs in the side drawer before giving up. She knew it was a program making the changes and she knew he was the one running it. If she'd read the security log, she knew he'd set her up and she'd be steamed.

When she flicked off the light, he crawled under the desktop and sat motionless, holding his breath as she passed on the other side of the cubicles. Her sneakers barely made a sound on the carpet. She exhaled loudly, frustrated he'd hidden his work so well. She had no idea he was listening from the floor. Papers rustled in her office. Zippers jingled on her bag. She called a cab and rustled around her desk a bit longer. The lobby door opened and closed behind her a few minutes later.

Cautiously, he slipped outside the cubicle, keeping his head low as he slinked around to her darkened office. He hit redial and told the dispatcher he was Gregg Turner, the boyfriend of the woman who'd just called. He'd take her home, so she wouldn't need a cab. The man on the other end recognized her name and cancelled the cab for 155 Franklin.

In his own office, the brown paper backing peeled off a landscape of Portland Head Light to reveal the CD she'd been looking for. Quickly into the computer, he copied the contents onto the CD Erica had handled without getting his own prints on it.

As the computer transferred the files, Brad picked up the phone.

"Hello," a gruff voice answered.

"I need your help."

"Why are you calling me this late? It doesn't look good."

"She rifled my desk. She knows what she's looking for."

"Did she find anything?" Herman asked.

"No. But I got her prints. I'm making the CD now."

The line went quiet. "Good. Follow her out and take care of her. Tomorrow we go to Marty."

"I'm not *taking care* of anyone. That's your job."

"You've got to earn your money somehow."

"I've earned my share a dozen times."

"The girl is your problem. I can take her side or yours. Doesn't matter to me. You want my help with Marty, get rid of her."

"I can't do that."

"You've carried that forty-five long enough. Time you fired it."

Brad remembered his practice with the bucket. Erica wouldn't let him get that close and she wouldn't stay still while he lined her up. Herman had professionals for this. Brad had never imagined shooting anyone except Herman.

"She's as much your problem as mine. Send one of your goons."

"You've got twelve hours. Make her disappear or I'll be in the office bright and early with another big white envelope."

"Do it and the forty-five will be pointed at you."

"She'll be easier, trust me. Take her out and I'll hold on to the envelope. Your call."

The line clicked dead.

Brad stared at the receiver until the CD drive popped open. She was stranded out front. She might be the practice he needed to get ready for Herman. She might also be the fastest route to prison. He pulled the .45 from his briefcase, grabbed the CD and ran out the door.

. . .

Erica was jittery being in the building after searching Brad's office. She talked to the security guard for ten minutes, watching the street for the familiar brown and white Boston Cab she'd called. When she ran out of small talk, she waved goodnight and headed outside into the warm spring air. She told herself no one knew what she did upstairs and that the cabbie had to be parked outside.

The cab wasn't on Franklin or Pearl. It wasn't like them to blow off an arranged fare. She stood on the dark sidewalk feeling like a target, a woman alone in the city at night, especially after what she'd found. Her driver probably got caught up with his last fare. He'd be along, but she'd feel safer getting away from the building. In three blocks she could mix in with the crowd around Faneuil Hall and jump one of the cabs that ferried tourists from place to place. She felt bad ditching her ride so she waited a bit longer.

She scanned the dark, empty sidewalks and blackened buildings. Rowdy voices cheered a few blocks over. A car coasted down the next block, disappearing from sight. She gripped her cell phone and started walking. The financial district around her was a mass of shadows punctured here and there by dim street lights. Weary cleaning crews were finishing their second or third buildings and sleepy security guards were settling in for an uneventful night. There was no one to tell Erica why the evidence she'd found pointed to her rather than Brad; why doing the right thing now meant implicating herself. Was Brad smart enough to know she'd be the one to catch on? Did he think anyone would believe she was a thief? Her reputation should make that decision clear cut.

Something heavy shifted on the concrete behind her. She flashed around, but the movement stopped. The look toward the dark corner was quick, almost frantic, but she'd seen something; an arm disappearing behind the column maybe. She turned toward the glass doors, now sixty yards away. Before she could take one step, something emerged from the darkness. A large figure, a man, moved through the shadows between her and the entrance. He circled a granite lined flowerbed. His face was in shadow, but his movements were familiar. He stopped between Erica and the doors, blocking her retreat to the security guard inside. He lurked silently in the gloom behind a column, waiting.

Adrenaline coursed through her, ever limb ready to flee.

She spun around, her feet tangling together as she abruptly broke into a walk toward the corner. Her pants allowed long quick strides and her sneakers made barely a sound on the sidewalk. At the corner, she scanned the street for help, casually, as if looking for traffic at this late hour. Nothing moved except the dark figure she glimpsed, leaving the column and approaching from behind. He stayed in the shadows against the building, avoided the lights at the corner and ducked behind a lonely car. She crossed toward the park and cut around a row of bushes that disguised the exit ramp from the garage buried below ground. If he followed her into the park, she'd race him three blocks to Faneuil Hall. She'd have a small head start and she ran every day.

She strode as fast as she could without breaking into a trot.

Her heart thumped in her chest and her feet yearned to run as she listened for the man behind her. A car door slammed two blocks away. Nothing moved nearby, there were no voices to run to, or from. She slipped her bag off her shoulder, clutching it in her hand as her feet touched the grass. Surrounded by shadowy hiding places, the attacker could be herding her toward a dark building or a parked car and a waiting accomplice.

She stopped.

She remembered the walk, Brad's walk. It was him behind her somewhere and he knew what she'd been doing in the office tonight. All the things going wrong around her had him in common. The break-in, her name on the access records, the erased tapes, the disappearing notes. Brad had everything to lose and he was protecting himself by blaming her. If she disappeared, he'd have a convenient scapegoat. He could even take credit for solving the theft.

She looked over her shoulder to see how close he was, but he wasn't there. She spun all the way around in the gloom, but he was gone. There was no time to wonder where. He was lurking nearby, sneaking ever closer.

Sprinting past her favorite bench, she jumped into the garden. Through rows of dormant bushes, up on top of a four foot cement wall, she jumped. She fell through the air, legs extended beneath her, both hands on her bag. The drop was farther than expected. She landed feet-first. Her knees buckled, toppling her forward down the ramp, leaving her sprawled on the concrete, looking down at empty parking spaces. She hopped up and in one step regained her balance and turned her energy loose, accelerating into a full run into the one place she knew Brad wasn't hiding, the dark garage.

The heavy bag flopped against her hip as she darted down the ramp. Her strides lengthened as she crossed the empty floor and raced down another ramp to the level below. Halfway down, she froze and stood still against the cold concrete wall. She stifled her breath down to soft shallow puffs of air. Her heart pounded and her lungs ached for more oxygen. Click. Scratch. Click. Scratch. Footsteps approached from above. Erica shifted her feet and eased down the ramp. The stairs were on the opposite end of the garage.

A patch of loose sand launched her sneaker down the slope, stretching her legs wide. The grating, scratching noise echoed through the damp musty air. She scrambled, regained her balance, and stopped long enough to hear the footsteps hasten toward her. She ran down two more levels, farther away from her pursuer, but deeper and deeper underground where she'd eventually be cornered. The bag was getting heavy now, too. The weight was slowing her pace and her shoulder ached. On the next floor, she decided to hide. She sprinted along the outer edge of the garage and lay down in a cluster of cars. Minutes passed. Each shallow breath brought more dust and dirt to choke her. With each passing second, she cursed herself for not getting on the elevator and riding up to freedom on the surface.

She waited.

Footsteps approached from the ramp. Erica hoped it was someone coming for their car, but patrons would use the stairs or the elevator not the ramp. She peeked out from underneath a bumper and saw Brad searching the parking area with a black gun in his hand, his face lit by weak fluorescent lights. He methodically checked inside and underneath each car, making his way down the row on the opposite side of the garage.

When he disappeared behind the little building that housed the elevator, Erica saw her chance. She lifted her bag and snuck toward him, hiding behind the building as Brad passed on the other side. At the end of the row he spun around and peered down the line of cars. He didn't notice the eyes behind the blue sedan.

There were few cars in the garage at this hour, but thankfully enough of them were clustered around the elevator to hide her movement. Brad moved slowly, venturing to each and every car on the floor, even those parked off by themselves. His thoroughness made his progress slow and predictable. Erica slipped behind a black Volvo against the far wall. Brad had already checked the area once. She wouldn't give him reason to return.

When he circled the small elevator building, Erica could hear his growls and frustrated curses. She waited until he searched halfway back to the ramp and then slipped between the cars, scooted to the elevator bank, and eased inside. She pressed the up button, counted to five, and pressed the down button. She stood in the center of the little room ready to jump though whichever pair of doors opened first.

A motor started somewhere below, the cable lifting a car toward her.

Trapped, the wait seemed endless. If the elevator came now, Brad would be at the far end of the garage with no chance to stop her. If it took much longer, he could intercept the elevator on a floor above. If he did, she'd be trapped in a four-by-four stainless steel coffin when the doors opened.

The room she was in wasn't much bigger. The concrete wall hid Brad and Erica from each other. He searched out there somewhere and she was trapped inside with no idea where he'd moved since she last saw him. The end walls and doors were mostly glass with a thin metal sheet underneath. She backed up against the concrete and switched her head back and forth from one glass wall to the other, watching the width of the garage. The enclosure muffled the sound of Brad's footsteps. She'd entirely lost track of him and could only hope he was on the ramp to another floor. Freedom would be here soon.

Ding.

Brad, by chance, had circled back to re-check some cars in the center of the garage and the ringing bell called him like a hungry animal. Erica stepped up, poised to dive inside at the first possible instant, not knowing he was rushing toward her.

The heavy car settled in place on the other side of the doors.

Brad's head popped into view. He raised the gun over the roof of a brown sedan and the instant it settled, the gun kicked up with a flash and a muffled roar. The wall of glass between them shattered as the first bullet passed through. Shards of glass rained down on the worn carpet. Erica dropped to the floor, smacking her knee and elbow on the tiles that outlined the small room. Brad fired again and again leaving no time to aim between shots. Erica clutched her bag to her head, and rolled away from the elevator hoping there was something solid enough inside the bag to slow the bullets.

Her ears rang with the reverberating reports as she huddled at the base of the concrete wall, lying flat and clutching the bag at her head. The bullets stopped. Shattered glass covered the floor. The contents of her bag were strewn all over from her rolling. She couldn't see Brad beyond the waist-high, solid wall and she couldn't hear anything over the high pitched ringing in her ears. She wanted to run, but Brad could be waiting for her to step outside. She crouched low and waited as the doors vibrated.

The scraping of the clip was barely audible and Erica didn't recognize the sound. Her eyes swung from door to door wondering where Brad would appear. The elevator doors slid open and as they did, the bullets started again. Pairs of bullets pierced the thin metal walls beneath where the glass had been. The first two tore through the worn rug, ricocheted up and lodged in the door jam of the elevator. Two more skipped right through the room and into the parked cars beyond, shattering the remaining glass in the door behind her.

Erica wondered how many bullets Brad had. They were coming slower now. He was being more careful. She peeked up and saw him pull the gun down and rush toward her between two cars. As he did, she took two running steps and leaped across the floor, landing halfway in the waiting elevator. She dragged her legs inside and heaved on her bag strap, hauling it past her so fast it smacked into the rear wall. She frantically pressed the lobby button from her knees, pressing hard as if that would close the door faster. A bullet whizzed by and clanked as the doors finally started to move. Erica hurled herself into the corner, protected from the bullets by the concrete wall and several layers of steel. Two more bullets clanked inside the far end of the elevator, leaving dark, round holes in the shiny metal. The remaining bullets struck the sealed outer doors as Erica was lifted away.

The ride up was slow, but Brad would be delayed when the next elevator arrived, heading down. He couldn't beat the elevator up four flights of stairs. She got off, hobbled up the ramp and outside on a sore knee. Several streaks of blood oozed through her tattered pants where the skin on her kneecap had been. She jogged off gingerly toward Faneuil Hall ignoring her burning knee and aching shoulder. The pain was forgotten when she saw a brown and white cab at the corner of State Street. She waved frantically, crawled inside and the cab sped away.

Chapter 48

Carlos scrawled the cab's plate number then flipped open his phone. "Hey, Boss," he said.

"What's going on?"

"He chased her into the P.O. Square garage. In eight minutes I counted fifteen shots."

"Fifteen?"

"Could've been more. They came fast," Carlos said, shaking his head in disbelief. "She's hobbling, looks like she fell, but he didn't score a hit."

"Fifteen shots and she's moving? Where is he?"

"She bolted into a cab. He's scrambling ass for his car."

"How'd she get away? He run out of ammo?"

"Don't know. You want me to do her?"

"No. I don't want you guys cowboying around the city. Let's leave this one to Brad."

"He missed her fifteen times – *Indoors!*"

"I know. He's useless. Anyone else hear the shots?"

"Nothing's moved here for a while. Can't say for sure no one's camped out down there, but I doubt it."

"Good enough for me. What about cameras?"

"Not sure."

"Go down to there and check it out then report the trouble. Make sure there's nothing to lead the cops to him or her. I don't want cops attached to either one of them in case we need to make a move. If he whacks her great, but I'm not expecting miracles. Just try and keep him out of jail."

"Got it."

Carlos couldn't understand why he was cleaning up after Foster rather than chasing the girl. Foster was more trouble than he was worth, but Carlos didn't protest. That didn't play with the boss. Carlos walked downstairs shaking like a frightened office jockey, scared by the commotion and ready to cling to anyone who could protect him.

The scene looked like Brad had been firing a machine gun. Ten shell casings lay in a group on the concrete about forty feet from the elevator. Eight more were scattered ranging from twenty-five feet to as close as ten feet from the glass door. Brad must have been running and shooting. Carlos got on his knees and searched around every tire to be sure he had them all. He couldn't do anything about the slugs, but the gun was untraceable.

Every pane of glass was smashed out of the elevator lobby. At least four cars had been hit. Luckily no cameras filmed the shooting spree. He picked up some make-up and business cards from the carpet where the girl had fallen. He stuffed them in his pockets and went back upstairs wondering how Foster could miss her in that tiny room. He'd hit everything else.

. . .

Erica fished ten dollars from her wallet as the cab double parked on Marlborough. Brad couldn't have beaten the jerky stop-and-go of the cab driver across town, but Erica nervously scanned the dark sidewalks for him anyway. Two young kids wobbled along in search of their next drink oblivious to Erica watching them through the glass. Farther up the block a more calculating figure leaned against a brick entryway. This man was waiting for something. His head was in shadow, yet she could tell he was intent on the happenings up and down the street.

The cabbie knocked the plexiglass for his fare. Her eyes shifted from the cabbie to the form outside and back.

"Change of plans." She gave him Gregg's address in the North End.

He hesitated, annoyed with the delay, but he must have sensed the fear in her face because he turned around and sped away without complaining.

Erica dug for her cell phone. She chose the speed dial for Gregg's house, but didn't dial. Brad knew about Gregg and he'd have ways of getting his address. He could probably get her mother's and Gregg's parents', too.

They turned off Sturrow closing in on Gregg's place. She let him approach knowing she couldn't get out. She needed someplace safer.

Her mother had taken her to a shelter once when she was four. They'd escaped her father for a week while the bruises on her mother's face healed. Erica never understood why she brought them back into that house. Years later Erica volunteered in the shelter to counsel other young women not to make the same mistake. Some had listened.

She dialed the number her mother must have dialed frantically all those years ago, a number Erica spent a good many nights answering.

"Safe Haven Crisis Center. Do you have an emergency?"

"I'm safe at the moment. Is Jan in?"

"Jan Tripp? She hasn't worked the hotline for six years. Who's this?"

"Erica Fletcher."

The woman didn't recognize the name. "Erica, do you need help?"

The cabbie pulled over and looked back. "Fourteen seventy-five, Miss." He eyed the rear passenger's side door expectantly.

"I need a place to stay for a few days. Can you connect me to Jan?"

Fifteen minutes later Erica stood outside a house that had the amenities she'd come to expect. There was an eight-foot stone wall surrounding the property with wrought iron spikes on top to discourage angry husbands. The cars were either in the garage or around back to keep them out of view from the street. There was a police station two blocks down, though this did little to calm Erica's nerves after seeing her name on the security computer.

The gate buzzed. Erica let herself in and closed it securely behind her.

Jan opened the front door and gave Erica a solid hug. "They say history repeats itself, but you're the last person I expected to show up here in the middle of the night."

Two inches taller than Erica, Jan was substantial, though her muscles had softened with years. Her expression was as serene as Erica remembered. She eyed the bloodstained hole in the knee of Erica's pants and then reached a hand toward Erica's elbow, sour at the way she carried it.

"Tell me this isn't what it looks like," Jan said, as she closed the thick wooden door and engaged the deadbolts.

"I wish it were that simple."

Shock registered on Jan's face when she turned. They both knew the tangle of emotions that surrounded being beaten by someone you loved. They'd both lived the horrifying reality and volunteered to help other women overcome hopeless situations. She knew what Jan was thinking, but Jan had never been shot at by her boss.

Jan led Erica into the living room doubtful anything could be more horrible than domestic abuse. Maybe she was right.

Erica described her last few years working for Brad, the break-in at her apartment, and her discoveries tonight with Stan. When she replayed her frantic run through the parking garage, Jan understood that she was lucky to be alive. She had nowhere to turn. Brad wanted her dead and he knew how to find everyone close to her. The police would probably join the chase in the morning and there was nothing she could tell them to make them understand. She hadn't had time to find the proof she needed. At least she was safe for the night.

Chapter 49

Brad burst out of the elevator and dashed over empty parking spaces on his way to the ramp. Halfway up, the cool air hit and he slowed before exposing the gun hanging by his side. A driver revved his engine and disappeared before Brad's eyes reached street level. The bushes were still, the sidewalks empty. He listened for sneakers jogging away. She'd go for South Station or Faneuil Hall. He couldn't decide which way she'd choose, and he couldn't hear her footfalls. She'd gotten lucky.

Down Congress and back into the park, he scoured the shadows with the gun ready. He needed to find her, get rid of the gun and get away from all those bullet holes downstairs.

The benches and shrubs around the fountain were clear.

Someone turned the corner at Franklin and walked down Pearl toward him. Brad doubled back over the grass into the park. He ducked behind the bushes, stuffed the gun into his waist band, covered it and kept walking. They passed each other with a row of fruit trees between them. Brad hastened down the path wondering if the man had been drawn here by the shots or if he was just heading home.

Had someone called the police?

Brad couldn't risk waiting.

He hustled through the park, over three blocks and up three flights of stairs to his car. He thought he heard tires squealing toward him several times before he hit the gas and took off in the Corvette. He accelerated for the first four blocks, hitting fifty on Congress, running the red as he cut across two lanes onto State, barely squeezing inside the curb. He heard the sirens for the first time on the narrow streets around Washington. Dozens of squad cars descended on the scene he'd left. He dropped down to the speed limit and cruised along Tremont toward Back Bay.

The lights were off when he parked half a block from Erica's window. No sign of life in the apartment. Coming here was a waste of time. She wasn't crazy enough to come home alone. She'd go somewhere else. Gregg's probably. If she was upstairs, being parked out here was admitting his guilt to the cops when they showed up. He had to do something fast. She knew about the scam; she knew it was a program and she knew it was him running it. Seeing him in the garage cleared up any doubt she had after coming up empty with the video tapes. At least right now she couldn't prove anything. She was frustrated in the office because she didn't find what she was looking for, but she was very close.

He had to end it now. Another day sleuthing around the office and she might have the proof she needed. Tonight he graduated to attempted murder and he couldn't give her time to prove he fired the shots. He weighed the gun in his hand. Discovered on him it could set her free. Discovered in her apartment, it could send her to prison.

Would a jury believe she tried to kill him?

The security system showed she was the one in the computer room. To anyone who believed she'd taken the money, attempted murder made sense. He thought about sneaking in and leaving the gun, but if she could prove she hadn't been home, he'd be helping her prove she'd been framed.

He cruised over to Gregg's apartment in the North End and parked facing an alley where three sets of fire escapes twisted their way up the side of the building. The lights were out, but at two o'clock, almost all of them were. He waited a half hour for her to show up, debating with himself whether she was already inside or not. This was the first place she'd come.

At three o'clock he slipped across the street. He climbed on top of the dumpster, careful not to kick the metal sides. From there he pulled down the ladder and made his way up to the third floor on the rickety metal supports.

216

Black paint chips stuck to his hands and the metal platform swayed, threatening to detach from the bricks.

He peered through the window on three. Nothing moved. The wooden windows were loose in their tracks so slipping the knife between them and prying the lock open was a snap. The counterweights were connected with ropes and pulleys in the window casing. They squeaked as the window rose, not enough to wake someone up, but enough so that anyone already awake would know someone was sneaking into the kitchen.

Brad's shoes touched down on linoleum.

The gun led the way in. The door to the hallway had a chain and deadbolt, both engaged. He'd take that way out if he had to shoot. Otherwise, he'd slip out the fire escape the way he came in.

The first room he checked was Gregg's. The sheets were pulled down, the quilt half off the bed. No mistaking he was sleeping alone. The second bedroom was piled with a bachelor's odds and ends: weights, books, a bicycle and a cheap desk with a computer that looked like it was never used. The couch in the tiny living room was empty. She'd vanished.

Brad slipped back through the kitchen, out onto the fire escape and climbed down as fast as he could steady his hands and feet on the rungs. He wasn't worried about noise anymore. He wanted to get home and figure out where to dump the gun. He jumped off the dumpster and trotted across the street to his car.

3:30 A.M. He'd come up empty.

. . .

Gregg slowly opened his eyes to rattling metal in the kitchen. He pressed his fingertips to the box under the nightstand. Fingerprints recognized, the end popped open and he withdrew the .357 he'd taken home from the farm. He eased the cylinder open, checked the contents and pushed it closed. The cylinder clicking shut would alarm any intruder. A pro would flee or hunker down.

He raised the bead to the center of the doorway and reached his feet to the floor. Hugging the wall he padded to the door casing. His back to the wall, he braced himself on the door jam and leaned his head outward, the .357 pointing to the table, the fridge, the window.

The window was wide open. Someone was inside.

He stalked into the guest room, the living room and back to the kitchen. Something banged in the alley. It sounded like a man jumping on the hood of a car. He leaned out the window and saw an outline rush out of the alley. A car started and drove past the far side of the building out of sight. The TV and stereo were in place. Gregg closed the window and wondered why someone would break-in and leave without taking anything.

. . .

Brad inched the door open and stepped inside, half expecting a swarm of blue shirts to envelop him, knock him to the ground and cuff him. He closed the door as quietly as he could and listened for intruders. His head was numb from twenty-two hours without sleep and the swirl of activity that began when he saw Erica hunched low in his darkened office. Finally home, he felt even more vulnerable despite the gun tucked in his pants, truly because of it.

The phone rang as if it had seen him walk in and wanted to talk. He ignored it, walking through the kitchen and into the bedroom. The LCD panel on the Digital Logger showed the number of the only person likely to know he'd just arrived home at 3:47 A.M. He clicked the record button and lifted the receiver.

"Nice work Bradley."

"I could've used your help."

"You don't know half of what I do for you."

"Like what you did to Vinny?"

"You screwed this one big. The cops are all over. Anyone see you?"

The man on Pearl Street came to mind. "No one but her," he lied. "She's a problem. If she shows up tomorrow, she's going to tell the whole world."

"She's a smart girl. She got there just a bit too late."

It sounded like Herman was agreeing to help.

"Be in my office first thing," Herman said. "We'll wrap it up."

"See you at ten."

"Idiot! Do you want everyone to know you were out all night? Get your ass in my office by eight. Have four cups of coffee if you have to. I want you looking traumatized, glad to be alive."

A few more weeks and he'd never listen to Herman again. He didn't bother to respond. Obedience was required. 3:58 A.M. Three hours to sleep if he was lucky.

"Don't forget that useless thing you've been carrying around in your pants. It might be helpful."

The line clicked dead.

Brad lifted the gun from his belt and wiped it down with a handkerchief. It was a throw-away Herman had given him. Getting rid of it would be a relief. He thought about cleaning it, but didn't know what kind of oil to use. Even if he did, he couldn't get it this late. He rubbed the prints off the remaining bullets and reinserted them into the clip. He wiped the outer surfaces over and over. He wasn't sure whether the dry cloth would remove his fingerprints so he rubbed harder and longer than seemed necessary. The rubbing eased his nerves. Finally he dropped the cloth and the gun into a Ziploc.

The gun might be the deciding factor that would flip the police, the judge, or the jury if, God forbid, this thing got that far. He rubbed the handkerchief over the gun a little more through the bag then tucked it in his top drawer and collapsed on the bed.

Chapter 50

Keenly focused from three cups of coffee, Brad sat upright in the tall leather chair watching the faces around the table. Herman had called this meeting hastily and gotten the team assembled before 8:00 A.M. He didn't look pleased that they'd been waiting ten minutes for Marty. Across the table Sarah looked bright and attentive. She couldn't know what was happening, but she was eager to get started. Being here in the boardroom for her first meeting with Marty thrilled her into silent awe. She sat with her hands folded trying to think of something intelligent to say.

Cathy Plummer, the new vice president of human resources, looked disinterested for someone who'd only been with the firm six months. She wasn't yawning, but she might as well have been. Late thirties, bland, and chunky, she held no interest for Brad. She stared vacantly over Herman's head giving the impression there wasn't much going on behind the pudgy cheeks. Not surprising she was still single and nearly forty.

Tension hung over the rest of the table. Each person felt special by virtue of their position. Herman and Brad needed the rest of them to buy the story. Cathy as head of human resources shot smug looks at Brad when she thought he wasn't looking. She could feel as superior as she wanted. She'd never know more about this case than he did, no matter how far the investigation went. For now, no one wanted to reveal what they knew. They tried not to look at each other, keeping their secrets to themselves, preparing to look unfazed when Marty officially released the news.

Herman looked angry. His only question: where would the blame fall? The answer was up to Marty and this disturbed him as much as Brad's failure in the parking garage. Herman thrived on the power to bend others to his will. He hated being subordinate to a simple man like Marty, who could only come to power one way. Herman had made it to senior vice president on his own. Unfortunately for him, he'd never rise further because he wasn't a Finch or a board crony. No matter, he didn't need the money.

Finally, Marty pushed through the door and took his seat at the head of the table. All eyes trained on him. He measured the faces around the table until he was sure he had command of his audience. No one spoke. Sarah was so entranced she wouldn't have moved if a snake slithered into her lap.

Marty began, "I found this news deeply troubling on several levels as I assume you all did. I find it very difficult to believe that someone would steal from our customers. This is a family company, always has been, always will be. This is the most fundamental breach of our duty. I take this very seriously. If what Herman says is true, there is no option but termination and prosecution.

"That said, I have to ask myself how something like this could go on for any length of time. Putting aside that I've been paying Herman, Stan, and Brad to prevent problems like this, I am even more disturbed by our choice of a suspect. Erica Fletcher is a model employee. If you're going to accuse her, you better show me solid evidence or your boxes will be on the move in the next re-org."

Herman moved to speak.

Marty silenced him with a raised finger.

"This will not be a witch hunt and it will not be public. You will work together discreetly until you've proven *to me* that further action is warranted. Herman and I will bring this forward. No one else is to discuss this with anyone outside this room.

"Is that clear?"

The audience around the table nodded solemnly.

Marty waited for each one, as if making a mental tally before allowing Herman to speak his mind.

"I agree that privacy and fairness are important," Herman began, "but I can't agree to let her come and go on company property while we're investigating. Brad caught her destroying evidence last night and if we let her back in, we're inviting her to continue."

Marty looked down at Herman incredulously. "You really believe this? This is Erica Fletcher for God's sake."

Herman's face was half hidden in his hands, one in a fist, the other hand on top, propping up his chin. He gave a slight nod, barely moving, content to let the question drop.

Cathy broke in. "We could quietly suspend her with pay while we investigate. If we don't find anything, she comes back like nothing ever happened. No one needs to know."

"How appropriate," Marty said, "since, most likely, nothing did."

Sarah's strong voice surprised Brad, "Something definitely happened, Sir. I've seen trades that have been tampered with. I've suspected for a while that someone on the IT team has been changing trades to siphon off customer funds."

"Have we met?"

"No, Sir. I've only been with the firm a few weeks."

"And in that time, three lousy weeks, you've discovered someone stealing from us and you've known it for some time?" Marty glared down the table.

"I believe so," Sarah said.

Shocked, Marty snapped a look at Herman. "How is this possible? I've been paying you and Stan for years to catch this sort of thing. And what? She finds it on her first day?"

"It's a complex scheme, masterfully done. She didn't leave anything behind. The trading reports were always in balance and the trades we audited were always clean. To be fair to Stan, I think there was an element of luck here." Herman had more to say, but didn't.

"She outsmarted all three of you," Marty paused. "That I can believe." Marty snickered at Brad. "What about you? You've always resented her screwing up your man-team. Are you leading this lynch mob or just along for the ride?"

"Sarah asked me for help last Friday. I didn't know anything about this before then, but after last night, I guess you'd say I'm ready to throw the rope over the branch."

"You've been braiding that rope for years. What makes last night so special?"

"She tried to kill me," Brad said as evenly as he could.

Marty stared, dumbfounded or disbelieving, Brad couldn't be sure. Didn't Herman tell him about the shooting? How could he leave that out?

"I caught her in my office sifting through the security tapes. I kept out of sight and waited until she left, then I took a look at the tapes myself. Every one of them is blank."

"You think she erased them?"

"I certainly didn't. Those tapes sit in my office and I change them personally." Brad explained how the tapes were used in sets to capture the activity in the computer room then explained how she'd been systematically removing tapes from the rotation, erasing them, and leaving them in his office with the spares. "She's doing something in the computer room that she doesn't want us to see," Brad finished.

The room fell silent. Each of them sensed Marty was about to be overcome by the evidence. Nothing more was needed to change his mind but a few moments to sift through the facts.

"Did you ask her to explain herself?"

"She wasn't in the mood to talk."

"What does that mean?"

"It means she saw me go into my office. She knew she'd been caught and her only chance was to stop me from telling anyone. She waited outside until I left the building."

"You're not going to tell me you're afraid of her."

Marty wasn't going to believe she was a killer, but Brad had no choice but go ahead with the story. He hoped everyone else was primed for it.

"She pulled a gun." Brad made the rectangular shape of the barrel with two fingers. "It looked like a .45 or a gun a cop would carry. I was half a block from the office and she cut me off. She pointed the gun at me and I ran the other way. The streets were deserted, not a single person to help and she was catching up fast, so I ran down the ramp into the parking garage hoping to lose her or get close enough to overpower her."

Marty was entranced. He had doubts but didn't interrupt.

Cathy seemed to have awoken from her stupor. This was news to her.

"She found me on the fourth or fifth level down and started shooting. I was lucky to catch the elevator up before she hit me. After that, I had a good enough head start to run a few blocks and hide until she left."

"What did the police say?"

Brad hoped Marty wouldn't ask, but knew he'd have to face the question eventually. "I didn't call them. I called Herman. I felt stupid for running from her and I still didn't know what was on the tapes. I wanted to see them before we involved the police."

"Good call," Marty said, seeming a bit surprised, but appreciative of Brad's concern for the firm's reputation.

Now convinced, Marty began handing out assignments. He tasked Brad with finding an independent consultant to review any malicious code Erica might have written. He tasked Cathy with keeping Erica out of the building. Herman and Sarah were told to focus solely on what Erica had been doing in the computer room.

The meeting broke and everyone went back to their offices, bound by Marty's order of silence.

Chapter 51

Stan tossed and turned incessantly through the night. At 2:07 A.M. he realized he needed to tell Sarah about his discovery and join forces on the investigation. The longer she worked with Brad, the more brainwashed she'd become. Unfortunately, Sarah was all about the glory. If he suggested they team up, she'd think he was weaseling in on the credit and she'd refuse without a second thought. All he had for incentive was what he'd learned that night: a few dates Erica scrawled, the blank security tapes and a security system that pointed to Erica as the culprit. Everything he knew would push Sarah further off track. He needed to get her turned around fast. Her jealousy and the lack of evidence were going to make that difficult.

Brad had done an excellent job setting Erica up, but Stan knew he was guilty and that was more than he ever expected of this job. The evidence was somewhere in the office and together they could find it. He wasn't sure how they'd convince Marty that his brother-in-law was a crook, but he'd worry about that later. First, he had to convince Sarah to help.

All morning, bits of dialog ran through his head. Nothing in his imagined conversations convinced her of Erica's innocence, so he lay awake searching for something stronger.

At 7:56 A.M. he found Sarah's bag on her office chair, her laptop running, but no Sarah. She wasn't in the cafeteria, the computer room or Gregg's office. On a whim he jaunted up to twenty-three and found her in the boardroom with an interesting cast of characters: Brad, Herman, Cathy and Marty. Cathy's presence meant this was serious trouble for someone.

Herman and Sarah together meant the trouble was related to an IA project. Brad's sorry carcass meant the person in trouble was from IT and by the expression on his face, it wasn't him. Stan thought about barging in, but had nothing to offer but his conviction. He swung by Erica's office instead, came up empty and parked on Sarah's desk by 8:25 A.M.

Fifteen minutes later Sarah rushed around the corner with a wide grin. When she saw him perched on her desk she stopped dead, her pride wiped away by an expression of shock. She cautiously circled to her seat as if she were intruding in her own office.

"What got you out of bed so early?" she asked.

"Early meeting?" Stan countered.

"Yeah. You?"

"Interesting group up there. You should have invited me."

She smirked as if Stan was useless in that context. He shook off the insult knowing this was the man he'd shown her, the old Stan. The guy who'd washed out and given up. That was going to change. He wouldn't fail Erica.

"If you were talking about Erica Fletcher, you're dead wrong."

"I can't discuss it."

"You're going to be embarrassed when the truth comes out. Not a great first impression on the almighty Marty Finch."

"If anyone's going to be embarrassed, it's you. Marty said so himself."

"I'm trying to help," Stan pleaded, hating the sissy voice he used.

"I like you, Stan. No one's trying to make you look bad."

He wished that was true. "I'm sure you stuck up for me in there."

Sarah looked like she was going to be sick. Of course she hadn't. She couldn't say so, but he didn't blame her.

"Don't let your feelings color your judgment," Stan said.

"Don't even go there."

She was insulted and angry at the insinuation. She wanted to explode, but something inside her wouldn't allow it, probably the same compulsion that had her lining up desk accessories.

"Brad's setting her up."

"The facts point to Erica."

"Brad's facts. Look at the access logs if you're interested in facts. The system says she was in the computer room a dozen times when she wasn't."

"What were you doing in the security room?"

"Saving your butt."

She laughed in his face, looking at him like a clown. "It's your butt that needs saving. She's been stealing under your nose and you're still sniffing around her like a puppy dog."

He hadn't taken this job seriously before Sarah arrived, but he knew she was wrong about Erica and it was going to blow up in her face. She was going to help Brad push this all the way to trial. By the time she figured out Erica was innocent, correcting her mistake would be messy and public. Firing a senior vice president for embezzlement would be front page news. The trust of every BFS customer would be shattered, the firm devastated. Hundreds of jobs would be lost, jobs Stan could have saved if he'd lived up to his responsibilities.

He tried to keep a steady fatherly voice. "Don't rush into this."

"I can't discuss this with you. Marty's keeping a tight lid on it."

"He trusts me. You know that."

"No, I don't."

"She's being framed. If you weren't so star-struck, common sense would tell you I'm right."

"You think you can read people in five minutes. You should try working a little longer than that."

"It takes a certain kind of person to steal. She ain't it."

"You don't know that."

"I went with her to the security room last night."

Sarah stood up in a panic. She glared like she was ready to whip out the cuffs and haul him away. "What were you thinking?"

"The access list's been doctored."

"You don't know what you're getting in to."

"I was there. Someone's screwing her over. It's got to be Brad."

Sarah got up and closed the door. She sat beside him like a parent about to have *the talk* with a teenage child.

"Accuse Brad and you have a big problem," she threatened.

He told her about the blank security tapes, the way the dates were misaligned and what that meant. They both knew it was Brad's job to handle them. Sarah listened without emotion. He couldn't tell whether she was ready to join him and help vindicate Erica or rush upstairs and use this information against her.

Stan wrapped up his case. "We need your help to prove it's Brad."

All he got was a cold glare.

"Brad Foster is a senior vice president not to mention that he's the CEO's brother-in-law. I'm not running off into your fantasy world. Don't ask me to."

"You're living the fantasy, buying his imperial crap. Just because he's got a big job and a big title is no reason to trust him."

"It's over Stan. She's suspended. She can't even get back in the building to pick up her stuff."

Stan stared back dumbstruck.

"We're going to prosecute," she said.

Stan got to his feet and made for the door.

"Not a word to her Stanley," she called after him, "or it's your ass."

Chapter 52

Sarah kept herself far enough from Erica's office furniture so she couldn't accidentally leave fingerprints. She wished they'd brought Stan for his knowledge of police procedure. The thought made her chuckle after his rant that morning, but she wasn't trained as a detective and she couldn't imagine Herman was either.

She stood awkwardly self-conscious in the center of the room, more unsure about this case than ever. Herman opened the door for Brad and a guy that looked about eighteen. The kid couldn't have looked less eager if he'd been asked to flush the fish from the company aquarium. Brad stood behind him, arms crossed, prodding him on. Hacking into Erica's laptop and opening it up for Sarah to peruse sickened the poor kid. He came from the help desk and like every other guy on this floor he dreamed about Erica. She'd probably helped him dozens of times when no one else would. According to Stan that was her way.

The young man sporadically clicked keys. Brad became disinterested after the first few unsuccessful attempts and picked up some papers from the credenza and browsed until Herman barked at him. This job belonged to internal audit. Chastened, Brad dropped the papers, averted his eyes and slinked out the door.

A knock sounded minutes later and a kid from the mail room swayed in, his body moving to a rhythm in his head. His ridiculously baggy jeans showed red boxers all the way around his hips. He dropped a bundle of folded moving boxes inside the door and fixed his eyes on Herman. When

Herman nodded the kid replied with a clenched fist in the air as if knocking on an imaginary door. He hiked up his pants and left. Faces peered past him until the door swung closed. Word was spreading and there would be questions to answer when Sarah left the room.

Sarah popped open a box to get started, but Herman sternly angled his nose toward the kid behind the computer. The clutter would take days of sorting and she was eager to dive in, but she'd have to wait until the kid was gone. He was the only entertainment available, so she moved next to Herman and watched the commands as he typed. The letters didn't spell any words Sarah recognized and they appeared on the black screen then disappeared faster than she could follow. He paused occasionally to strategize and still the commands made no sense. After the fourth or fifth such pause, he stood up and handed Sarah a sticky note with Erica's new password, one Erica would never know. He'd found nothing and it was no secret he hoped Sarah and Herman wouldn't find anything either.

Sarah patted his shoulder and thanked him.

He dropped his eyes to the floor and shuffled out.

When the door closed, Sarah took up her box and started carefully sifting through the piles on the desktop. The white pages held nothing but computer gibberish; lots of semicolons, parentheses, and oddly long words with too many consonants. Some of the handwritten notes in the margins made sense, but she could never turn this into any sort of a case. When she finished her first folder and placed it in the box, Herman cleared his throat. She looked up to find him watching with a smirk.

"If you were stealing big money. I mean big money, would you leave the evidence on top of your desk?"

Sarah's face reddened and Herman paused to revel in his superiority.

"That'll take days to sift through. Just stuff it in a box." As he said this, he leafed through books one at a time, holding them upside down and shaking them. Whether he expected something to drop from the pages or he was just being excruciatingly thorough was unclear. When he finished a shelf, he piled the books vertically and moved on.

Sarah didn't bother looking inside the folders now. To match Herman's precision would take weeks and to find what they were looking for required expertise she didn't have. Instead, she lumped the files and papers from the desk into three heavy boxes and stacked them by the door. Finally, she could see the desktop. She pushed the pictures and accessories to the corner, shut down both laptops and stacked them off to the side. Now that she had a clean workspace, she opened the next box on top and was free from bending to the floor for every item she packed away.

The first drawer she opened was stocked with anything you'd need for an overnight at the office. Sarah packed a box with deodorant, aspirin, nail polish, shampoo and dozens of other essentials. Erica had surprisingly little memorabilia for someone who'd been with the firm so long, like a soldier on deployment. Sarah stacked a few framed photos on top of the toiletries box and moved on to more files. Armloads and armloads went into new boxes.

Behind her Herman ruffled through file cabinets as methodically as he'd gone through the bookshelves. He smiled when he noticed her watching. "Not what you pictured?" he asked.

"Not exactly."

"The hard work starts tomorrow, sifting page by page."

That job would be Sarah's. She grabbed another stack of files from the bottom drawer. As she measured the gathering mass of work ahead, she fumbled and something heavy slipped from her hands and clunked solidly against the wooden drawer. When the manila pile lifted clear, she dropped everything, releasing a cascade of files that scattered at her feet. She wailed, frozen in place with two inches of papers covering her shoes.

Herman jumped to her side urging her to keep quiet. He saw the black handgun lying at the bottom of the drawer and kicked it shut. He trained his eyes on the door, posing at attention nearly a minute, expecting someone to burst in, but no one did.

Sarah grabbed the phone and dialed, but before she could finish, Herman pressed the switch hook.

"Who are you calling?" he asked.

"The police. Last night in the parking garage – this is the gun."

Herman held out his hand for the receiver. He dialed a number and spoke firmly, "Where is he? No. I need him now. Pull him out. No. Right now! Send him to Erica Fletcher's office on twenty-two." And he hung up.

One minute later Marty Finch walked in.

Herman pulled open the drawer for him.

"Anyone touch it?" he asked.

"No," they said in unison.

"You've got my attention," Marty said. "Find anything else?"

Herman indicated the stack of boxes packed by the door. "It'll take weeks to sift through all that."

Marty nodded, his face darkening as he decided what to do.

Sarah still had the urge to pick up the phone and dial 911. "The police can match this gun to the bullets from the parking garage. They can tell us what happened," Sarah urged. It was the right thing to do.

Marty eyed her a second then exchanged a sharp look with Herman.

"Herman, go find some plastic to wrap this thing up. We'll stick it in the safe." Marty rested a hand on her shoulder and waited for the door to close behind Herman. "Sarah, this is big news; the biggest news in this firm's history. I don't want this getting out until we're ready to answer every possible question. Understand?"

"No police," she said halfheartedly.

"Finish your work," Marty said. "Then we'll talk."

Marty walked to the door and twisted the knob, inspecting the lock as he did. "This won't do," he said. He eyed the piles against the wall and the laptops on the desk. "I've got a secure room next to my office. I'll have all this moved there. Your work will be safe until you're done."

Sarah wondered who he was protecting.

Chapter 53

Erica's horse followed Gregg's off the trail and into a patch of tall grass by a small pond. The big brown Morgan held steady for her to dismount and seemed to know Gregg would leave her to graze nearby. Even if delivering young women to this romantic hideaway was routine for the horse, it was anything but for Erica. A light breeze blew ripples over the water and sent downy white clouds drifting overhead. Erica nearly forgot the terror of the last forty hours as she lay back in the grass and let the bright sun force her eyes closed. The breeze played in the grass and the horses munched and snorted. Her favorite bench in the park paled to this place. There were no voices, no pavement, and no cars. Something tapped in the distance, a woodpecker perhaps. Erica homed in on the sound feeling her chest rise with each inward breath and then melt as she released it.

Gregg sat at attention next to her watching the woods for trouble. He had an understated power about him and he took to the role of protector without fanfare. He'd tried to hide the shiny revolver under his arm, but she'd felt it the first time they embraced. Being around men had always put her on edge, but everything about Gregg was comforting. Even the gun was reassuring in his hands, a powerful force he'd wield on her behalf. She reached for his hand without opening her eyes. She trusted Gregg without a hint of fear. His determined pursuit had been worrisome for a long time, but now his steadfastness had become contagious.

She lay at ease for the first time since her last visit to the farm. Gregg was upset that she was going back to the city, but she had no choice. Left alone, Brad would build an ironclad case against her and when she did return, she'd be headed for prison. She had to prove Brad's guilt. The evidence she needed was in Boston and that's where she needed to be. Gregg hated the idea, but she'd made her decision.

When it was time to go, Gregg prepared the horses and helped Erica up into the saddle. They roamed down a wide section of trail among the pines and followed lush green fairways back up the slope toward the barn. They'd ridden five miles and never left the Turner's farm. Erica had never imagined a place so vast existed in Massachusetts. They emerged from the trees a half mile below the barn and she gazed off at the far edges of the fields as they dismounted and walked the horses the rest of the way up. Gregg showed her how to groom the horses and then they went inside to shower and change for the trip back to the city.

Gregg followed the flow of traffic back to Boston rarely passing anyone. He stayed centered in his lane, sternly focused straight ahead, eyes avoiding Erica in the passenger's seat. The slow driving was his protest. If he thought the delay would give her time to change her mind, he was wrong. She knew he was angry and that worried her more than anything she'd face in Boston, but she still needed to go.

The impasse held for the final half hour of the trip. Gregg wanted her to go home with him and nothing short of that would do. He couldn't understand that she wasn't dainty and helpless like Claudia and Dianne. She might never be the kind of woman Gregg needed, but she wasn't changing and she wasn't letting go. He'd have to adjust.

Watching his sharp features she felt a new fear. Their relationship had changed radically in a short week. He was important to her now. She was clinging to him and anything that upset him, anything that pushed them apart threatened to make her crumble. The thing she feared most was telling him about her father. Her childhood would be so foreign to him after the storybook life he'd led. She couldn't tell how he'd react. He might be incredibly compassionate or detached like he was now. She'd have to find a way to tell him eventually, but it wouldn't be anytime soon.

The car stopped at the alley behind Erica's apartment. His eyes begged her not to go, but her door was open, her feet already on the sidewalk. She kneeled over the seat and brushed his lips with hers. The short goodbye turned into a dangerously long embrace in plain view. She took a long, melancholy breath and backed into the alley, her eyes following the car as it powered away.

Two hours on horseback had stiffened her muscles more than if she'd run the entire distance. A long, hot shower had relaxed her, but the uneasy ride with Gregg had magnified her tension and intensified the pain in her legs and butt. Three teenagers walked by and paused to look at her alone in the alley before moving on. When they disappeared, she pushed ahead, tuning in to every voice and footfall.

Each step to her back door was painful and she stopped on the landing to loosen up. She massaged her quad through her new running suit ever vigilant for any movement behind her in the alley. The apartments above were quiet, their occupants off at work this time of day. She rested a sneaker on the small concrete stoop and stretched. After a few reps on each side, her leg muscles felt flexible again and she stepped through the back door into the hall. The lobby was empty, the twisting staircase and the floors above quiet. Instead of going up, she passed through the corridor and out the front door for a quick run.

There on the sidewalk, she hoisted a leg to the railing for one more stretch and scanned the street. Down the block, a car came to life. The Corvette's exhaust grunted mightily above the hum of the city. She began lifting her other leg to the railing, but suddenly broke off in a trot away from the Corvette coming toward her. She jogged at an easy pace. The traffic forced the Corvette to stop twice before the corner and she moved well ahead.

How long had he been waiting for her to come home? He'd made a huge mistake in the parking garage and he was trying to fix it now. The threat of losing everything made Brad desperate to catch her. He'd do anything to stop her from telling the truth about that night. Why had she let Gregg drive away? His gun would be comforting now.

She turned the corner toward the river and once she was out of sight, she broke into a full run and dashed across the street to the shelter of the parked cars on the other side. She ran down the sidewalk as Brad broke free of the traffic at the corner and pulled closer. A shot now would be difficult. He'd have to match her pace, shoot through the passenger's side window, and avoid hitting the parked cars between them, all while driving. He wasn't likely to hit her, but even a lucky shot could kill. She watched the Corvette creeping up behind and at the same time looked for places to hide. There wasn't a cop anywhere on the street. Barely a soul was out.

Her legs ached as she bounded faster down the sidewalk just several yards ahead of the car. She spurred herself through an intersection ahead of a blue pickup that lurched across behind her. The signal changed. The red light would stop Brad and give her a moment's breath. Her strides shortened as she looked back. She'd almost stopped when the Corvette ran right through the red light, slowing only to let the pickup cross in front.

The passenger window was open and pulling even. Erica darted for a van up ahead. When she reached it, the soles of her sneakers slapped the ground and she screeched to a stop, hidden by the boxy gray vehicle. She crawled to shelter behind the rear wheel and watched the Corvette stop opposite her and then move on, carried away by anxious drivers that honked from behind.

Erica squatted, breathing heavily.

She needed to get off the street. In this light traffic, Brad could be waiting up ahead or circling around from behind. She couldn't know which. She jogged three more blocks then veered off into the park toward the river. Fortunately, it was late afternoon and the lunchtime crowds had headed back to work. If Brad was there, he'd be easy to spot. She watched the path up ahead for any signs of him as she jogged at an easy pace. The openness of the park gave her a great view of the wide river and Cambridge beyond. She was exposed, but Brad would have to leave his car to get near her.

. . .

Brad parked his car ahead of a delivery truck so Erica wouldn't see it as she came up the path. He picked a bench on her normal jogging route and waited, hidden by a newspaper.

The blue running suit appeared one hundred yards away. The short dark hair bobbed along the trail that led to Brad's feet. He strained to see what he knew to be true. She was coming right to him. He slipped the .357 from under his windbreaker, cocked it, and laid it in his lap. He peeked around the paper again to check her progress. She turned away from him toward the river. Soon she'd disappear behind some trees. Too long a shot. Herman had screamed at him to get close this time, so close it was impossible to miss.

Brad carefully let down the hammer, shoved the gun in its holster, and hurried across the open grass to the trees. Few people ventured inside the tree line and the head high bushes were too thick to see through. Hidden inside, he trudged his way through until he could see the path along the edge of the river. He chose a large tree to hide behind and crouched there sheltered from both directions with a good view of the path below. Seconds passed. No one appeared from either direction. This was the only way out unless she saw him and turned back. But she couldn't have. He'd been hidden by the newspaper and then the trees.

He picked his way through the bushes toward where he last saw her, careful to stay out of sight, but close enough to maintain a good view of the path in case she sprinted by. At the next curve, a splotch of blue appeared. She was resting on a bench facing the water. Brad scanned the path for onlookers. No one was close enough to identify him or catch him when he ran. He closed twenty more yards for a clearer shot and luckily, she didn't hear him rustling in the bushes.

He lifted the gun and focused on the sight as it drifted in and out of the blue sweatshirt. He couldn't keep it steady until he braced his forearm against a tree. The sight settled on the patch of blue and held. Herman would have told him to get closer, but he had her. POW. The sweatshirt jumped and settled back on the bench. His shot had hit its mark. He lined up again to be sure. POW. Again the swatch of blue jumped as the slug passed through. This time, it fell to the ground.

Brad holstered the gun and ran even before she came to rest. The bushes swiped at him, stinging his face and arms. He broke into the open grass and sprinted for his car, a mere sixty yards ahead, poised to speed away.

When he neared the center of the lawn, too far from the trees to turn back, two large figures emerged from either end of the delivery truck. Each extended a palm as a warning to stop. When he saw the guns, he turned up river. After two long downhill strides, he saw a much larger man burst from the tree line. He was well over six feet tall and almost three feet wide at the shoulders. He closed the distance between them so fast Brad knew he couldn't outrun him. The officer stopped twenty yards away and stood with his 9mm aimed at Brad's chest, ready to fire. Brad stopped and looked down at his motionless feet.

Slowly he raised his hands over his head.

"You shot my dummy, Man," the officer hollered.

...

"We've got him and the gun, Sir," Officer Lewis squawked through the tiny speaker. Erica hoisted herself up from behind a stone wall. Two officers stood up on either side and escorted her across the park. She pulled the tiny radio from her ear and brushed herself off as they went.

Erica had been listening to the surveillance reports even before she stepped out her front door. Gregg had been listening from the communications van. The play-by-play of the officers guided her near enough to lure Brad into the ambush without giving him a chance to shoot, although it had gotten dicey a couple of times. She could see Gregg standing with the officers outside the communications van. He looked pale, stressed from the last ten minutes, but relieved to see her coming up the hill unharmed.

Sergeant Douglas, a roundish man with a curly clump of reddish-brown hair on each side of his head, greeted the group as they approached. "Congratulations, Ms. Fletcher. Believe it or not, that's about as smooth as these things go."

Officer Lewis handed Brad off to his partners and joined the team by the van. "You make excellent bait."

"Thanks, I think." She patted his huge shoulder. She could see kindness in these men and she couldn't have been more grateful they were taking Brad away, probably for life.

"He means, you did an excellent job," Sergeant Douglas corrected.

Erica looked at the men circled around her. "I'll sleep better tonight. Thanks to you guys."

Sergeant Douglas handed her a business card. If she saw anyone suspicious hanging around or even if she just got nervous, he'd have a cruiser to her apartment in two minutes. He was grateful for her help. It probably meant a promotion for someone on his team. She didn't say so, but it was Stan Nye they both had to thank for putting this together.

She thanked Sergeant Douglas and reminded him about the call to Sarah Burke. He promised to call right away then turned to Gregg with his hand extended. "I know it was hard to sit back and watch, but you should be very proud. That's an incredible woman you've got there."

Gregg agreed. The anger was gone. He looked drained and maybe disappointed that she didn't need him as much as he'd hoped.

Erica slipped off her sweatshirt and opened her protective vest revealing the moist T-shirt below. The sergeant took the vest and left Erica and Gregg standing together on the grass.

Chapter 54

Sarah crossed Sturrow Drive and found Stan on a bench more or less where he said he'd be. At three o'clock in the afternoon, the trip from the financial district had taken a full twenty minutes, time she couldn't spare and appease Herman's appetite for constant progress updates.

Stan hopped up off the bench when he saw her coming and bounced along toward her. Nothing dampened his spirits.

"Thanks for coming right over," he said.

"You know why I came."

"Confident are we? You want to up the stakes?"

Stan couldn't know about the gun. "Sky's the limit," she said.

His eyes traced her figure top to bottom and popped up to meet hers. His interest had been obvious for awhile and it was flattering, but he was a bit too short and way too unfocused. Nothing meaningful would ever happen between them. What he wanted was clear, but he didn't have the guts to ask. Too bad for him. She was so positive she was right, she would have agreed to anything for his side of the wager. No way Stan could change her mind about Erica in five minutes, not with the gun in the safe.

When he didn't answer she said she wanted lunch delivered to her desk every day for three months. He hesitated then asked for dinner and a movie every Friday for two months. She agreed and they walked along the grass toward a cluster of activity about a half block away.

"Should I start the clock?"

"Not yet, there's someone you need to meet first."

Faces in the crowd grew clearer as they approached. Gregg mingled with a dozen men. Some wore blue Boston Police uniforms others were large and fit, plainclothes detectives maybe.

Stan introduced Sergeant McKenna, a young man in blue with a jovial attitude she didn't attribute to policemen. He was one of the Boston Police Department's fastest rising stars.

"Sarah works with Erica and me," Stan said. "She's very interested to learn what happened today."

"Pleasure," he said without the brogue she expected to accompany the upturned nose. "It's been an exciting day. We've learned quite a lot."

Sarah wondered how much eight dinners and movies would cost.

Stan tapped his wrist on an imaginary watch to start the countdown.

"It seems Mr. Foster was making some unauthorized withdrawals and trying to pin them on Ms. Fletcher," McKenna said.

"Stan told you that?" Sarah asked.

"Mr. Foster proved it to us."

Sarah couldn't imagine how.

McKenna described the stake-out of Erica's apartment and how Brad chased her from there into the park and then shot the mannequin dressed in an identical running suit to the one Erica was wearing. Brad's intent was unquestionable. Any jury would make the connection to the fraud he'd perpetrated at work. They'd know the incident in the parking garage was his first attempt. Brad Foster was going to prison.

Sergeant McKenna shifted and Sarah spotted Erica among a group of officers. They treated her like a hero. They believed her. McKenna believed her. Stan idolized her. Still, the story was hard for Sarah to reconcile with the gun. If she could have asked McKenna, he'd have said the gun was another part of the frame-up. What would Herman say?

McKenna stood silent. She looked past him toward Cambridge across the river. She couldn't acknowledge her own investigation, the gun, or even Erica's suspension from work. She asked the only question she could. "Where's Brad now?"

McKenna indicated a squad car at the curb.

She turned toward it, but Stan had hold of her elbow. "What time will you pick me up Friday? I'm thinking Italian. Chinese might be good, too. You can pick the movie."

She whirled toward him expecting him to drop her arm and back away, but he stood close and held her glare with an intense look of his own. This wasn't the goofy clod she'd joined a few weeks ago. His intensity immobilized her. He'd put this whole thing together to prove Erica was innocent; to prove her wrong. He concocted the bet to bring her here, to keep her from driving too far down the wrong road. He could have embarrassed her, but he didn't. He'd saved Erica and Sarah a lot of heartache.

It seemed the goof-off had found his inspiration. There was fire behind his eyes. His fingers locked them together a foot apart. She thought he might pull her in for a kiss. The realization that she might not pull away made her smile and this broke him from his trance.

"What?"

"Do you mind letting me go? I'd like to talk to Brad."

McKenna perked up at this. "Can't do that. He's headed for booking. You can see him tomorrow at the station."

"Don't even tell me you still think she's guilty," Stan said.

"I didn't say that."

"You didn't have to."

She canted her head toward the cruiser. Herman would change his mind once he heard what the police had to say, but it wasn't her place to tell them anything. Stan was way out of bounds. If he wanted to blow his career spouting off about company business that was fine. She wouldn't, not until she talked with Herman.

Chapter 55

Erica stepped inside and immediately felt their eyes swing on her from the other end of the boardroom, their instinct to jump up and pounce barely restrained by an affinity for decorum. Marty looked surprised but rational from the head of the table. Herman glowered as Sarah led the way in and sat to Marty's left. Erica sat beside her, glad to have the table between herself and Herman and a clear path back to the door.

Herman exchanged prodding looks with Marty. Absent his leadership, Herman began, "Sarah, you're aware Ms. Fletcher was suspended. You mind telling me why you risked your job to bring her here?"

"I know she's innocent. I've brought her in to help me investigate."

Herman's hands clamped down on the table. "I don't care what she's told you. If you've let her touch those files, you're both headed for the back seat of a police cruiser."

He'd have Erica in a cell next to Brad's if he could.

Sarah raised her hands to calm him. "We didn't touch anything. We came straight here, but trust me, the police won't take her anywhere."

"You were ready to call the police yesterday," Marty said.

"That was before I talked to them–"

Marty went white.

Herman jumped from his seat and slammed his fist on the table, "What!" He was so angry he fumbled for words. "What the Hell were you thinking?" If not for the table between them, he would have grabbed Sarah by the throat. He hulked above his chair, fuming then shot a look at Marty.

Marty took a bit longer to consider the ramifications, but his tone was just as menacing. "If this is in the paper tomorrow, you're through."

Sarah held her breath.

Herman was unsure where to look.

"I think I can help," Erica offered.

"That's the last fucking thing we need, thank you very much," Herman yelled. He turned to Marty, huffing to regain composure. "I think we should reconsider that item in the safe. It might be time to turn it over to the authorities."

Erica turned to Sarah who clearly knew what they were talking about, but didn't explain. She offered only a shrug.

"Don't play dumb," Herman said, glaring at Erica. "It's too late. We found the gun in your desk. Not a very good hiding place for someone as smart as you."

"I shot at Brad? That's a laugh," Erica hissed.

"Don't play with me."

Herman's snide sarcasm reminded her of Brad.

"Do you know where Brad is now?" Erica asked.

Neither man made a sound.

"That's what Sarah was trying to tell you. He tried to kill me. Twice! First in the parking garage and again yesterday outside my apartment."

"We don't have time for this bullshit," Herman started.

"The police don't think it's bullshit. They have the whole thing on tape and they've locked him up. I don't expect he'll be leaving there anytime soon. You're going to have to find me a new boss."

"Why would he do that?" Marty asked almost to himself. "I know he blamed me for saddling him with you, but I can't imagine he'd shoot at you." Marty's mumbling trailed off.

Being up on twenty-three, Marty was insulated from Brad's dealings around the firm. He must have trusted his brother-in-law implicitly and no matter how carefully stated, the message was going to be hard to hear.

"This is going to be a shock," Erica began, "but Brad was stealing from the firm. I'm sure of it."

Marty wheeled toward Herman for reassurance. Neither he nor Sarah offered a word of support, so Erica continued herself. "He was switching around the surveillance tapes and erasing them to hide something he was doing in the computer room. Whatever it was, he was using my credentials."

"What credentials?" Marty asked.

"My building access card for one. The security system shows me in the computer room at times I wasn't there. That's why he needed to erase the tapes. Otherwise you'd see him on camera not me."

Marty cupped his mouth to hide his expression and nervously tapped the fingers of his free hand. He'd come here expecting an indictment of Erica and this was turning into something else entirely. It wasn't going to be an easy transition to make or to explain at home.

Herman watched Marty thump the table for nearly a minute. When he couldn't wait any longer, he craned his neck so far around that Erica could barely see his face. "I have a real problem with this. You know what we found yesterday. You heard Brad. And now she's telling us Brad was framing her. This is all he said, she said. Just as likely she set him up and now she's taking advantage while he's not here. It comes down to a question of who we believe. I don't like having her involved in this investigation one bit. Frankly, Sarah's out of her mind for suggesting it."

Marty turned to Sarah. "Why do you want to include Erica?"

"She's the first person I brought this problem to and she knows more about the work downstairs than anyone. If we want to get this closed quickly, she's the one to do it."

Marty nodded his agreement, but said nothing.

Herman scowled at Sarah. "You came to me because you thought she was the embezzler. Now you want to give her a chance to cover it up?"

Marty halted the discourse by holding up a single finger. "Herman, I tend to agree with Sarah. Erica can help us determine what happened here. She never struck me as the outlaw type. Just look at her. If the police have Brad in custody, I think we should take any help she's willing to give. What will it take to convince you?"

"Are you serious?"

"Damn right! We've searched her office. What harm can she do?"

"We found a gun for God's sake. What more do you need? I can't let a thief and a murderer loose in the building, not on my watch."

"Anyone could have put that gun in there including Brad. If the police say he tried to kill her, I'm inclined to believe them."

"Over me?"

"Yes."

Herman slumped, just perceptibly. The room was quiet while he considered his next move. "I want to check her financials," he said inflating to full stature again. "If we did that, I'd be comfortable letting her see what we have."

"Ok with you, Erica?" Marty asked.

"I have nothing to hide."

"It's settled then. Herman will do the financial screen and Sarah will show you what we've gathered to date. Take the work home with you and stay out of the office until Herman's research is done. I know that sounds harsh, but it's safest for everyone."

Staying away from the office would make her feel safer, too.

"Good. Anything else we need to discuss?" Marty asked.

Herman raised half out of his chair.

"One thing," Erica said firmly. "I don't think Brad could do this alone. The evidence has been extremely well concealed for a very long time. I'm convinced he had help, maybe high up."

"Are you saying Brad's incompetent?"

"Let's say he's adequate and our thief is brilliant. I just don't think Brad could have kept this hidden from me for this long."

"Aren't we full of ourselves?" Herman snipped.

Erica ignored the quip and addressed her thoughts to Marty. "This involves more than just programming. There were lots of complaints and other evidence that needed to be covered up. I'm sure Brad had help. I wouldn't rule out anyone at this point." Erica rolled her head toward Herman as she said this and he nearly exploded.

He said nothing, but his face reddened and his eyes looked like they'd launch from their sockets.

Marty didn't seem all that surprised.

"I suggest we search Brad's office and his apartment, check his phone records and see who he was talking to. It might lead us to his partner. If we do it quickly, we might catch him before he runs."

"We're not the police," Herman growled.

"That didn't stop you from searching my office," Erica said.

There was a big difference between searching company property and an employee's apartment, but there was a lot at stake for Marty and his family. Solving this case quietly meant everything to Marty, but Herman was convinced Erica was guilty and didn't want to hear anything new. If Erica was going to solve this, she'd have to go elsewhere for help. After that morning, she was comfortable with the police for the first time since she was four years old.

Sarah interrupted to Herman's chagrin, "Stan has connections with the Boston Police. He can help us get Brad's apartment searched, but that means we'll have to let them know what we're looking for."

Marty stiffened at her mention of the police. He might have had his own key to Brad's apartment, but he didn't offer it.

All he said was: "Do it."

Chapter 56

Brad paced around his cell with the lawyer's words ringing in his ears. Assault with a deadly weapon with intent to murder, no priors except a drug offense, probably one-to-two unless they connected the attempt the day before. If the jury believed he'd tried twice, he'd get five-to-ten. The videotape was a killer. It showed a blurry, blue figure in the foreground and Brad leaning against a tree, shooting it twice, and running away.

The prosecutors would argue premeditation. The police had time to mount the camera, set out the dummy and wait. Brad wanted to argue entrapment, but the lawyer didn't see how setting out a dummy invited him to shoot it. The trial would be short, a maximum sentence likely. Brad's lawyer already wanted to make a deal for two years. If he knew about the embezzlement, he'd have offered the deal already.

The guy wasn't worth two hundred an hour. The most important thing he'd done was call Herman, something Brad couldn't do from his cell. The bail hearing followed in record time, but the bail was set at one hundred fifty thousand, another sign the lawyer was failing him. Brad would pay any amount to get out. He had the money. He just couldn't get to it.

Time was everything now. Sarah and Stan saw his arrest in the park. By now they'd be ripping his life apart, searching his office, his apartment, his car. The notebook! Brad grabbed the bars as if he could pull them apart. His bag in the trunk held the audio tapes of him talking to Herman and the notebook. The tapes weren't very specific, but they'd be enough for the cops to identify the players and the basics of the scam. Once they had that, the numbers in the notebook would start to make sense. Vincent's telephone number, Erica's bank account number, and his Swiss account number were all listed inside. The notebook linked him to murder, embezzlement, and conspiracy. If they found the right Swiss bank, the money from his account would be confiscated while he sat helplessly in this musty cell.

At least the money in the farmhouse was safe. He hadn't left a single clue to its whereabouts. The tight stacks would be there in the wall when he got out. He just hoped he'd be young enough to enjoy them.

Sharon and Marty refused to help. They could afford the bail, but not the embarrassment. Brad had the money, too. The lawyer could get his account number and code from the bag in the Corvette, but once he had it, he could take everything. Brad thought of people he might send to the farmhouse, but he imagined each of them ripping the walls apart, taking the money and flying off. Every scenario left him alone in the cell.

"Foster, you have a visitor," a voice boomed down the concrete hall.

Brad didn't know if Marty and Sharon had come through with his bail or if Sarah and Stan had come to grill him. The guard escorted him to a series of booths facing a plexiglass wall. He sat opposite a stiff man in a brown suit, late fifties with a long, narrow face.

The man picked up the phone and introduced himself as Russell Egan.

"What do you want?"

"I'm here to help."

"Sharon and Marty send you?"

"No, a mutual friend. You called him, I believe."

Brad recalled the first time Herman whispered a tip about a stock that was going to tank. Every moment since had run straight downhill to this cell. Payback was coming. Herman was about to save him five-to-ten.

"I can get you out, but I have some conditions."

"I'm listening."

"Never contact my client again."

"Done."

"I'll argue your defense and you'll follow my instructions precisely."

Brad agreed, but no matter what Russell said, he was leaving the country. No lawyer could win this case.

Thirty minutes later, Brad watched Russell hand his passport over the counter. The original was in his bag in the Corvette's trunk. How Russell could get into an impounded vehicle without his permission was beyond him, so he assumed the passport was a phony.

Russell's car was a long black sedan with tinted windows. Brad stretched out on the plush, back seat and watched Russell fight his way onto the expressway.

"Where are we going?"

"Providence. They'll be looking for your face in Boston."

"How about papers?"

"All set and waiting."

Brad wondered how long it would be before the police found the bag in his trunk. They hadn't opened it yet or they wouldn't have released him. When they eventually played the tapes, they'd launch a man hunt for Herman Richards and Brad Foster. Brad would have started a new life as Jean-Claude Verrier by then. That would be justice. Herman would get what he deserved and Brad would end up with twenty million in cash.

Russell drove faster than the speed limit, but not fast enough to attract attention. The pace bored Brad. He imagined himself on a warm sandy beach watching well-tanned young women parade past in colorful bikinis. He wouldn't settle right away. He'd sample a few islands, anywhere with a steady stream of tourists. Rio would be his first stop.

Russell turned off the highway and stopped the car alongside a river trimmed with intricate stone work. Pedestrians walked within a few feet of Brad's window.

"We're going to dinner," Russell announced and stepped outside.

Brad hadn't eaten well in jail, but the sudden stop had him feeling out of control. "Why here?"

"The food's good. Trust me, you'll like it."

"Can't we eat at the airport?"

"Do I need to spell it out for you?"

Apparently he did.

"I can't help you skip bail. I'll lose my law license. We're going to part ways publicly. We're going in together and leaving separately. After I've been gone awhile, you come outside and I'll pick you up."

They passed a dozen empty parking spaces on the walk and Brad had a feeling Russell was taking the cloak-and-dagger a bit too far. Russell turned down a side street and pointed to the next corner. "When you leave, go to the corner and turn right. I'll be waiting halfway down."

Brad wondered if he'd really be there, but being ditched in Providence was far better than the cell he'd come from. He followed Egan into the restaurant. If he disappeared, Brad would find his own ride to the airport.

Three women in long summer dresses sat at the bar. Beyond them, couples chatted at small tables scattered around the room. The men were dressed much like Russell, in suits or at least ties and the women wore light summer dresses. Brad's faded jeans and torn shirt were all wrong. On a younger man the look might have worked, but at his age the outfit smelled of gardening or worse, prison. He'd buy some new clothes when he landed.

Russell chose a seat just a few steps from the door even though the restaurant was half empty. The stream of footsteps at his back made Brad edgy, but he enjoyed dinner despite the lousy seat. Russell was well traveled and suggested several places for Brad to visit. Brad discussed his flights around France and Italy and watched several couples at tables nearby. He didn't notice how quickly Russell ate until he pushed his empty plate forward and dabbed gently at the corners of his mouth. Brad's plate was half-full when Russell announced, a bit too loudly, that he had a late appointment and needed to go. He slipped two hundred dollars across the table and whispered, "Give me twenty minutes."

Russell stood up and extended a hand to Brad as the waitress approached from the bar. "I'll see you Monday. It was good to meet you, Mr. Foster."

"Was everything ok?" the waitress asked.

"Wonderful as always. I'm late for an appointment, but my friend will take good care of you." Egan winked at the waitress and marched to the door.

Brad filled twenty minutes watching faces around the restaurant. He focused on the three women at the bar. What would they say if he asked them to run away with him to live on some exotic beach halfway around the world? Would they believe him? Could anyone drop everything and move on a whim? He knew it was too late, but he romanticized about the opportunity he could offer. How many women would jump at the chance for a life of leisure? He remembered women he'd dated and wished he could take with him, but there was no time.

He left the two hundred on the table without waiting for change and found Russell in the car where he said he'd be. Brad decided he'd be safer up front and climbed in. Russell didn't protest. He shifted into gear and they were underway.

Chapter 57

Sarah felt a flash of panic when Herman closed the heavy wooden door. Staffers were leaving the office in droves and by the time this discussion was over, there'd be few people left to witness her exit. Thoughts of physical harm were irrational here in the CEO's office. Marty was a gentle old guy, smaller in stature than she. Still she was wary.

It was Herman's glib look in the doorway that had her on edge. She'd been to visit Brad earlier and been told he'd made bail. Frightening that he could be arrested for attempted murder – witnessed by seven police officers and videotaped – and released the next day on bail. Power had its privileges. Erica's theories about Brad's partners seemed conservative. His network covered his mistakes in the office and on the outside as well.

Erica had gone back into hiding when she heard the news. No wonder. He'd tried to kill her twice. He'd stolen her work and planted evidence in her office. How far did his influence stretch? She wondered if Herman's persecution of Erica was driven by his investigative instincts or an obligation to Brad. Gooseflesh rose up on her arms as Herman circled behind her and took a seat on the corner of Marty's desk.

"Do you know where Erica is?"

"I haven't seen her since this morning. You told her to leave pending the background check," Sarah said.

"Good thing I did." Herman took a few pages from the desk, leaned over and dropped them in Sarah's lap. He operated with frightening efficiency. In just a few hours he'd summarized Erica's financial life into a stack of laser-printed pages.

The first thing Sarah noticed was the size of the direct deposit: almost double her own. The balance wasn't significant though, and a search through a few months of statements yielded the explanation in the form of a significant check to Northeastern University. Her 401(k) was typically meager for someone her age. Nothing looked that surprising, nothing to warrant Herman's excitement, until she reached the final page of the stack. The checking account was in a different bank than the one that received her direct deposit. The page showed only two transactions. An initial deposit of one hundred dollars two years earlier and a ten million dollar deposit two weeks earlier.

Herman smiled broadly when she looked up.

"I was just as surprised," Marty said.

"We'd like to give her an opportunity to explain before we call the police," Herman said smugly.

Herman wanted to do this personally.

Marty probably harbored some secret hope that she'd give the money back, help the firm avoid the negative press, and save his embattled career from imploding. They stood waiting, expecting her to jump from her chair, run out and drag Erica to justice. But it didn't fit. The ten million was deposited weeks ago, but its appearance, like the gun in her desk drawer seemed too convenient, too careless for a woman as smart as Erica. Stan's assessment was starting to make sense. She wasn't the type. The man who was had just vanished from a jail cell.

Herman and Marty seemed angered with her unwillingness to flip-flop.

Herman put a heavy hand on her shoulder rousing her from her thoughts. "Sarah," he said, jolting her to attention. "This will go better for all concerned if you help us. With everyone in the same room we can figure this out. We don't want a public spectacle, but this needs to be resolved. There's no avoiding it. We need your help to bring her in."

To cover this up, she wanted to say. "Why? So you can lynch her?"

"Surely, you don't still believe she's innocent."

"It doesn't fit. She's smarter than this."

"We won't know until we talk to her."

"There's much more to this than ten million dollars. Someone planted the money like they planted the gun."

"Ludicrous! Who'd give her ten million dollars? Certainly not me," Marty said.

"You think Brad gave her ten million? Sounds extreme. I know you want to believe her. And yeah, it's easy to believe this is Brad's fault. He's a gruff character. Unfortunately, the facts say otherwise," Herman said.

"Only your facts," she blurted. In the open air the words had more stinging realism that she expected. The gun was found in the office with Herman in the room. The financial review was Herman's doing. He was pushing Erica's guilt on Sarah and it seemed everything he touched pointed to Erica. Sarah couldn't believe Herman was involved, but his objectivity was doubtful. She imagined Brad and Herman were friends since they were both V.P.s. They'd stick up for each other no matter what.

Herman went silent.

Marty looked like John Kerry trying to decide which side of this issue he should jump to.

Herman didn't wait to find out. He walked toward Sarah. She expected him to break into a fit of rage, but he stood back and crossed his arms.

He began in a gentler tone than she expected. "You need to figure out whose team you're on. We're trying to bring this thing to a close and we could use your help. I don't know what she said to you, but shake it off. You need to wake up and take an objective look at the facts."

Exactly what she thought he needed to do.

The lack of emotion in his voice was scary. He desperately wanted Erica in the office. He wanted to scream, maybe even grab her by the throat, but he managed a calm, even voice that betrayed none of what he was feeling. She was more afraid of him now than when she came in. The bald-headed chameleon disguised his thoughts and emotions better than she thought possible. He was playing a game, justice was secondary. She couldn't imagine what he'd do to Erica if he got his hands on her.

She took a deep breath and addressed Marty. "I think it's time to call for help. We need someone who has the authority to track the money that left here and find out where it ended up. I can't believe Erica would do this, just like Herman can't believe Brad would do it. I think we need to let the money – all of the money – connect the dots."

Silence.

Neither man looked at the other, nor made the slightest of movements.

"Ok, Sarah," Marty said after a long pause.

Herman gasped, incensed at being overruled again.

"We'll get you the help you want. I'll make the call myself if that will make you feel better, but I want you to talk to Erica and see what you can do about getting her in here. Agreed?"

Sarah nodded, unsure how she'd deliver on her end of the deal or even if she'd try.

"I'm counting on both of you to keep this thing from exploding in my face. It this gets out in the wrong light, it will be catastrophic for BFS. This may be just a job to the two of you, but this company has been in my family for over a hundred years. You can't imagine how important this is to me. I want to get it right no matter how many people we have to drag in here."

Chapter 58

The afternoon traffic was light south of Providence and soon the car circled along the exit ramp and sped down the access road to the airport. Russell picked up the phone and dialed. "We're almost there," he said without a greeting.

Brad strained to hear Herman's voice on the other end, but couldn't make out the instructions he gave Russell. The car slowed and made a hard right turn into the long term parking area, passing the shuttle bus as they entered. It was a vast lot, open to the elements with a massive grid of cars stretching away from them in every direction.

"Why here?"

"Ask the boss."

This would be their final meeting. Herman had changed Brad's life forever. After skipping bail he could never return to his family or his country, but he had the wealth to retire happily in seclusion as long as he lived. He'd always thought he'd want to kill Herman at this stage, but right now he'd be satisfied to board the hop to LaGuardia and fly off to France. The past few days had degenerated into chaos. Herman had bailed him out, but Brad had made him rich. He deserved what little help Herman gave.

The sedan followed the edge of the lot almost to the airfield. Twin jet engines blotted out all sound as a plane thrust off the runway and up into the clouds. Russell stopped the car and pointed toward the door. When Brad closed it, Herman appeared from beside a boxy white sedan.

"Thanks for–" Brad began, but was cut short.

Herman barked as he closed in on Brad. "Never call me again."

When he got close enough, Herman poked him hard in the chest. The force backed Brad up against Russell's car. In the stillness between takeoffs, there was no one he could yell to for help. Brad's chest hurt from the two-fingered poke. How much damage could Herman do with his fists? Brad had fantasized about meeting Herman man to man, but now, standing inches from the monster, he regretted ever having the idea.

"I needed help."

"You think I didn't know that?" Herman moved closer until Brad held his breath, expecting a fist to the ribs.

Herman watched intensely. "You couldn't handle that little bimbo."

Brad didn't know where to look. "She was working with the cops."

"After you let her get away."

Herman was right. Brad had screwed up and nothing could change that.

"You need to disappear. There's a passport and some cash in the trunk." Herman stepped back and popped the trunk of the white car, never taking his eyes off Brad. "Don't show up in the states again. Got it?"

Brad nodded, breathless, hoping the confrontation was finished.

Herman gestured in the trunk and Brad recognized his own brown leather bag deep inside. Russell had indeed handed over his real passport. Brad circled Herman cautiously. The bag was freedom if Herman hadn't seen the contents. He stretched into the trunk for the bag, knees touching the bumper. He clutched the handle and pulled it toward him.

Crack.

A hole appeared in the trunk's carpet and a rattle whizzed and clinked through the undercarriage. The ragged hole in the carpet stupefied him. Fire burned in his chest. He clutched instinctively and felt warm blood pour through his shirt and cover his hand. He coughed violently as the sticky fluid pooled in his lungs.

Crack.

The second shot struck bone in his ribcage, thrusting him, chest first, into the trunk and slamming his head into the lid. He collapsed inside and the pain was no more.

Chapter 59

"Slow up," Sarah said when Stan pulled a few feet ahead.

Rushing down Milk Street to meet McKenna, Stan was possessed by the challenge to solve this case. The relaxed happy-go-lucky dreamer was getting things done. He'd set up the sting in the park. Now his friends from the Boston PD were searching Brad's apartment and nothing could keep him away. It would have taken Sarah a week to organize the search. Even her gait was holding him back. She knew now why female officers didn't wear two-inch heels in the field.

Stan crossed Federal Street against the light and turned around on the opposite curb, frustrated that she hadn't crossed behind him. He waited for several cars to pass and the light to change. Chivalry was winning out over eagerness, but just barely. They hurried up Devonshire together and turned into the bland ten-story block of concrete where Brad lived. When the elevator doors opened on the fourth floor they were met by a large uniformed officer outside the door to Brad's apartment.

"Sorry folks, official police business. You can't go inside."

Stan's chest puffed out involuntarily. "I'm Stan Nye. Sergeant McKenna called me over."

The officer left them standing in the hall and disappeared inside so quickly they couldn't see past the door. McKenna must have been nearby. He popped into the hall almost immediately and shook Stan's hand. "Some case you threw me."

"What are buddies for?"

"Was this guy into anything else? Drugs maybe?" McKenna looked nervous. Strange. He'd been a Boston cop for years if he'd been in the academy with Stan. This white collar stuff shouldn't spook him.

"Doubt it. What's going on?" Stan asked.

"I'll give you a look," he said, pulling two pairs of rubber gloves from his pocket. "Put these on first."

Stan took them without hesitation.

Sarah turned up her nose.

McKenna was adamant about the gloves. He was stretching the rules having civilians on scene, especially civilians with a connection to the crime. The internal audit roles meant nothing to McKenna or his superiors. If not for Stan's relationship, they'd be suspects like everyone else at BFS.

He urged them not to touch anything and risk rubbing out a print.

They agreed, pulled on the tight-fitting gloves and McKenna led them inside. Nothing in the room had been left undisturbed. The couch had been sliced end to end, every cushion ruined, stuffing spilled all around. The coat closet was completely empty, its contents unceremoniously dumped in the corner behind the door. Stray items from coat pockets had been tossed in a pile a few feet away.

McKenna followed a winding trail through the debris and into the kitchen where every cabinet had been emptied. Cereal, crackers, uncooked pasta and sugar had been dumped on the floor, empty containers tossed aside. The refrigerator had been tipped over, its panels pried loose to prove there was nothing hidden in the insulation.

"What are you going to tell him when he comes back?" Sarah asked, stunned the police could do this sort of damage searching someone's home.

McKenna laughed out loud. "We didn't do this. I'd be docked ten years to pay for this. The place was trashed when we got here."

Whoever tore this apartment to pieces had a secret he was desperate to keep. Erica had guessed they'd stolen two hundred million, enough motivation to rip the place apart and plenty of money to pay to have it done.

McKenna nodded toward the door. "It was picked, not forced."

"Did you find anything?"

"A huge pile of everyday junk," McKenna grunted.

The bedroom had received more severe treatment than the other rooms. The carpet had been sliced and pulled back on each side of the bed, clothes everywhere. Two phone cords dangled near the bed. One from the wall and one from the phone, but they were both male. They couldn't have been connected to each other. Something had been there.

"I guess that's what we're down to," Sarah said.

"What's that?" Stan asked.

"What's missing. Anything worth taking is gone."

"Computer?" Stan asked.

"Didn't find one. Not a single CD or a disk, not even a notepad. Someone made sure we weren't going to find anything he left for us."

Stan made a note to check with IT later. They'd check his computer, phone records and search his office if Marty would allow it. McKenna was eager for an invitation, but didn't ask and they didn't offer.

Whoever tore the place apart had taken anything Brad could have used to leave a message. They left no paper except a few magazines and they were ruffled as if they'd been flipped through to make sure nothing was handwritten in the margins. Any clues Brad left behind had been hauled away. Any hiding place he could have dreamed up had been torn open or busted into. How much noise had these men made? They'd been inside for hours to be so thorough. These men were professionals and they weren't afraid of being caught.

"Wasn't his car impounded?" Stan asked.

Brilliant. They couldn't have gotten into the car. If Brad had left anything behind it would still be there.

McKenna dialed his cell and made arrangements for them to see the car. The threesome was gone within minutes.

261

Chapter 60

The shock of Brad's release slowly lost its grip on Erica. If anything happened to her, the police would suspect him immediately. Trying again would only add to his sentence and he knew it. He'd be looking for a lawyer or a place to hide.

From her seat on the couch, Erica traced the veins that cemented the massive stone wall together. She had complete anonymity behind the wall, but her reason for hiding was gone. Her packed bag rested by the coffee table, but she couldn't bring herself to take it up and go. The last time she went home, Brad chased her into the park and tried to kill her. Erica's instinct told her Brad had a partner, a smarter man pulling the strings, one who'd kill her with the first shot. That feeling had her stuck on the couch.

Her hosts were becoming restless, too. Jan's feet shifted in the doorway. Sam, the retired-cop-turned-volunteer-security-guard, reclined at his post in the hall and covered his dozing as best he could. A tiny earpiece squawked out the call of a ball game. Their protection deserved a woman who needed it and Erica hoped her stay wasn't forcing a truly desperate woman to live in fear on the outside.

Jan came around to the couch and rested a feathery touch on Erica's knee. "What's got hold of you?"

"Who is more the question."

"No need to rush out there before you're ready."

She'd traveled crowded city streets since birth, but now walking out in public was terrifying. She couldn't escape the feeling that she'd be in someone's crosshairs the second she stepped outside. This man would be a professional and he wouldn't miss. Staying hidden seemed simple enough, but letting other people fight for her felt cowardly.

She picked up her cell and dialed Sarah for news, but Sarah didn't answer. Erica left her number and dialed Gregg.

She eyed her bag as the phone rang. He'd be worried. He'd ask her to stay with him and she'd go. He made her feel safe. After witnessing the brutality between her mother and father, she never thought she'd run to a man for protection, but here she was, listening to the third ring, anxious to hear his invitation.

The phone connected, but instead of relief she was shocked into silence. "It's about time you called. We were beginning to think you forgot about Mr. Handsome." She didn't recognize the menacing voice.

It was the right number. The caller-id at Gregg's would show her cell number, but the man professed to have something far more important.

"Who are you?" she asked feigning confidence.

"That doesn't matter."

The voice didn't sound like anyone from work.

"I know what you're thinking," he said. "Where's Lover Boy?" Distant voices and a loud crack sounded over the line. Then a tortured howl faint at first then so piercing she yanked the phone from her ear. The sound was unmistakable. Gregg was in severe pain. She called his name, but his hoarse scream faded into the background.

There were at least two voices in the room with him.

"What are you doing to him?" she asked.

"No permanent damage. Yet. Cooperate and you'll be together soon."

"What do you want?"

"Unwavering Obedience. Do what I say and you'll see him again. Get out of line and I'll send him to you in small bloody pieces."

The voice was steady and cool. Violence was part of his lifestyle. He'd have no qualms about hurting Gregg and the scream proved him capable. He must have gotten the gun away from Gregg. At least Gregg wouldn't be tempted to pull it and shoot his way free. She doubted he could aim at another man and pull the trigger. He could shoot animals, but he wasn't cruel. Pulling the gun would only get him killed.

She'd gotten him into this. He didn't know anything about the theft. They'd taken him to get to her, but she had nothing to give them in exchange. Brad had already proved his guilt. Why did they need her?

"What do you want?" she prompted again.

"A little cooperation is all. Stay where you are. When we meet I'll tell you exactly what you need to do. Until then, don't call anyone, not BFS, not the cops and not the feds. Stay right where you are."

The line went dead and Erica stood up.

She was safe. They couldn't find her at Jan's, but what about Gregg? She could be at his apartment in ten minutes, but what then? They'd overpowered Gregg and probably had him tied up. Even if she could surprise them, she couldn't overtake armed men.

"What's wrong with Gregg?" Jan asked.

The guard pulled off his earphones and stepped halfway in.

"They're hurting him."

"Who?" Jan asked.

"They're working with Brad. They're in Gregg's apartment."

The old man wouldn't be much help against the thug on the phone. Even the three of them together would be helpless while Gregg was held at gunpoint. Gregg was being hurt because they wanted Erica. Adding the old man's life and Jan's to his was unacceptable.

Jan suggested the police.

The man had ordered her not to call, but what choice did she have? A hostage taker wouldn't be good to his word. They were in Gregg's apartment. In twenty minutes they could take him anywhere in the city and she might never see him again. Calling the police made her queasy, but it was all she had.

Erica wrote out Gregg's address and Jan called a police captain she knew well. He promised they'd go in quickly and quietly.

Erica paced nervously as Jan hung up.

The police would be there in five minutes.

Chapter 61

Sarah's hopes were dashed when they found Brad's car showroom clean. It could have been that way when it was towed in, but more likely the men who'd ravaged Brad's apartment had visited the impound lot. Even the glove compartment was empty. Sarah's hopes were buoyed later when Pete Harrison arrived at the office. A substantial FBI agent with extensive contacts and the savvy to navigate a tricky political situation, he gathered more information in twenty-four hours than Sarah and Stan could have uncovered in weeks.

The trio made its way to Marty's office to present what they'd found. Pete had convinced Marty to exclude Herman and Cathy from the meeting, something Marty would never have done for Sarah or Stan. Going without Herman felt right, but Sarah had a nagging desire to call him as they passed near his office. Herman had been driving for a quick conclusion to the case. Without him, they'd navigate a straighter path to the truth, but when he found out she'd gone to this meeting without him, there'd be trouble their working relationship might never recover from.

They settled around the boardroom table and Pete began.

Stan gauged Marty's reaction as he listened. Stan's contacts with the Boston PD had been indispensable and Sarah had to admit his insights had been right on from the start. He knew Erica was innocent. He proved it and he was big enough not to make points with Herman and Marty at Sarah's expense, even after she'd been a jerk. He was a decent guy and he was good at his job, even if he spent most of his time goofing off. He'd swindled her into buying dinner for eight weeks. She'd dreaded the idea at first, but she knew why he'd done it and she was warming up to it.

Marty listened intently as Pete explained the complicated nature of the plot and why he assumed Brad had a partner. The accounts had been linked to social security numbers of people that had been dead for three to ten years. Regular deposits were made in their names all across the country. Pete handed over a long list of deposit dates in cities Brad could only reach by plane. Most of the dates were in red to indicate that Brad had entered the BFS offices at least once that day according to the security system. Pete's team would visit the banks and view the security tapes to try and identify Brad's partners, but that would take time. Brad could have sent the deposits by mail, but the three of them were convinced the amounts were too large to have been sent in unsupervised. In a few weeks, they'd have grainy photos of Brad's accomplices.

Marty shook his head noncommittally. He may have been shocked that his brother-in-law had been stealing from his company. He may have had new doubts about his young wife. He may have been thinking ahead to the consequences for him. Sarah couldn't be sure, but he was taking it in. Herman had undone her work with Marty twice before. This time they'd hammer it home until there could be no doubt in Marty's mind.

Pete continued.

The money had gone from these bank accounts to a single bank in Turino, Italy, again suggesting a cohesive plot. The bank had been cooperative but unfortunately had little to offer. Marty crossed his arms as Pete explained how the withdrawal records had been falsified. Cashier's checks had been written, but the check numbers had been dummied. Tracing the money would require finding the physical checks among the hundreds of thousands returned to the bank. Sifting through would take months. Getting access to the checks might take longer. To complicate matters, the bank manager had recently died when his car went off an embankment and exploded. Pete believed it was a professional hit to clean up the money trail.

Sarah pointed out Brad's trouble shooting Erica and the likelihood that he couldn't have killed the bank manager himself.

The steady drone of facts was irritating Marty. Whether it was the pace or the message Sarah couldn't be sure. Undeterred, Pete dribbled out a monotonous flow, building his case piece by piece as he would for a jury.

Marty couldn't take more. "Where's this going?" he said finally.

"Brad Foster wasn't alone. He took the money from customer accounts and he went to Italy to withdraw it, but someone was helping him connect the dots in between."

Marty leaned forward and spoke in a hushed tone as if he believed his own boardroom could be bugged. "You think someone else inside the company was involved?"

"Absolutely," Pete said without hesitation. A bold statement Sarah couldn't have made herself.

The words slapped Marty. Not only was his brother-in-law stealing from his family, but another of his trusted employees was in on it, too. "Who?" Marty's pained face suggested he'd rather not know.

"We're working on that. He needed help covering up customer complaints. That help could have come from client services, IT or internal audit. We'll start there and work out through Brad's contacts."

"Are you talking rank-and-file or leadership?"

"Both. At least one of them would be high up in the firm."

"What about the gun in Erica Fletcher's office? Was she in on it?"

"Definitely not. I saw the police video and he was trying to kill her. I have no doubt the gun was planted."

"What about the money? Was that planted, too?"

"I believe it was."

Marty looked at Pete like he was insane, but Pete explained that the thieves had taken two hundred million dollars without a trace. They were too smart to leave ten million in a checking account. Ten million is a lot of money, enough to be persuasive, but not too costly. Deposited in an account with just two transactions, Erica might never have known it existed.

"So what now? I can't leave a criminal walking the halls and I can't do anything without tipping them off."

"We'll start with Brad's phone records. With your leave, we'll track every call made from his office, the security room and the computer room."

"Certainly."

"We didn't mention Brad's apartment," Sarah offered.

"What about it?" Marty asked.

"I've never seen anything like it. They pulled up the carpets, pried the covers off the appliances, they even emptied the food containers. It was incredible. Someone was very worried about what Brad might have left behind and they made sure we weren't going to find anything."

Marty nodded and stared down at the table a moment. He was convinced this time. After a long pause he lifted his head toward Pete. "I'll get you whatever you need here at the firm. Anything you need."

"Confidentiality is critical," Pete said.

"Understood. Not a word except to our V.P. of human resources and our V.P. of internal audit."

Sarah didn't want to give Herman another chance to change Marty's mind. She wanted to object, but indicting her boss without evidence was career suicide. Pete objected for her and Marty agreed to leave them out of the loop for the time being.

Marty dismissed them, staying in his chair until they'd gone.

Outside, Sarah congratulated Pete on incredible progress in the last day. He'd taken Erica's list of suspicious transactions, traced it back two years and followed the money all the way to Italy.

She wanted to tell Stan she'd been wrong about him, but she knew where that would lead. They'd be having dinner every Friday for the next two months. That was enough.

They hustled off to get started on Brad's phone records.

Chapter 62

Erica imagined a dozen uniformed men storming Gregg's apartment and finding him bound to a chair, his captors fleeing down the fire escape, guns blazing. She strained to hear the other half of Jan's conversation with the police captain. When Jan reassured him that this wasn't a prank, Erica was terrified. She'd called Gregg's apartment and someone there was hurting him. She hadn't made a mistake. She hadn't imagined it. The police arrived ten minutes later. Why hadn't they found him?

Jan ended her conversation with an apology, hung up and told Erica they'd found nothing. The apartment was clean and neat. No one was home. No sign of a struggle. Erica was going to have to pay for the damaged door.

They must have gone to the wrong address. The men couldn't have gotten Gregg out that fast. How could she help him if they had?

When Erica's cell phone rang moments after the police called, the coincidence escaped her. She answered expecting Sarah, but was greeted by a dreadfully anguished howl. The tortured voice was quickly replaced by a hostile one, yelling in her ear. "Weren't my instructions clear? I said no cops. I meant no cops. A minute ago four men in blue busted their way into Greggie Boy's apartment. Good thing we weren't there. Someone could've gotten hurt and Lover Boy is first in line."

They were near enough to see the activity on the street, probably within a block of Gregg's apartment, but she couldn't call the police again. They might not go back. If they did and this maniac saw them, he might kill Gregg and take off.

"Listen carefully this time," he said. "Go to your apartment. There's a checkbook taped under the middle desk drawer. Get it and go to the Bank of America on Dartmouth Street. I'll meet you there."

"I don't have a checkbook under the desk."

"It's there and it's got quite a balance."

"I don't know what you're talking about."

"Listen. Go home. Get the checkbook. Go to the bank. Now!"

What was he talking about? If the checkbook was there, he could get it himself. Would she be incriminating herself by going to the bank? Was this Brad's last ditch effort to blame her? It was obviously a setup. They wanted her not the checkbook, but what choice did she have?

Before the man hung up, he rattled off a string of warnings. They had Gregg and they'd be watching. If she asked for help from the police or anyone in the bank, Gregg would get a bullet to the temple.

She put the phone down and took two steps toward the door.

Jan jumped up to block her, but Erica pushed past and left her open-mouthed on the steps. She couldn't risk another call to the police. Motoring back into the city, moving steadily deeper into the caller's trap, there was no question that this was the right thing to do. A year ago she never would have imagined risking her life for a man, but Gregg had awakened something in her that went beyond compassion; something she'd never known.

This is what her mother had done for her. She could have left her father anytime, but getting away with Erica proved difficult. She had sacrificed so much and Erica had been less than appreciative. As a child, Erica had belittled her mother's efforts to provide for them. She realized now that there had been plenty for one. Caring for Erica had complicated her mother's life from the day she was conceived.

She shook off her embarrassment as she parked and walked up the stairs to her apartment. She had to pull herself together by the time she reached the bank. They'd call her and tell her what to do then. She needed to be thinking clearly. These people had planned this through. They'd be leading her into a situation she was never expected to survive. No doubt they'd underestimated her, but she'd need a miracle to get Gregg out unharmed.

The old door pushed in, sticky as always. The apartment was dark and quiet. Most of the neighbors were at work. Weeks ago at this hour, Melanie would have been chopping vegetables to the sounds of some band Erica had never heard of. She missed her. The bond between them had been financial at first; a way for Erica to help someone who needed a boost. Melanie had her degree now and Erica would probably never see her again.

She kneeled in front of the desk and patted the underside of the drawer. The bulge was about where she expected. She ripped down the large envelope and found a brand new plastic case inside. She fanned the crisp pages. Nowhere had it been written on.

The hair suddenly straightened on the back of her neck. Her shoulders stiffened and she had the conflicting urges to scream and to hide. Her body sensed an invisible danger. The urge to turn around proved irresistible and as she did the man on the other side of the counter slowly came into view.

He hadn't made a sound, yet here he was in the middle of the apartment with a gun trained on her. The muzzle looked oddly thick and as he side-stepped the counter, she saw the silencer. The man could shoot her and leave her here to die and no one would be the wiser.

"Finally obeying orders I see," he sneered.

It was the voice from the phone.

She gave a faint grunt as he approached. He didn't look like a thug. He was big enough. A good five inches taller and about a hundred pounds heavier than her, but his fair skin and wispy hair gave him a delicate appearance. He told her to stand up. The calm depth of his voice was more menacing than if he'd barked the command.

"This withdrawal's the only thing standing between me and payday. If I were you, I wouldn't do anything to screw it up."

His focus on the blue checkbook belied the fact that he'd done nothing to hide his identity. If he planned to let her and Gregg go free, he wouldn't have allowed such a clear view of his face. If he wanted the checkbook he could have taken it and gone. He might want the money, but he wanted her more.

He ordered her hands on the desk, feet spread apart.

She complied, put the checkbook on the desk and felt the silencer press against her temple.

"Let's not get silly. I can easily find another dark-haired chick to carry your license into the bank."

They both knew she'd never been to this bank. She wasn't sure if she dipped her head and signaled submission or if he knew she'd realized the position she was in, but then she felt his belly press into her back and his free hand brushing over her ribs. If she'd thought to bring a weapon, his groping would have uncovered it. He lingered pleasurably over his work probing every inch of flesh. When he was done he took a step back and she turned to face him though she couldn't meet his eyes.

"So far, so good. Keep it up and you'll live."

She was convinced he intended to get his money and kill them both. There was too much at stake. The whole scam was too well planned to leave behind someone who could identify him.

Standing there with the gun aimed at her chest he gave her a new set of orders. "Before we go you need to remember a few things. If we drive into a bunch of police at the bank, Lover Boy's going to buy it within a half hour. You'll never pin anything on me because I didn't get involved until today."

She could tell he was lying, but it didn't matter. She had no idea who he was and no way to connect him to Brad or BFS. An investigation might turn up a link, but that wasn't a chance she could take. She couldn't risk Gregg's life, not even for her own. This man would lead her to him. Her chances would be slim, but it was the only hope for both of them to survive.

"We have people in the bank," he continued. "Don't talk to the guards. Don't use the phone. Don't pass any notes. Collect a cashier's check for the total amount. Make it payable to cash and get out of there.

"If you keep me waiting too long, I'll drive away and it's over. You'll never see him again. Not alive anyway."

Chapter 63

The steering wheel brought a feeling of control in spite of her predicament. The four-block drive offered little hope of surprising him by either crashing or flipping the car. He wasn't buckled, but she couldn't manage more than fifteen miles per hour in the heavy traffic around Copley Square. The man rode behind her in the center of the back seat, the gun balanced low on his knee, aimed at her ribcage. Any shot would rip through her torso. There was no way to escape the line of fire on the way out the door. Years of karate had honed her reflexes, but she couldn't see him behind her. Snatching the gun without being shot smacked of impossibility.

They approached the bank on Dartmouth Street. Once inside she could find safety with a guard or call the police for help, but he knew she wouldn't abandon Gregg. That's why he was going to send her in alone.

"A simple withdrawal. Nothing more," he said as she exited the car.

She crossed the wide sidewalk through a stream of harried commuters.

Most faces in the bank seemed oblivious to her presence. A decent-looking guy in a golf shirt watched her fill out her withdrawal form. She lined up several positions behind him and waited. Half the people in line talked into cell phones or listened to an iPod. The other half gazed absently around the marble room. The scrawny guard in the corner wouldn't last fifteen seconds with the guy out in the car.

People filtered up to the tellers, completed their business and headed home. The man in the golf shirt gave a long glance in her direction before pushing through the revolving doors and out into the street.

No one else paid her much attention. There probably wasn't an accomplice in the bank, but she couldn't be sure. With the man in the car outside there was nothing she could do anyway. If she waited for help to arrive, he'd know something was wrong. If someone followed her out, it would be obvious with the car parked so close to the door. There was no way to help Gregg without getting back in that car and letting the thug lead her to him.

The teller called 'next' three times before Erica made her way down the row. After reading the withdrawal slip the young woman shot a look at Erica and left her station. She offered no explanation, but returned quickly with a somewhat older man in a dark blue suit. He scrutinized the forms, tapped on the computer screen and spent a good while comparing Erica's face to the photo on her driver's license.

Finally convinced, he asked how she'd like the money. He grimaced at her instructions, but stood back as the teller tapped a few commands on the computer and printed the check. After nodding through several warnings about the nature of her check, Erica declined their offer of an escort, thanked them and pushed through the revolving doors.

Unsympathetic faces rushed past, blocking her progress at every step across the wide courtyard. Halfway through the crowd, she spotted the car, but sunlight gleamed off the windows and hid the man she'd driven here. When she approached, the rear door opened. A different man sat in back, thinner and angrier than the man from her apartment. He had a quickness in the way he motioned her into the seat next to him.

She slid in.

The heavier, wispy-haired man started the car and pulled away. The door locks clicked. She tugged the handle instinctively, but the child locks kept her trapped in for the ride facing the muzzle of another silenced handgun. Strange they hadn't asked for the check.

The guy watching her wasn't as careful as the driver. He held the gun within reach and he twitched so nervously he was sure to be easily distracted. The driver flowed along with traffic, obeying the lights and being sure not to draw any attention. Erica eyed the driver next to them at a red light. She thought about mouthing a message through the window, but changed her mind when she felt the muzzle press into her knee cap. She kept her eyes forward for the rest of the ride across town.

Jan was miles away in Brookline; the guard at the bank a faint memory. Erica was on her own, scanning the men for hints of where they'd come from and what connected them together. The guy in back had a military style buzz cut. Brad would never have survived the army, though someone else in the group might have.

The car turned off Kneeland Street into the leather district and pulled up to a heavy garage door set into a windowless brick wall. The driver got out, opened the door and drove into a loading dock sized for a single vehicle. The man in the back seat held her there until the car was turned off and the garage door was lowered and securely locked behind them. The wispy haired man opened Erica's door and ushered her out and up the stairs.

He locked the car and pocketed Erica's keys.

Gregg would be somewhere inside.

She had visions of them both lying together heavily bound with the building ablaze around them. No one would be in the old warehouse to hear their screams. They'd die together in agony.

The man from her apartment trotted ahead, off the loading platform and through a door at the back. The twitchy guy led her in the same direction, one hand gripping firmly above her elbow, the other leveling the gun on her midsection.

Chapter 64

The door opened into a metal framed stairwell with poured concrete steps. Erica descended as carefully in her sneakers as she would in three inch heels, slowing the skinny guy behind her. By the time she stepped through the door into the room below, the bigger guy was nearly across the room and about to turn the corner out of sight. The musty basement was one huge storage room divided by thirty rows of shelves that ran toward the far wall. The lighting was dim enough so she could hide if she could break free.

The skinny guy knew what she was thinking. He kept his distance, the gun trained on her from behind. He prodded her straight ahead into an aisle where the packed shelves hemmed her in. If she ran, she could only go straight ahead and he was ready to put a bullet in her back if she did.

She negotiated the clutter under the single row of lights, watching the stacks for a break big enough to dive through. Unfortunately, every available space was filled with white boxes labeled with names and dates, possibly case files from a law firm. Filled with paper, the thick file boxes would stop a bullet. If she could get a shelf between them, she'd be safe long enough to figure out what to do next. Getting free was the problem. There was nowhere to turn and the shelves were too high to climb over.

A dim light glowed at the far end of the room where the wispy haired guy had gone. The guy behind her stepped up close as they reached the corner and grabbed her arm as they turned. The gun jabbed into her ribs as a reminder not to run, then floated behind her spine out of sight. They passed a dozen long narrow aisles off to the right. Every six feet a new chance to bolt, but every shelf was packed and every aisle too long for her to sprint through before being shot.

Feet shuffled ahead. Muffled voices. She was running out of time.

He marched her down the length of the room by the arm. They turned past the last long shelf and she stood stunned by the three men that faced her. Gregg sat rigid in a chair, the near side of his face battered and swollen. His eyes pleaded with her to get away. The wispy haired guy stood behind him. Herman Richards stood on the other side with a nasty snarl that brought the desperate scenario into focus. Herman had masterminded the scam and kept it from being discovered until she stumbled into it. She knew Brad wasn't smart enough to do this alone. Herman had quashed the complaints Brad couldn't handle and together they'd kept their work from Marty. When they realized Erica knew what was happening, Brad was sent to kill her. Where he'd failed Herman was determined to succeed.

She'd have been better off if she'd taken Brad's advice and quit BFS.

Herman couldn't let her out alive now that she'd seen him. The check in the pocket of her jeans had given her hope. She'd told herself they wanted the ten million, but her subconscious had known better all along. The check was meaningless compared to what they'd stolen. It had served its purpose now. Erica had come quietly to meet her demise. Now they were both trapped.

The man behind her sensed her urge to dash and raised his gun for her head. The men around Gregg took a step back from the line of fire.

Like a trigger, the sight of the muzzle sprung her into action, her training taking over like a reflex. Without a thought, she had his wrist in her outstretched arm then jerked and twisted it before her. Before he could tug free, she thrust her palm into the back of his elbow with everything she had. The joint, forced to bend the wrong way, gave with a horrid crack, its owner howling in pain. The gun fired past her, the bullet striking the far wall and ricocheting somewhere into the storage area.

She wrenched his wrist. As he clutched his elbow in agony, she yanked the gun away. The compact Smith and Wesson fit her hand well. She torqued her captive's elbow, thinking she could trade him for Gregg, but

Herman and his partner grabbed for their guns. They were too close to Gregg. She couldn't risk hitting him with a wild shot, but they had no such reservations about their comrade. They raised their guns to fire even though he and Erica were only a foot apart.

She spun him around as a shield, raised the gun over his heart and fired twice from inches away. The silenced shots failed to drown out the cracking, tearing sound of the bullets ripping through his chest. Slug and bone alike tore out the other side and slammed into the concrete wall.

Herman dodged away from the gore spurting toward him.

Either shot alone would have been fatal, but oddly her former captor stood upright after she let him go, his body blocking Herman's angle for an instant before it crumpled to the floor.

The wispy haired guy aimed and fired. Paper exploded near her head. She raised her gun, but he ducked behind Gregg and she couldn't shoot. He saw it in her face and his fear vanished. He lined up a careful shot and Erica ducked behind the shelf and ran along the outer wall the way she'd come in.

Slugs smacked the shelves, the concrete wall, and the floor.

Herman jumped clear of the shelves and fired down the aisle. She fired wildly over her shoulder, hitting the ceiling. Slugs chased her. A clip dropped to the floor. Another slammed into place.

She darted into an aisle and stopped to listen.

Voices echoed at the back of the room.

There were dozens of aisles that ran the width of the room, but only two than ran the length, one against each wall. She couldn't stay among the boxes. They'd have both main aisles covered and she'd be trapped until they closed in. She had to find another way to move around.

She wanted to go back to Gregg, but they'd shoot her before she got close. She needed help. She needed to tell someone that Herman was behind this. That's what Herman was afraid of. That's why he hadn't shot Gregg already. She couldn't prove he'd taken the money from BFS, but she'd seen him here with Gregg. If Gregg disappeared and Erica got away, Herman would be on the hook for murder. She hoped Gregg would be safe as long as she was free.

Erica crept to one end of the aisle and peeked down toward Gregg. Herman was crouched behind the desk, ready to fire if she showed herself. She crept to the other end and found the wispy haired guy doing the same, but he'd wheeled Gregg clear of the shelves knowing she wouldn't shoot if she saw him. They wouldn't wait much longer before coming for her.

The door was a few aisles back.

She moved to the center and started pulling boxes off the bottom shelf and burrowing her way through from aisle to aisle.

Herman must have heard her working. He hollered, "Get back here Erica or there won't be much left of Gregg."

The words froze her. She wanted to run to Gregg, but realized that's exactly what Herman wanted. He was taunting her to step into view. Erica prayed she was right, pulled another box off the shelf and crawled through.

The shifting boxes drowned out the sound of the men behind her. They could be coming closer, but this was her only chance. She wouldn't last in the main aisles and she couldn't stay where she was.

When she dug through the next aisle, she saw the door. She crept to the corner and waited under the dim light with one eye visible beyond the shelf supports. The wispy haired guy sat behind Gregg, trained for any movement. He waited patiently. No one had followed Erica here. They had the building to themselves and they were content to wait for her to step out and make a mistake.

She waited two minutes for him to turn his head toward Herman.

When he did, she hopped the width of the aisle, jerked the door handle and burst into the stairwell. The commotion behind her could have been bullets zipping after her or the men running to catch up. She couldn't be sure and she didn't slow down to listen. She sprinted up three flights, finding every door locked. On the fourth landing, she kicked the door just inches from the lock and the flimsy trim shattered. The door burst open and she ran across the wide aisles toward the back corner and the opposite stairwell.

The splintered frame would tell them where to look.

She wished she'd thought to kick in the doors below, but now she had to keep moving. She ran across the floor, out the door and into the stairwell.

She went down this time. She kicked in the door and stopped inside. Quiet now, she hoped they'd search the floor above. That would give her time to find help.

There was a desk in the corner similar to the one Herman had been hiding behind. A beige phone sat apart from piles of forms at the center.

She dialed 911 and the phone connected.

Recorded voice prompts played. Didn't the city have enough money to answer emergency calls live? She dialed one for English and waited.

A dispatcher picked up and asked if she had an emergency.

"We've been kidnapped."

"Are you ok?"

"They're trying to kill us! We need help now!"

"Where are you?"

"A warehouse in the leather district."

The woman paused. "Forty-two Beech Street?"

"I don't know. It's an old warehouse. We need help!"

"Relax, Mam. Help is coming. Are you safe?"

"They're armed and they're searching the building for me."

"Get out of sight. We'll be there in three minutes."

Erica told her it was Herman who'd brought her there, but the phone went dead. She wasn't sure if the dispatcher had heard or not. They had the address, but Herman must have figured out what she was up to and yanked the phone wires from the basement.

He'd be in a hurry to finish this and get out.

Footsteps trotted across the floor upstairs.

They were searching. They would have split up. One would be with Gregg while the other looked for her. She checked the clip. Four bullets left. Not enough to battle both of them. She needed help fast. She needed the police to know exactly where to find her.

She rummaged through the desk until she found a pack of cigarettes and matches. She took the matches to the window and dragged three boxes of files over. The window wouldn't open, so she heaved a heavy box at it. The pane cracked, but the box fell back inside. She heaved it again and the box

280

stuck there, half in, half out. A kick toppled it forward and sent it plummeting for the sidewalk leaving behind a hole opened to the outside world. No one was on the sidewalk to see it fall.

She dumped the other two boxes of paper files in a heap by the window, fluffed them as best she could and lit them. The old paper whooshed into flame against the concrete wall and up past the window. She added a few more boxes to be sure the police would see the smoke, but not enough to spread over to the shelves and burn the whole building.

Smoke filled the room and she hunkered at the end of a shelf to wait.

A minute later the door opened about eight rows back.

He came straight for the fire, cautious, but driven to find the source of the smoke. She let him stand near the desk for two seconds, thinking of ways to put the fire out before she sprang.

"Freeze," she said, the gun extended, her torso still shielded by the shelf.

He turned his head toward her, but didn't swing the gun in her direction.

He wouldn't have given her the opportunity. He would have shot her without warning, but she couldn't bring herself to kill him so cold bloodedly. What she'd do with him if he surrendered, she didn't know.

No matter. He didn't.

He dove for cover and she shot wildly over his head.

He'd found her. Only a thirty foot long shelf separated her from a professional killer and she only had three bullets left. The smoke stung her eyes and the fire drowned out any movements he made on the other side of the room. She ducked her head out on each side of the shelf to keep him from sneaking up on her.

She peeked out again and a bullet zipped past. She fired wildly. She hadn't even seen the sights on the barrel, just waved the gun out there and pulled the trigger. She wasn't thinking and she was going to get herself killed.

Two shots left.

She unscrewed the silencer. The least she could do with her remaining shots was to attract some attention. She steadied herself and tossed the silencer down the aisle, tumbling past a half dozen rows of shelves.

CJ West

He darted out around the end, running past the fire, thinking she was running for the door and that he'd get behind her before she reached it.

She let him run right to her before she moved. He was in the open and she was covered behind the shelf, but this was her last chance. She had two shots left. If she missed he'd be right on top of her with a loaded gun. She'd be dead in two seconds. She hoped he'd have to stop to shoot.

She opened fire from just eight feet, hitting him twice and filling the room with the report. Stunned, the bullets ripped into his chest and spun him sideways. He dropped face first on the floor without firing a shot.

She stepped over and kicked the gun from his hand, expecting him to spring up, but he lay lifeless on the concrete. Blood leaked onto the floor, but not nearly as much as she expected. A tremor shook through her. Her hands and arms defied control. She'd killed two men and her shaking nerves were voicing their displeasure.

He lay still much like her father had lain on the linoleum thirty years earlier. Her mother was only twenty-two then. Erica wanted to vomit after killing a complete stranger bent on killing her. What had her mother felt after killing the man she married? How much more painful had it been for her to stand over him? Erica was the only person who knew what they'd been through, and she'd never really helped her mother cope.

What kind of daughter was she?

She flung the empty Smith and Wesson into the fire. She opened the dead man's gun and counted at least six bullets left in the clip. She headed for the stairwell. Only Herman was left down there with Gregg. Help was coming. She just needed to keep Herman in the building and keep him from hurting Gregg until the police arrived.

Chapter 65

The flimsy door wouldn't stop a bullet. Erica crouched low, reached her hand up to the knob and inched the door open. If Herman were watching, hopefully he'd shoot high and she could roll out into the stairwell before he realized his mistake. The hinges opened silently. The basement was still as she held the door open and peeked past, toward where she last saw Gregg.

Nothing inside responded to her movement at the door.

She scampered in and hunkered down between the two shelves opposite the door. The door clacked closed. She waited, listening, afraid to breathe. Herman knew she would come for Gregg. He'd be waiting for her to slink in or for his partner to come back and report he'd finished her. If she could imitate his bravado on the walk back toward the desk, the bold footsteps might draw Herman out into the open. He had to expect his thug to win.

She considered trying, but didn't leave the safety of the shelves. Walking right up to him was the quickest way to get herself and Gregg killed. Better to confront Herman on her terms.

If Herman was hiding, he'd be lurking among the shelves, waiting to sneak up on her from behind. Erica moved down the rows of shelves away from where she'd last seen Gregg. She kept to the end of each shelf, peeking her head into each aisle. The boxes she'd pulled off the shelves were still in the aisles. Nothing else was disturbed. Nothing moved ahead of her or behind as she looped all the way to the end of the room, along the far wall and back toward Gregg on the other side.

There was nowhere for Herman to hide among the boxes unless he was shadowing her movements. She hadn't heard a single footfall and she hadn't made much noise herself. Herman had to be back with Gregg.

It took three minutes to creep the length of the room. When Gregg finally came into view, he was alone. His hands were duct taped down to the arms of the chair, his feet bound together. They'd even taped over his eyes. The chair was wedged between the desk and the cement wall as if he'd been searching for something to free himself, but been frustrated because he couldn't see and couldn't reach the desktop with his hands bound.

His head was turned toward her as if he'd heard her coming. She didn't dare step away from the cover of the last shelf and cross the length of the room in the open. She ducked between the shelves and walked the aisle, slowly and silently as she could. Her head shifted ahead and behind to search for Herman, the gun leading the way down the aisle to Gregg. She reached the far end and craned her neck into the aisle. The door from the stairwell was still closed. Gregg was focused on her again, now from just ten feet away. She hadn't been as quiet as she thought.

"Where is he?" she whispered.

"Gone."

"Where?" she breathed.

He stretched his chin toward the far wall.

She'd just come from there. He wasn't lurking among the shelves. Could he have given up and left? They'd both seen him. They knew who he was and what he'd done. How could he expect to get away? Maybe he knew the police were coming and decided to run.

She stepped tentatively from the cover of the shelf to the desk, her back to Gregg with the gun aimed toward the far aisle.

She couldn't free him and keep the gun trained across the room. Reluctantly, she turned her back to the shelves, wheeled Gregg back a few feet and stepped around behind the desk and rummaged through the drawers for something sharp. Taking a rusty old pair of scissors from the top drawer, she set the gun on the desk and started working to free his wrists. The dull scissors chewed rather than sliced. Her mind ticked off every second she worked, warning her that she was standing in plain view, focused on Gregg rather than the danger that could be ready to pounce. She clamped down on the scissors, slowly tearing through the tape.

Gregg jolted backward and howled.

His wrist broke free of the tape and he clutched his shoulder. Blood immediately painted his fingers bright red.

Erica wheeled for the gun, but before she could reach it, searing pain ripped through her right shoulder and threw her forward, sprawling her on top of the desk.

The telephone exploded into two dozen plastic shards.

Erica clutched the gun in her left hand, turned and fired blindly. She fell, landed sitting with her back to the desk with nothing between her and Herman. Visible now, he stood at the far end of the room using the shelf for cover. He fired a fourth time in their direction, luckily missing them both.

Erica aimed and fired twice and he retreated behind the shelf.

A bullhorn blew a warning from outside. The police wanted them out of the building, but the shouted warning provided little relief. The police might take minutes to come inside. Erica and Gregg could be dead in thirty seconds and the call would make Herman far more desperate.

Erica dropped the gun on Gregg's lap, grabbed the chair with her good arm and pulled Gregg toward the cover of the shelf. She'd use the long aisle to keep him at bay until help arrived. Herman heard the movement, ducked out and fired. Erica picked up the gun from Gregg's lap and returned his shot with a wild one of her own. She needed help and she cursed herself for forgetting to remove the silencer. The report would have brought the police rushing in to help.

At the cover of the shelf, Erica held the gun in her weak hand and twisted off the silencer as quickly as she could. She didn't waste a bullet to alert the police, but her next shot would tell them exactly where she was. She considered throwing the silencer down the aisle, but guessed Herman was smarter than the man she'd killed upstairs.

"It's over, Herman. The police are outside. There's no getting out of this now," Erica yelled.

"Not with you two alive," his voice boomed. "But telling my story is going to get much easier in a minute." He was still somewhere on the far side of the room.

Erica looked down at Gregg. He was bleeding badly, still blinded by the tape with one hand fastened to the chair. The scissors were on the floor across the room. Too far to run out in the open and get them. There was no way to get him up the stairs without getting shot.

Blood dripped on his jeans, her blood. Her triceps was torn, blood running down her forearm and dripping down from her elbow. Her arm hung lifeless. She could use her hand, but barely. With nothing to stop the bleeding, she ignored the wound. She needed to get Gregg outside to the paramedics. He was covered in blood and he was looking pale and weak.

They huddled behind the width of one shelf. If Herman rushed them, she couldn't move Gregg and return fire. She opened the clip. Three bullets left. Gregg needed a safe place to hunker down. Herman would be moving soon and there'd be no way to know which direction he'd come from.

Erica rushed away from Gregg to the far end of the main aisle.

She shifted the gun to her weak hand and yanked on the first shelf, rocking then tipping it over with a crash, cutting off the aisle so Herman would have to climb over the boxes to approach. She did the same to every aisle, save the one in the middle. Soon the room looked like a maze with every avenue blocked. Herman was still out of sight.

She wheeled Gregg to the one open aisle and tipped over the third shelf, creating a shortened aisle for them to hide in. The blockage protected them from Herman, but allowed a view over the boxes to the stairwell on the opposite side. When the police came, she could call to them. If Herman came down the aisle, he'd be completely exposed. If he chose another aisle, he'd have to noisily climb over the boxes. If he went around one of the ends, he'd be stuck in the main aisle, blocked in by the overturned shelves.

Erica fired two shots. She only had one left, but the report filled the room and set the police and Herman in motion.

Herman's feet shuffled on the opposite end of the room, no doubt looking for an aisle to sneak down and finish them. He paused in each aisle, confronted with the mess she'd left to block it off. She could hear his calculations in the long pauses in his steps. He knew time was running out. Soon he'd figure out where they were.

The footsteps fell silent. He was coming.

Erica left Gregg in the corner, shielded by the fallen boxes on one side and the undisturbed shelves on the other two. She stepped to the end of the aisle and stood quiet listening for Herman's approach.

Seconds later she heard a scratch on the concrete floor. He was coming, but she couldn't afford a look. She had just one bullet left. He'd have a full clip. He was coming down the main aisle from her left. With the gun in her left hand, she'd have to expose herself completely to shoot. She'd wait for him to be right on top of her. She couldn't miss, but if he got a shot off, neither could he. She had to be quicker.

Sweat poured from her brow. She didn't dare wipe it. She waited, barely breathing. She could hear the steps now, shoes softly touching down, steadily closer. When she imagined he was only a few feet away, she burst out into the aisle, gun leading, arm outstretched, her eyes searching for the sight and her target. He wasn't three feet away, it was more like twelve.

Startled by her sudden appearance, he flinched, his gun aimed over her head a second before he regained control. She fired before his gun came level. The bullet ripped low through his chest, but he didn't fall. He wobbled, trying desperately to line up a shot, but his arm wavered with the pain, defying control. She charged him full speed, dead into his sights with just one good arm. His first shot whizzed over her head. He didn't fire another.

She buried her shoulder into him and he dropped, slamming his head on the concrete floor, immobile from the shock. She wrested the gun away and stood over him.

Erica was finally free.

The paramedics swarmed around Gregg a minute later.

Holding his hand in the ambulance and listening to the steady beat of the heart monitor, she knew for the first time how completely her world had changed.

Chapter 66

Melanie, Sarah and Stan followed Gregg and Erica up the slope for the last attraction on their tour of the Turner's farm. Stan and Gregg lugged heavy picnic baskets while Erica listened to Melanie chat away about her new job with the Boston Globe. They passed the sturdy pine that Erica and Gregg spent two evenings underneath and climbed a set of makeshift stairs up to the plywood decking that would be the main floor of the new house. No walls had been framed and the concrete foundation for the barn had yet to be touched.

A sheet of plywood over three sawhorses formed the picnic table. There were no chairs. Sarah spread two large blankets over the plywood table and the men opened the baskets and began laying out the food. Erica noticed Sarah's hand on the middle of Stan's back and a wide smile passed between the two women. It seemed the Friday night dinners were turning into something more.

Back at BFS, Sarah and Stan were running internal audit together until they got a new boss. They were both relieved to be rid of Herman and co-managing had gone well in the first month. Erica and Gregg had agreed not to press charges or speak to the media. Marty paid handsomely for their silence and both retired quietly from the firm. Pete Harrison had found Herman's Swiss accounts and was helping Marty give the money back to investors. Pete and his bosses had agreed not to go public. The group at the picnic would never know how much that had cost Marty.

Stan asked Erica what she'd do now that she didn't need to work for a living. Programming computers seemed pointless. Odd after she'd poured four years of her life into learning so much about technology, but she realized she wanted to have a real impact in the world. She wanted to help people. She'd figure out how later.

A car drove up and Carolyn and her fiancée stepped out and walked over the grass. Erica jumped down and jogged across the field to meet them. She held her mother there like she did that day in the courtroom. Mother and daughter connected like never before. Tragedy had ripped their lives apart. Carolyn had struggled to repair her life from the moment Dale Fletcher hit the floor. She'd worked hard, raised her daughter and now she was enjoying a new life with a new man. Erica had been running away from her life ever since that day thirty years earlier. She'd never realized how hard she was running until Brad started chasing her.

Standing in the grass with her mother, Erica spun around the gold band on her left hand to show her the diamond ring she'd kept hidden all morning. She'd finally stopped running from Gregg.

Author's Note

I hope you enjoyed watching Erica come to terms with her past and deal with those in her present that wished to do her harm. You may notice that the cover photo is taken from Post Office Square Park, facing Franklin Street. If you're in that area, you may want to visit some of the places Erica frequents in the book.

For your added entertainment, we've created the Taking Stock Character Contest. Two lucky winners will appear in an upcoming CJ West novel. Winners will share dinner with CJ and a guest. Over dinner, CJ will create one character based on the lives and characteristics of the two winners. For more information, visit www.22wb.com/contests.htm.

To win, solve the code on the next page and find CJ at the appointed time and place. The rendezvous only occurs once each year. Please check the website before going to the rendezvous to make sure the contest hasn't already been won. We'd hate for you to make the trip and not be there to greet you. Good Luck!

As always, we'd like to know what you thought of this book.

Contact CJ at: CJ@22wb.com
                              or
                    22 West Books
                    P.O. Box 155
                    Sheldonville, MA 02070-0155

Thanks for reading!

Taking Stock Character Contest

Win a role in an upcoming CJ West novel. Details available on the previous page and at http://www.22wb.com/contests.htm. Good Luck!

Rendezvous Code:

103	68	12	69	23	20
77	66	9	61	7	72
54	6	71	5	3,032	64
75	5	65	21	62	33
4	34	78	4	88	63
667	86	90	9	6	2
9	34	64	7	83	1
7	46	1	67	69	63
64	129	60	11	172	124
336	11	265	13	261	61
109	37	2	131	58	41

Printed in the United States
84577LV00002B/415-468/A